Women's Studies in India

Women's Studies in India

A Journey of 25 Years

Edited by
Madhu Vij
Manjeet Bhatia
Shelly Pandey

Women's Studies and Development Centre
University of Delhi, Delhi

RAWAT PUBLICATIONS
Jaipur • New Delhi • Bangalore • Hyderabad • Guwahati • Kolkata

ISBN 978-81-316-0634-6

Published by
Prem Rawat for **Rawat Publications**
Satyam Apts, Sector 3, Jawahar Nagar, Jaipur 302 004 (India)
Phone: 0141 265 1748 / 7006 Fax: 0141 265 1748
E-mail: info@rawatbooks.com
Website: www.rawatbooks.com

New Delhi Office
4858/24, Ansari Road, Daryaganj, New Delhi 110 002
Phone: 011 2326 3290

Also at *Bangalore*, *Hyderabad*, *Guwahati* and *Kolkata*

Typeset by Rawat Computers, Jaipur

Printed at Chaman Enterprises, New Delhi

Contents

Part II
Expanding Horizon: Touching Multiple Concerns

Part III
Taking it Forward: Retrospection and New Areas

Foreword

Malashri Lal

The Women's Studies and Development Centre at University of Delhi celebrates an eventful period of 25 years. One of the first four Women's Studies Centres established in 1987 under the aegis of the University Grant Commission, the 'WSDC' as it is fondly called, has shown consistent commitment to the environment of change that has brought empowerment to the women of India. It is a matter of pride and satisfaction that WSDC has demonstrated a strong engagement with issues concerning women that have been prioritized by the Government of India through its various ministries and departments, and also participated in public debates on policy.

The formative years (1987–2000) of the WSDC were spent under the stewardship of its founder director Prof Susheela Kaushik, an eminent scholar in Political Science. The 1980s marked 'second wave feminism', a time for 'theorizing' in academia and awareness raising in society. Understandably, this phase coincided with the public discourses on feminist issues and the beginnings of policy making in India that were directly linked to the advancement of women. The path-breaking report *Towards Equality* (1974) had convincingly shown that societal advancement must integrate with the well-being of women and therefore policies must look towards social formations from their perspective. At the Fourth National Conference of the Indian Association for Women's Studies held at Vishakhapatnam in December 1988, the participants from the Women's Studies Centres and Cells decided to undertake a common research project so as to arrive at comparable data leading to a national perspective that proved vital to women's studies and development. A research-cum-action project on "Girl Child and Family in India" was decided upon. The choice of the subject was linked to the activities that led to the declaration of 1990 as the SAARC Year of the Girl Child as also by the paucity of data on girl children. The WSDC was the lead partner in the country-wide project on the girl child, involving 22 Women Studies centres across India. The findings of this project were published as a book in 1993 titled *Family and Rights of Girls*, which contributed towards government policy on the girl child.

Yet another issue particular to the Indian political conditions was the representation of women in decision-making bodies of the government. Prof Susheela Kaushik's able guidance brought forth doctoral dissertations and in-depth researches on the panchayati raj movement. She wrote analytical articles that commented on the power structures in rural communities and the need to bring women into the local political hierarchies. The passage of the 73rd Constitutional Amendment Act, 1992, which granted 33 per cent reservation to women in the panchayati raj institutions (PRIs), not only endorsed the significant analysis that was conducted by women political scientists but also gave a new direction for fieldwork for WSDC members and students. The next several years were spent in training women panchayat leaders in association with NGOs, all of them driven by the challenge to make the newly elected women confidant leaders and not mere 'rubber stamps'. This was an important demonstration of the sisterhood spirit of women's studies organizations, specially in North India, who wished to dispel the stereotype of the rural woman as an appendage to her husband's will and incapable of thoughtful leadership. Prof Susheela Kaushik, functioned as the Director of WSDC for 13 years with the able cooperation of Dr Manjit Bhatia, a celebrated political scientist with multidisciplinary interests. As the only permanent faculty at WSDC, she carries the history of WSDC in her work and her memories.

When I took charge of WSDC as the next Director in 2000, the initiatives from before were enhanced and new dimensions addressed from the perspective of Humanities and Law. It was a privilege to be appointed to the position and I remain grateful to Prof. Susheela Kaushik for the strong foundations she had given to the Centre. During my tenure of six years, the focus turned to expanding the scope of WSDC to the colleges so as to incorporate more field activities and raise wider awareness of contemporary concerns. With supportive funding from the Department of Social Welfare, several colleges instituted Women Development Cells (WDC), which conducted short courses, field surveys, workshops, awareness campaigns and research projects. It was a high point in each semester when the central WSDC met with the WDC representatives over a day-long brainstorming session and this large group of almost 150 persons could share experiences and propose new ideas. Significant achievements through this network were project reports on diverse subjects such as call centres which had been newly introduced in Delhi, and Census 2001 data analysis on the girl child that had shown for the first time the crisis of the 'missing woman' in the skewed sex ratio of 933. It came as shock to the public that Delhi, specially its affluent areas such as Hauz Khas, had shown the worst discriminations.

Such data analysis propelled the creation of women's studies networks across six locations for which WSDC, Delhi was the lead partner – Kurukshetra, Shimla, Jaipur, Lucknow and Mumbai. Through conferences and research alliances, significant new material was released in the public sphere, in the context of 2001 National Policy for Empowerment of Women. The proceedings of a major conference, held in collaboration with the Indian Institute of Advanced Studies, Shimla, were published as a book *Women's Studies in India: Contours of Change* (2002), which had contributors from around the country, including the lyricist Gulzar, and IAS officer Ms Sarojini Thakur, then Secretary, Women and Child.

WSDC also ran a Counselling Centre for five years, and initiated two short-term courses, viz., 'Gender Studies' for Undergraduate students in six colleges and 'Gender and Society', a certificate course for postgraduate students. The active networking between colleges in Delhi and centres throughout India was kept up with the publication of the WSDC newsletter, annual reports, periodic handbooks and two full-length books on women and law. The international project "Higher Education Link" through the British Council was conducted for four years.

During this period WSDC also took up international research projects. Dr Manjeet Bhatia won the funding for an international project from British Council that she completed in collaboration with Dr Ann Stewart of Warwick University.

The year 2004 was a landmark year for the University of Delhi as it approved the Ordinance XV-D: Prohibition of and Punishment for Sexual Harassment. The ground work, based on the Vishakha judgment, was coordinated at the WSDC along with the inputs from several professors from Departments of Law, Sociology, Political Sciences and others. The University of Delhi was the first in the country to adopt an ordinance on this issue.

WSDC received high ranking from UGC during this period and additional funding made possible the recruitment of three faculty members with commendable research skills: Nilima Srivastava, Meenu Anand and Manjeet Baruah, whose work was ably complimented by the office staff members and librarian, Renu Rani. With others in the unit and the network in colleges, these years at WSDC were marked with high levels of activities in teaching, training, outreach and extension, documentation and publications. Also, UGC's programme for Women Managers in Higher Education, chaired by Dr Armaity Desai, built a vigorous, countrywide network.

The next Director of WSDC Prof Vibha Chaturvedi (2006–2011) from the Department of Philosophy consolidated the gains of research and social activism and provided contexts for larger academic frameworks in women's studies in India. Significant documentation was done under the project 'Feminist Theories and Practices' from the Ministry of Women and Child. The important realization that emerged is that women's studies in India have roots and trajectories that are different from the 'western' models which provide the vocabulary of feminism. Looking back to the social reform movements of the 19th century, it becomes apparent that the matrix of caste, class and gender creates overlapping identities that elude simple affiliations. Philosophical traditions through ancient texts, interreligious issues, the impact of history and the country's enormous diversity are just a few factors that make Indian feminism distinctive. The project reflected this diversity, taking in its purview Indian contexts for women, e.g., Gandhi and women, life writing, ostracism of widows, domestic workers, political participation, and rural agricultural communities. Linking theoretical formulations to current conditions, further research was undertaken on the Women's Reservation Bill in which it is proposed to reserve 33 per cent seats of the lower house of the parliament and legislative assemblies, for women. The Bill was not passed, and remains pending, in direct contrast to the women's reservation in PRIs which became an Act in 1992. In closely argued discourses it was shown that women's representation in local communities is acceptable as identities are more closely matched with the voters, but at the national level, the woman's identity gets blurred due to several intermingling factors of caste, class and religion. Issues such as this require closer analysis in the Indian context which may be competently addressed by a multidisciplinary women's studies group rather than by a single academic department. The WSDC through its projects attempted to formulate literary theory in conjunction with practice that might throw light on contemporary problems and also impact policy decisions.

Another major project concerned the girl child in the context of a mid-term review of the 2001 census in 2006. Haryana and Delhi were selected for close analysis. The new aspect of the questionnaires implemented in the field was interviews with the men, especially fathers of girl children, with the objective of finding out their gender positioning. The theoretical basis of such enquiry was the prevailing view that men are the decision-makers when it comes to family planning, and women and potential mothers submit to their decision. The project was published as a book titled *Girl Child: Changing Perceptions*, with the major recommendations, which have been incorporated as a chapter in the book. Some important researches on the issues of domestic violence and honour killing were initiated during her tenure. The findings of domestic violence research were published in the *South East Asia Research Journal*.

WSDC also expanded its international research base and was given major funding by the Indo-Sri Lanka Foundation for two projects on 'Gender and School Curriculum' and 'Gender and Decision-Making in Public Arena'. These projects conducted comparative studies between India and Sri Lanka on exploring gender in the school curriculum and the gendered realities at the decision-making positions.

Following Prof Vibha Chaturvedi's tenure of five years, the next Director appointed was Prof Sushma Batra from the Department of Social Work for one year 2011–12. Her enormous field experience and hands-on approach gave a distinctive character to the WSDC; one obvious manifestation of it was the celebration of International Women's Day by bringing many women NGOs under one roof to display their visions activities and outreach.

The next director was Prof Madhu Vij from the Faculty of Management Studies. During the brief period of her stay of one year – 2012 to 2013 – she strengthened the ongoing programmes in teaching and research and actively planned for the celebration of 25 years of WSDC. The present book was formulated under her guidance, leading to important recovery of early material which provides historical records not only for WSDC but also for the story of women's studies in India. During her tenure, Shelly Pandey, one of the editors of the book, received the prestigious M.N. Srinivas Memorial Prize, awarded by Indian Sociological Society for her article in *EPW* (which is also a part of the book).

During this period, the WSDC remained highly preoccupied with implementing the provisions of Ordinance XV-D. The WSDC is the location of the Apex Committee for the Sexual Harassment Cases and the Director is the member-secretary of the same. The number of cases of sexual harassment that are referred to WSDC has been rising over the years, hence the work relating to inquiries and reports has increased manifold. The WSDC, taking its mandate with seriousness, has regularly held meetings of the Apex Committee and conducted inquires as required. During the tenure of Prof Madhu Vij, WSDC has been proactive in spreading awareness about women's safety in and around campus.

The current Director Prof Bharati Baveja took charge in July 2013. Being from the Central Institute of Education, she is likely to take up the important cause of linking school education with higher education, analysing curriculum, and giving policy advice on aptitude and development of student potential.

The journey of the Centre would not have been possible without the remarkable cooperation and contribution of Dr Manjeet Bhatia. The Centre has had six directors so far and Dr

Bhatia has worked closely with all of them. Dr Bhatia's abled support made the journey of each Director more enriching. She is truly the spine of the Centre and her support in research, teaching, administration and extension activities has been exceptional.

The mapping of 25 years of WSDC provides an enriching array of activities that have contributed to women's studies in three significant directions. First, the location of the Centre has brought intricate engagement with colleges and departments with vital everyday issues of safety, security and empowerment being addressed. Second, WSDC's role as part of UGC's country-wide network of such centres gives it a national relevance as a consultative body that may, in conjunction with others, impact policy decisions in the government. Third, WSDC has an important contribution to make to Women's Studies as an academic discipline in universities by sharing its research and publications with global partners. The legacy of directors of WSDC, and their teams, keeps up the trend of participative engagement with emerging trends and issues. The present book is a tribute to the large numbers of students, teachers and well-wishers who have kept this Centre energized and productive. Women's Studies, by its very philosophy, is located beyond the individual. Its aim is to transform society for ensuring dignity to women through various institutional tools such as teaching, research, policy advice and extension programmes. WSDC has fulfilled such a mandate and deserves warm congratulations for the 25 years of dedicated service to the University of Delhi and to the nation.

Professor Malashri Lal
Dean of Colleges
Dean, Academic Activities & Projects
(Former Director, WSDC)
University of Delhi

Introduction

Women's Studies: A Journey of 25 Years

Madhu Vij, Manjeet Bhatia and Shelly Pandey

Women's Studies in India is born out of feminist movement and academic concerns. The thrust was initiated by the release of the *Towards Equality* report in 1974. The report highlighted some of the stark realities of the status of women in India, like the decline in sex ratio, higher mortality rate, and decline in rate of economic participation of women. It also brought to light the regressive practices of dowry, prostitution, media representation of women and legal disparities.

There were many institutions, individuals, activists and academics that took cognizance of these revelations and worked at different levels to address them. A study group at Delhi University emerged in this background to deliberate on such issues, the complete absence of women's issues in the subject disciplines of the university was highlighted and the biggest challenge was to bring them in higher education.

The Research Group on Women's Studies, Department of Political Science, University of Delhi organized a three-day national seminar from 21–23 April, 1985 at Delhi to deliberate on the guidelines for initiating women's studies units in Indian universities. The seminar was co-sponsored by University Grants Commission (UGC) and Indian Association for Women's Studies. Besides scholars from various disciplines a number of eminent women's studies specialists and academics also participated in this seminar.

The eminent scholars deliberated on the purpose and objectives of incorporating women's studies in the university system. The concern of the participants was not only the development of women but also making university education more meaningful and relevant.

It was decided at this national seminar that independent centres, equidistant from all the departments, should be created at universities. Alternatively, all departments should have women's studies units. There was general agreement that women's studies should have multidisciplinary approach.

In the University of Delhi, Women's Studies & Development Centre (WSDC) was established in April 1987 in the Department of Political Science and soon got shifted to a cubicle above the Indian Coffee House (now Nirula's is housed there). Struggle for adequate space lasted long, till the university decided to house all the research centres in one building and WSDC got its present location in Academic Research Building after more than one and a half decades.

This Centre was one of the first four centres sponsored by UGC in late eighties. The initial mandate of the centres was to play as catalysts and raise awareness of women's issues in higher education. The Delhi University Centre was deliberately not housed in any department least it gets dominated by one subject discipline perspective. It associated itself with colleges through their development cells and departments through the progressive teachers in implementing the UGC mandate. It regularly involved colleges in raising women's issues and celebrating International Women's Day. With the help of teachers it lobbied with social sciences and humanities' departments to include women's perspectives in the course curriculums.

The Centre also joined hands with independent research centres, such as CWDS and women organizations and marched on roads to raise awareness and hold protests on women's issues. Some of these were: women's representation in media/advertisements, women's political participation in elected bodies, violence against women/girl child, and women and political participation.

Towards Equality report had clearly established the low status of Indian women. There was dearth of knowledge about women.

Empirical research was required to build the knowledge about women. Knowledge building took the shape of unearthing women's roles in daily chores, agriculture, culture, environment and also their exclusion from institutions. Such revelations led to felt need of further research, policy interventions and women's empowerment. WSDC was the active participant in the all these interventions.

Idea to do a national level research on girl child was born at the All India Women's Studies Conference. The Department of Women and Child, Government of India, sponsored this project in collaboration with 22 Women's Studies Centres, including the Delhi University's. This research project was one of its kinds that collated the national level data on girl child. The Centre then took up research as its main objective and did several research projects along with counselling, lobbying documentation, curriculum development, publication, networking, and organizing seminars and workshops.

Some of the areas of research which have been taken up by WSDC are: women and political participation, women and election, rehabilitation of children of the prostitutes, girl child and family, gender in school curriculums, domestic violence, sexual harassment, honour killings, gender audit, feminist theory and debates.

Through its seminars, conferences and workshops the Centre has further contributed towards understanding several burning women's issues. Some of the issues of these engagements had been women and access to land rights and other productive resources (with ICHR, 1988), role of women in Indian National Congress – 1985–1947 (with Maitreyi College, 1987), mobilizing women for equality through education (with NEHU, Shillong, 1989), dialogue for continuity and change in India (with USEFI, 1991), child labour in beedi-making: legislations and practices (1994), women in bureaucracy (1995), regional consultation on National Policy on Women (with DWCD, 1995), women and cultural icons (2004), women, science and society (2006), mainstreaming of women in work and political processes (2008) and in the name of honour: matrimonial practices and women's subjugation in South Asia (2011).

Apart from issues pertaining to women's conditions in India, the seminars and conferences also focused on the Women's Studies as a discipline, like Women's Studies Network: Issues and Agenda (2001), Feminist Theories and Practices (2003), and Women's Studies: Achievements, Challenges and Future Directions (2013).

The Centre widely networked locally, regionally nationally as well as internationally. It also closely worked with other teachers and student activists on many fronts. One such front was opened by the Vishakha judgment. The Centre played an active role with other Delhi University teachers and students to make the university's policy against sexual harassment. Today, the Centre houses the secretariat of its Apex Complaint Committee against Sexual Harassment and its Director is the member secretary of this body. On many other issues, WSDC has lobbied with government and also collaborated with other organizations for shadow gender reports at international meets and conferences.

The Centre grew in its stature and had international visitors and collaborations. It had Fulbright scholars, UGC fellows associated with it from time to time. It started taking up international projects along with national and regional ones. WSDC engaged in two international projects through British Council involving Warwick University and SOAS, University of London. It also collaborated with Towson University, USA for organizing a seminar on women leadership and community. It has done two projects with Indo-Sri Lanka Foundation, Focusing on the comparative analysis of gender issues in both the countries. The Centre has also welcomed visiting scholars from Canada and London in its journey of international links.

By late nineties UGC wanted universities to take over their Women's Studies Centres and maintain them. Some of the state universities found it difficult to find funding and those centres suffered for a period till active teachers restored them. Whereas some other state university centres had cakewalk and could become part of the university immediately and enjoy the permanency. Now, there are 158 UGC Women's Studies Centres in the country at different levels of development. It has become a huge family now.

UGC had been changing its mandate for these centres from time to time. It now wants university-based centres to become departments and offer degree courses. Only those centres that were supported by their universities could do that. The Delhi University Centre could start different levels of add-on courses. It started with a certificate course in women's studies at undergraduate level in 2006 and added postgraduate and research level courses in subsequent years. Women's Studies Centre at Jawaharlal Nehru

University started with offering an optional course and is now offering research degrees. Many other centres offered MPhil in women's studies, including Gauwhati and Beharampur centres. Kurukshetra University and Panjab University centres along with centres in south like one in Hyderabad University could become departments and offered MA degree.

UGC has given a fillip to women's studies in the Twelfth Plan period by increasing its grant to these centres. Increase in grant could make address the problem to quite an extent and ensure some continuity in its programmes.

WSDC in its journey of 25 years had developed many local, regional, national and international links. Scholars got associated with the Centre in various research projects, seminars and workshops and also contributed to its academic and extension activities. This book is an acknowledgement of this association and the journey of the Centre's work through some of the available written works of the scholars associated with it. Included articles are neither the full representation of the work of WSDC nor of scholars. Editors have tried to include writings from different phases of the Centre and bring it close to the current one. These articles are placed in three broad phases – early, middle and current one. The book is, therefore, divided into three sections. Each section reflects the issues of different phases that Women's Studies Centre at Delhi University has gone through. The first section of the volume discusses the early days' questions and agendas of Women Studies like emergence of Women's Studies as a discipline and the issue of girl child. There are three essays in this section.

The first essay is by Susheela Kaushik on 'A Blueprint for Research, Curriculum and Action in Women's Studies'. In this she clearly writes about the contribution of Women's Studies for other subjects, disciplines, and its challenges to established concepts and theses. Lack of empirical data on women, only a few individual scholars taking up research and lack of macro studies were some of the early challenges. Until the UGC-supported centres were established the universities were slow in taking up this new field of research. These centres emerged as best placed to pool in resources to create this new knowledge base for the discipline of Women's Studies. The paper also highlights the utmost importance, especially in case of Women's Studies, of the link between research and classroom teaching.

In the second chapter, Veena Poonacha raises very relevant and critical questions around Women's Studies in her article, 'Women's Studies in Indian Universities: The Changing Parameters of Struggle'. It deals with issues of Women's Studies as a subject discipline and yet fulfilling the need of academic arm of women's movement. Some of challenges this article highlights are the problem of finding common ground among different shades of feminist commitment; changing context of welfare state in the era of globalization; rise of religion and other ethnic identities which is 'subtly eroding feminist radicalism'; and implications of growing divide in theory and practice.

In its early days WSDC was involved in a national-level project on the girl child and again in 2008 another project was done on the same issue. The third chapter is by Vibha Chaturvedi and Nilima Srivastava. This is based on the recommendations and suggestions which came forward in the research study done by WSDC in 2008 by involving six Women's Studies Centres from North India (Delhi, Kurukshetra, Jaipur, Shimla, Jammu and Yamuna Nagar) on 'Attitudinal Difference towards Girl Child in Selected Districts of North India'. The purpose of bringing this chapter in this section is the Centre's continuous engagement with the issue of girl child in India since its inception. The chapter highlights some of the issues pertaining to the girl child in India such as less preference for girl child by parents or greater chance of the girl child facing withdrawal from education or health facilities in the event of a choice between the boy and the girl child.

The second section deals with the multiple concerns that the Centre gradually touched during the end of 20th century and the early years of 21st century. This section includes essays pertaining to the various perspective of gendered violence and gendered culture.

Malashri Lal's essay on 'Women, Literature and Culture in India: Multiple Perspectives', reflects women's position in multiple contexts like, home, body politic, mythology through Indian literature, etc. The unique aspect of this chapter is men's way of portraying Indian women through their writings. This essay indicates that family, society, violence and caste together provide a combination which is particular to the literature of India. The another further argues that patriarchy has created hierarchies of power in the forms of family, community and caste, within which men and women are equally caught. She further says that fragmented actions have not yielded any significant gain for rectifying the disadvantageous position of woman, hence, the collective action should be taken up for feminism in India.

Sanjukta Dasgupta's essay on 'Women in India: Terror and Trauma in the Sacred Space' deals with the space inside home. She has taken two concerns of women's subjugation in home – unpaid domestic labour and dowry demand. She chalks out how identification of housewives is constructed with the perfection with which they perform household work. This work is romanticized as love of a woman towards her family regardless of what she wants. The second issue she deals with is the dowry – rather indirect dowry – as she explains how the school teaching, as a profession, makes women more attractive in the marriage market. A woman school teacher can very well combine the work in the paid labour job market and unpaid labour in the home.

The essay by Zarina Bhatty discusses the gender inequality among North Indian Muslims through an ethnographic account of their life cycle rituals and ceremonies. She argues that although strongly disapproved by Islam, rituals play an important role in everyday life of Indian Muslims. These rituals reaffirm and strengthened gender discrimination. This essay portrays the everyday life experiences of Indian Muslim women, which reflect a departure from the status of women in Quran.

Esha Niyogi De in her chapter studies the role femininity takes in Rabindranath Tagore's play, *Raktakarabi/Red Oleanders* (1924). Through this essay Esha explains that the images of women and the feminine in this work, and allied writings by Tagore, were part and parcel of his lifelong conceptual pursuit to rethink human collectivity in a world riddled by empire, capital and orthodoxy. What Tagore struggled to achieve through his imagination of the feminine was a polyphonic voice that critiqued western masculine imperialism and at the same time it was self-critical about the male nationalist perspectives proliferating in his colonial context.

Sukrita Paul Kumar and Malashri Lal's conversation with the flimmaker Gulzar on the question of women in his films throws light on a filmmaker's conscious and subconscious position vis-à-vis women. This essay shows how Gulzar has not referred woman only as the heroine of the romance but also projected her in a variety of roles, such as friend, sister and beloved. Gulzar emphasizes the responsibilities of the actors (both male and female) in the film industry, where they have to understand the damage they might bring to the cause of women by generating an image of woman as object. Gulzar also highlights that how through films even dignity of the woman can be projected, where the self-esteem of the women is kept up.

Ann Stewart and Manjeet Bhatia undertook a joint research project on domestic violence while the law in India was being made. The chapter 'Interventions to Tackle Domestic Violence in India and the United Kingdom' is the outcome of this joint research project of WSDC and Law Department, University of Warwick. It discusses the strategies the voluntary sector and state have evolved to respond to the survivors of domestic violence both in India and the United Kingdom. It brings out interesting comparison of such responses, like experiences of NGOs, police and lawyers in both the countries.

Amrit Kaur Basra, in her article 'Anti-Sikh Riots of 1984 Revisited: Gender, Violence and Politics of Representation', which is based on extensive research through the use of oral testimonies, along with other authentic recourses, recounts the events and discusses the failure of administrative machinery and loss of political will to contain riots or even delivering justice. Suffering of women and their orphaned children is still lurking large in some resettlement colonies. Though the community has moved on, it has kept the fight for justice alive against all odds. The article brings out that the aftermath of anti-Sikh riots had bearing not only on Sikh community but also on the emergent politics.

The third section of the book discusses the new areas which the Centre has been dealing with along with a retrospection of some of the older issues as well because certain questions remain alive even in today's context of Women's Studies.

The first chapter of this section is by Manjeet Bhatia that discusses gender inequality drawing on the concept of equality. The paper offers rich literature on the issue of inequality and establishes the gender inequality through various examples from Indian context. The paper also describes the feminist critics of equality. The author offers two levels of gender inequalities – constructive and implicative.

Tanya Caulfield's essay 'Happliy Unmarried' looks at the single women's lived experiences in Delhi. This chapter explores the ways in which single women shape and negotiate their existence on non-traditional lines of conduct as socio-economically independent women by rejecting patriarchal values and ideologies. Based in the context of Delhi, the paper argues that many women negotiate independent socio-economic situation in order to remain unmarried. Though it has been narrated as complicated and complex, the single womanhood indicates towards locating definition of South Asian femininity to establish lives free from many perceived constraints of traditional expectations.

The next essay by Lucinda Joy Peach discusses the portrayal of women in Indian and US magazine advertisements. She says that though culturally both the countries might be different, there are still many similarities in the way these advertisements objectify women. These advertisements depict women as sex objects, promote the beauty myth and encourage unhealthy behaviour, which have negative consequences for the status of women. This essay also talks about the impact of western ideals and norms on Indian cultural understandings of gender and how their manifestations must be seriously assessed.

The essay by Mary E. John is a feminist invitation to rethink the nation-to-globalization narrative that structures prominent approaches to India's post-independence history. This chapter argues that the long history of the women's movement in India from the 19th century onwards has been fundamentally international in scope within which the 'nation' occupied a troubled position. John has suggested that the future of the women's movement in India – and elsewhere – would be better appreciated within a 'post-national' as against a 'global' conjunctural analysis.

Krishna Menon's article on 'Dalit Feminism and the Question of Violence' echoes the challenges posed by Dalit feminism to the feminist movement in India to address the caste-based realities of violence and sexual regulations. This paper explains that how the caste-based purity and protection consider Dalit women as unclean and polluting but good enough to have sex with. This makes Dalit women more vulnerable to the patriarchal oppression by the upper caste men as well as men of their own caste. The essay reinforces the arguments of Dalit feminists that the social location determines the perception of reality and to understand the lived experiences of Dalit women there is a need to come out of the frozen definitions of feminism.

In her article, Shefali Moitra tries to reach the basis of axioms of liberal and radical feminists. With the help of mathematician interested in meta-logical questions, she explores, if logic has human face, is there any pure logic deviod of any axiom, and where do liberal and radical feminists surface in this exploration?

Madhu Vij's essay on gender and microfinance discusses some empirical evidence of the current trends regarding the microfinance sector with a special focus on empowering women. A small but intensive survey was done on the various dimensions of the microfinance sector in India. Different views and experiences were expressed but all agreed that microfinance had played a very positive role in boosting the confidence and self-esteem of women leading to women's empowerment. Also, all the major organizations agreed on the social transformational role that microfinance plays, at least in the Indian context.

Shelly Pandey's essay attempts to locate gender in public transport through an ethnographic study of Delhi Metro. This chapter talks about the relation between gender, public space and power. It shows that how the ladies coach of Delhi Metro has provided private space to women in public transport. Thus, a distinct power dynamics has been created, which has reproduced or transformed the internalised meaning of public space for women. It begins by analysing the gender in the public transport in the past and then it brings the changing meaning of public transport for women in the urban location.

Chantal Maillé, in her article 'Feminist Perspectives on Honour Killings and Domestic Violence', discusses perspectives of seeing 'honour'-based crimes as special crimes or as crimes that violate women's rights in the context of South Asian communities in Canada. The paper brings out that Canada has to move away from stereotypical representation of cultures, especially in dealing with violence against women.

Women's Studies in India is evolving in many directions and WSDC remains committed to knowledge generation and addressing women's issues through teaching and research. There will be many more phases in the future journey of WSDC, in which WSDC would thrive with students, teachers, scholars and activists coming along in its journey.

Part I

The Beginning: Reflection on the Early Days' Perspectives

1

A Blueprint for Research, Curriculum and Action in Women's Studies

Susheela Kaushik

Women are an integral part of every social construction, and any study of a community, be it through social sciences, humanities, pure sciences or technical sciences, would definitely involve a basic component on women's issues. Women's Studies thus gains in significance and contributes to the enhancement of higher education, its objectives, contents and methods; as the initiator and enabler of a critical assessment of the social structures and processes, it acts as a conscience keeper for the nation. Its impact needs to be felt beyond the educational system in the wider social dynamics of a desirable humane, egalitarian and equal society.

Defining Women's Studies

The discipline of Women's Studies seeks to conscientize both men and women by helping them to understand, recognize and acknowledge the multidimensional roles played by women in society. In this, Women's Studies follows basically the same approach as many other social sciences. The issue of poverty and the problems of the economic disadvantage used to be treated essentially as the agenda of social workers in the early years after independence. However, following appreciable research on certain dimensions of economic deprivation and the formulation of the concept of 'poverty line,' poverty status became very much a part of not only economics but also of political science, sociology and other academic subjects.

Women's Studies, in turn, can be defined as a comprehensive literature that embodies its concern for women's equality and development and seeks to find explanations and remedies for the unequal position of women in society. It is a method of research and analyses which enquires into the origin and basis of discriminatory practices against women. At the same time, it is a critical instrument for analysing the social reality thereby leading to further development of social sciences.

Women's Studies is an academic discipline, with its own identity and autonomous existence. It points out the need for re-examining traditional and inherited knowledge as well as promotes aspects of contemporary research from the gender/woman's perspectives. It has, over a period of time, developed its own theories based on feminist concepts, and evolved its own methodology that is distinguished from the varied precepts and methodologies adopted by 'mainstream' disciplines.

Theories and Methodologies

Ever since the publication of *Towards Equality,* 1975 (Report of the Status of Women Committee) there has been a spurt in research, seeking to enquire into the status and living conditions of women, exploring the theory of patriarchy and women's oppression and collecting data and devising appropriate strategies. By the eighties and nineties, Indian researchers had not only enormously contributed to the knowledge on women's rights and position but also lobbied vigorously for a set of policy measures and social action, and made laudable effort to publicize their findings. They had also actively initiated steps through NGOs and non-university-based research institutions to transform their findings into realistic social utilization. The researchers were thus vitally linked to the Women's Studies movement.

The present conditions derive from this context. In research and documentation, some penetrating questions about Women's Studies and the intervention of feminist perspectives in various fields have led to a rethinking of theories and methodologies. Many existing hypotheses stand re-examined and even reversed. Many traditional tools of analysis have been set aside for new tools that reach out to women in particular. Women's Studies has clearly demonstrated that the 'personal is political,' thereby making the researchers look into issues and practices that were hitherto considered as 'private'. Such enterprise has thereby demolished the public-private dichotomy in analysis. In questioning the epistemology of many words and expressions, old definitions have been subjected to review. Now, words such as employment, wages, poverty, intra-household disparity, citizenship, political participation, and the like, are interpreted through women's experience. Likewise, concepts of marriage, man-woman relations, socialization, etc., have come to acquire new meanings in the light of gender awareness.

Women's Studies has, by its empirical research and models, helped to awaken sensitivity to acts of discrimination, violence and crimes against women. It has brought attention to the poignancy of women's deprivation by way of health, food and nutrition, and education. The existence of forces of patriarchy and gender inequality in society are noted, showing how women have been treated primarily as consumers, sex objects or reproduction machines. Research in Women's Studies has clearly pointed out to the huge wastage of human resources in ignoring the potential of women, and indicated the need for chanellizing the productive talents of women for the betterment of society.

Being a study of the issues relating to women, who constitute an integral part of society, Women's Studies has, by definition, an interdisciplinary thrust. It has, therefore, contributed to and strengthened interdisciplinary approaches in social sciences. The contemporary relevance of Women's Studies has been reinforced by an insistence on the realities of women's lives and, by extension, called for a review of community structures.

Moments in History

The publication of *Towards Equality* is a landmark in modern times. However, scholarly awareness of women in India dates further back. Ever since Raja Rammohan Roy (an intellectual who combined his research with social action to herald a liberal outlook) and Swami Vivekananda (who analysed the religious base of women's subordination), the women's question has been brought into the centre of thinking and socio-political action. Dr Ambedkar was a proponent of equality. E.N. Ramaswamy Naiker focused more than any one else on the social origins of familial oppression and asked to break the private-public divide that had been the solid foundation of India's feudal, patriarchal order. However, his views were not systematically collected into a full document and therefore could not inspire widespread research. Nevertheless, in the context of women's status, Naiker's thoughts triggered local action and awareness.

The post-independence years in India have been marked by political developments that affected the adoption of the Hindu Code Act and the postponement of a Uniform Civil Code. Debates that ensued clearly showed the need for deeper knowledge and greater awareness of the injustices done to women. *Towards Equality* thus became a pioneering research statement about the origins of women's present-day status of subordination and dependence. It has been followed by innumerable micro studies and a few macro studies which brought out various other facets of exploitation and found root causes in religious precepts, rituals and customs, economic devaluation, social and political insecurity, and non-recognition of women's roles.

Women's Studies Research

Being a new field for research, the initial days of Women's Studies were challenging. With very little available data by way of economic and statistical inputs, many researchers turned to history and anthropology. Informed of the political and theoretical tools, they sought to uncover changes that came about over centuries leading to the decline in women's status and the consequent insult and injury to women. In the initial years such research was undertaken mainly by a few institutions like the Centre for Women Development Studies (CWDS) and Indian Social Studies Trust. But soon, some individuals based in the university system, women and men from media and other constituencies of learning picked up the cues. The university system made a slow start. The Research Unit on Women's Studies

(SNDT University) in 1974 and Tata Institute of Social Sciences marked the beginning of university-based work. However, it was not until UGC supported centres started functioning in 1987 that the universities became sensitized to the research undertaken by their own scholars in their individual capacity.

The Women's Studies Centres, both within and outside the university system ever since, have undertaken a range of work – both theoretical and empirical. Some areas covered are in the nature of evaluation and social auditing, data collection and documentation, theoretical formulation and policy orientation. So too, the sources have varied from archival to grassroots. Involving students and teachers, such action research combined field investigation and field work, social research and social action. Not only did women at the grassroots benefit from such engagement but the investigators too could better comprehend social reality and collect data through empirical surveys. At last research was not just lofty theoretical models. Instinctive and personal experiences at grassroots had a valid place. Such enquiry could unveil many hidden developments and demystify religion, economics and social practices. It was found that ground contacts would benefit the researchers and their subjects. By taking the findings to the people, social action could be propelled. Women's Studies research thereby acquired an active, catalytic role.

Micro and Macro Studies

The expression of Women's Studies in universities and outside was, in the beginning, mainly in the form of micro studies, confined to small areas – both geographically and theoretically. This was bound to be so, as most projects were individual enterprises, with meagre financial resources or none. Personal motivation was the compelling energy. Many researchers lacked networking support, information on ongoing research elsewhere, data, awareness of new theories and methodologies. The publication of *Indian Women: Change and Challenge in the International Decade, 1975–85* by Neera Desai and Vibhuti Patel, was the first (and perhaps till now the only) volume that sought to give a bird's eye view of ongoing research and methodologies. Though in subsequent years many bibliographies and directories have been compiled, they provide limited insights. They are also confined to specific themes rather than Women's Studies as a whole.

Micro studies served (and still do) an important role by way of collecting fresh data and highlighting problems which constitute a local aspect of a wider problem. In a nation as pluralistic and regionally varied in its historical and sociological inheritances and practices as India, a series of micro studies could serve a valuable purpose. Many M.Phil and Ph.D. theses are examples of such attention to particularity.

However, their usefulness in arriving at an all-India picture remains limited. From the point of view of policy framing and action the chart must be larger. One way would be to put these micro perspectives together to arrive at a macro picture to help theoretical models. Such a merger will, perhaps, be better achieved when the micro studies form part of a broader collaborative project. Associated with various Women's Studies and Resource Centres all over India, these projects can also attract grants. A nation-wide research, particularly action research, creates public enthusiasm and awareness. In turn, many students, teachers, librarians, statisticians and university authorities would be drawn into an academic mass movement. The instance of the macro-micro action research project on Girl Child and Family in which 22 Women's Studies Centres participated and analysed 13,200 households, interviewed 39,600 respondents (with one-third of them being directly the girl children in the age group of 7–18 years), is a successful example for such collaborative research. Based on the same research-cum-action methodology, with a common questionnaire, common training of investigators and analysers, the project had produced 22 regional reports as well as an all-India report. The study had triggered not merely policies, but also social action by the government and other agencies, individuals, university-based Women's Studies Centres and NGOs.

One can cite many other such collaborative studies such as Functioning Women in Panchayats, Child Labour in Beedi-Making, Conditions of Women and Children in Displacement, etc. Such collaborative works, combining the benefits of micro studies with those of macro research, can help in fulfilling an important need in Women's Studies in India. There is an increasing lament that Women's Studies has not worked out a theory of its own; instead it still follows only the western theories many of which are based on premises that are not valid for India. Western feminism is seen to be essentially Anglo-Saxon, white, middle class and 'housewife'-oriented. Indian researchers and undergraduate students often apply them and find themselves stonewalled by the practical realities and the innate and inherent values they confront in their field area. They encounter differential wisdom in many Indian concepts and practices, though cited within patriarchal reasoning. Researchers have surmised that the western theories are often based on individualistic experiences and materialism, while the Indian concepts are community/ socially-oriented and aspire beyond to touch collective and spiritual bases. The dilemma of methodological choice can be turned to an advantage. Innovative, culture-specific Indian theory could evolve through micro researches within a macro understanding.

The university-based Women's Studies Centres are best equipped to construct such a knowledge base. They can, additionally, pool the resources of experts from a multidisciplinary context of various departments.

Curriculum and Teaching

One basic platform for bringing about a focus on gender issues is the classroom – whether it is in schools, colleges or professional institutions. Most social transformations have been effected in this country through classrooms. Looking back to the national movement or to recent social reforms agenda, students and teachers have been the most effective agents. Through syllabi and examination requirements, desirable change can be initiated.

Women's Studies and its values of gender equality and gender justice can be best brought to the younger generation through the curriculum. Such curriculum needs to be based on the theories, findings, data and methodologies that the research in Women's Studies has developed. Incorporating the output of research in the syllabus and updating the same at frequent intervals is thus a necessity. The teachers will keep themselves recharged with latest additions to the corpus of knowledge and also be equipped to crosscheck their own values and practices.

Women's Studies has occasionally forced the educational system to be self-reflexive about syllabus, textbook content and pedagogy. Impelled by the gathering energy of gendered analysis, school textbooks in particular are being reviewed frequently for their elitist and communal bias in terms of class, caste and religion. It is to the credit of Women's Studies that it has persuaded academics, the textbook writers and boards of studies to understand that the syllabi should be examined for gender gaps and gender biases. Moreover, the historical contribution of women and other neglected sections of the population is highlighted in the classrooms by sensitized teachers. Today, many educators agree that traditional values related to concepts of equality, rights and justice are to be revised from the point of view of gender and grassroots experience. By aiding this process, Women's Studies practitioners can bring about a veritable revolution through curriculum design.

As pedagogical methods are reviewed, one of the challenges before academic planners in higher education is how to constitute a link between research and classroom teaching. This is all the more important in the case of Women's Studies. One way to actualize the link would be to undertake, on a national plane, the following:

- Series of seminars;
- Formulation of new syllabi/model syllabus;
- Incorporation of Women's Studies themes in the syllabi of various courses as well as frequent updating of course content;
- Bring research findings into textbooks, teaching and examination system;
- Orientation and Refresher Courses in Women's Studies so as to enable teachers to have updated information and its theoretical contexts;
- Publication and dissemination of research;
- Devising different pedagogy in Women's Studies, which would include paper-reading sessions/discussions/seminars in classrooms; and
- Short field trips during vacations and reports on the same will give students first hand knowledge, on-the-job training and empirical learning. Such work can be a part of the internal assessment.

In advocating such new pedagogic practices in curriculum design and its delivery, a few obstacles are to be anticipated:

- Bureaucratic and procedural difficulties in revising curriculum;
- Vested interests in the form of publishers, authors and even teachers; and

- The inertia/unwillingness of teachers to keep up with updated knowledge systems and demonstrate new scholarship.

Solutions can be found. Here are a few suggestions:

- Overcome resistance through seminars and orientation/refresher courses where men and women teachers should participate;
- Overhaul the present procedures for syllabus making and the examination system; and
- Float independent interdisciplinary courses which allow space for research, term papers, field trips, training in feminist research methodology, seminars, etc.

Research is also basic to training and capacity building, both of which are strengthened by practical contact and impact analysis. It is demonstrable that research provides expertise as well as guides training programmes based on felt needs. Policy planners have realized that research data is often the most effective mid-course corrector. For achieving the strategic needs of women and meeting the long-term goals of the women's movement, research has proved an invaluable tool for enhancing schemes such as *Panchayat Raj*, micro-credit, skills upgradation and other managerial training. Women's Studies is the best available academic means for promoting sustainable patterns of gender equality and justice.

To sum up, education in general, and higher education in particular, is viewed as consisting of four major components – teaching, research, training and community action (extension). Women's Studies, more than any other discipline, involves all the four fields. As a new discipline, research is fundamental to it as it brings fresh insights, theories, approaches, methodology and a gendered worldview. The Women's Studies Research Centres, NGOs, individual scholars, the school and the university systems are in the continuous process of sifting diverse material. But it is within the university system, where the four components inform, feed and interact with one another, that a sustained and mutually beneficial process can be formalized.

2

Women's Studies in Indian Universities

The Changing Parameters of Struggle

Veena Poonacha

Describing the political impulses that led to the development of women's studies scholarship/programmes within and outside the university system, this paper underscores some of the changing parameters of the struggle confronting it. These challenges arise partly because of the current policies that support privatization/globalization of education and cutbacks in state spending, and partly because of the growing conservatism in the universities. Both these trends have serious implications for the future of women's studies in the university system, its disciplinary boundaries, theoretical frameworks and its political potential. Elaborating on these challenges, the paper raises the following questions: (1) What has been the contribution of women's studies scholarship/programmes in the university system to the growth of

This is an abridged version of the paper entitled 'Women's Studies in Indian Universities: Current Concerns' in *Economic and Political Weekly*, 28 June 2003, pp. 2653–58.

activism? (2) Does the current explosion of theoretical works on women dilute the political content of women's studies? (3) Despite the expansion of women's studies programmes in the university system, why is it that the radicalism of women's studies scholarship is seemingly on the decline? These questions have, undoubtedly, been debated over the years, but they are vital because of the resurgence of masculine values in all areas of civil society and the virulent silencing of women and their values. Additionally, despite the inroads made by feminist scholarship, women's studies still remains marginal to the predominantly patriarchal set-up of the academia. These patriarchal structures continue to influence feminist scholarship by determining the criteria for scholarship and also exercising controls over appointments of personnel in women's studies departments.

Entry of Women's Studies into Universities

Pioneered by the SNDT Women's University, Mumbai, women's studies entered the university system at a point of time when there was discussion on the relevance of separate institutions of higher education for women. Through, research, documentation and action, women's studies was expected to give new direction to university education. Its founders envisaged that it would help to breach the academic isolation of the universities and make them instruments of social transformation. Additionally, women had increasingly recognized the need to reclaim space to conceptualize and articulate their knowledge and experiences from the standpoint of their lived experiences. Without such validation it was easier for patriarchal societies to enforce the subordination of women (Poonacha, 1999).

National and International Call for Women's Studies

From this tiny step forward, women's studies grew in the university system mainly because of the pressure exerted by the women's movement. Conceding that there was evidence that the status of women in the world was low, the United Nations declared 1975–85 as the International Women's Decade and organized the World Conference on Women in Mexico (1975). The World Plan of Action formulated during the conference called for research investigations, documentation and analyses into those processes in society that create structures of gender inequalities. This initiative taken by the United Nations was in keeping with the vision encoded in the various international documents on human rights such as the Universal Declaration of Human Rights (1948), the International Covenant of Civil and Political Rights, and the International Covenant of Economic, Social and Cultural Rights (Fraser, 1987: 1–68).

In India, the National Commission on the Status of Women was set up to examine the status of women in the country and their problems. Responding to the findings of the *Towards Equality Report* (1974), the Government of India drew up a Plan of Action. The research component of the plan was expected to uncover the prevailing inequities in society. Taking up the challenge, the Indian Council of Social Science Research (ICSSR) pioneered women's studies research to bridge the existing knowledge gaps on women's status and to develop intervention strategies. Responding to these developments, the University Grants Commission (UGC) established Women's Studies Centres/Cells within the university system.

Women's Studies Departments in the Three Decades

The rapid expansion of women's studies programmes within the university system suggests a measure of their acceptance by the academic community. This however serves to hide the subtle ways in which feminist thought and actions are sabotaged. For, apart from the perennial shortage of funds and bureaucratic tangles, their existence seems to depend upon the goodwill of the UGC and the predominantly male university managements. This is not to imply that its theories, research methods and legitimate critique of mainstream disciplines are taken seriously. Dismissed as polemical, the radical politics of the discipline is eroded. This, however, is not to imply that there are takers for research on gender issues. Influenced by the agenda of funding agencies, there is a proliferation of research on gender issues that do not necessarily subscribe to the central vision of women's studies. Treating gender as one more category of enquiry along with other categories of class, caste politics, these studies do not question the assumption of male domination that underlies mainstream disciplines.

Additionally, the institutionalization of women's studies has created its own compulsions of meeting certain standards of theoretical sophistication. These standards are largely determined by male academics and in trying to meet these standards, women's studies scholars tend to forget that the political aims of women's studies scholarship. Women's studies, thus, becomes another discipline – a venue for career growth rather than a potentially explosive political agenda.

When such a potential revolutionary discipline is introduced through official decrees, there is the additional danger of its subversion. Many of the departments have been opened in areas that did not have a history of women's oppositional politics. This means that very often the criterion for the appointment of faculty members in women's studies departments is that they are women and are willing to shoulder additional responsibilities. Indubitably, these women accept the additional charge from a commitment for women, but they are often unable to appreciate the political content of the discipline; or even if they do, they are not able to draw upon the rich experience of feminist activism to gain insights and creatively enrich their teaching/research programmes.

An equally contentious issue is whether women's studies should develop as a separate discipline or if it should be a part of the mainstream disciplines. Arguments for and against both these positions have their strengths and weaknesses. To make women studies a separate discipline is to acknowledge its unique history as well as its theoretical and methodological insights. Nevertheless, it could also lead to its marginalization. Similarly, attempts to mainstream women's studies have met with marginal success. In a survey conducted by the Research Centre for Women's Studies (RCWS), SNDT Women's University, Mumbai, it was found that despite the presence of a strong women's movement in western India, the discipline had made very little indent in the mainstream disciplines. It was not given due importance in the curriculum and the classroom teaching practices left much to be desired. Additionally, it had made no impact on mainstream disciplines. At best, women's studies perspective was viewed as one of the many mutually exclusive perspectives; at worst it was dismissed as the ranting of disgruntled women (Agarwal et al., 2002).

The Growing Divide: Women's Studies and Gender Politics

Given its historical roots as the academic arm of the women's movement, it is not unreasonable to expect that women's studies would retain its link with the movement. This interface of theory and action is under stress partly because of the changes in its theoretical framework and partly because of the prevailing political climate. At the outset, as women's studies challenged and criticized the pretensions of 'grand' theories and demonstrated that the universal claims underlying such theories were deceptive and based on false abstractions. This critique of 'grand' theories translated itself to the emphasis on political action, avoidance of abstract theorizing, based on an understanding of the experiential basis of knowledge (Barrett and Philips, 1992: 1–9). During this period (i.e., the 1970s), women's studies theorizing sought to understand the roots of women's subordination. Was it biologically ordained or rooted in the process of gender socialization? What was the economic basis of women's subordination and sexual division of work? Could women's subordination be traced to production or reproduction systems? The emerging feminist voices, because of their different ideological and theoretical underpinnings, came up with different explanations. Broadly, it identified the prevailing production, reproduction and sexual relationships as the foundational basis of women's inequalities.

These theories were based on the assumption of a fixed female identity, which subsumed other forms of competing identities. Therefore, feminist political action sought to ensure better legal protections for women and stringent implementation of law while dealing with gender-specific crimes of rape, domestic violence and dowry deaths; it also aimed at enabling women to access the existing goods and services in society. The political confrontations of the women's movement aimed at making the state more accountable for the welfare of women. The dilemma for feminists was the basis on which to ground their political action: if they asked for gender-neutral laws/social policies on the ground that women were the same as men, the prevailing socio-economic inequalities would prevent them from realizing the formal equality granted in the Indian Constitution and in the various instruments of human rights; if they asked for special protections on the basis of women's differences, the existing gender roles would be justified.

By the 1980s, feminist theorizing increasingly questioned the androgynous model of human nature; it aimed at recovering women's culture and critiqued masculine ideology by pointing to the interconnections between women's subordination and the destruction of the environment. These ideas infused the various environmental, peace and anti-nuke movements across the world. This rich variety of feminist thought percolated into art, culture, religion and literature to resonate in multiple voices. Women of colour and from developing countries pointed to the ways in which race, class and gender intersected in complex ways to modify their lives. These ideas breached the private/public, mind/body, nature/culture divide in western theorizing (Lamphere, 1987: 11–33). It indicated that the habit of thinking in hierarchical binary opposites was responsible for the 'othering' of women, races and ethnic minorities. Women's studies scholarship has reached new theoretical heights. It has problematized the concepts of sex, gender, power, identity, agency, etc.

Paradoxically, these developments also challenged the foundational assumptions of feminist thought of the 1970s. Giving up the overgeneralizing and overambitious models of liberal, radical and Marxist/socialist feminist analysis, women's studies scholarship opted for an analysis of the local, culturally-specific and particular. Drawing closer to the post-structural/postmodern positions, these studies became deconstructive. Seeking to destabilize, subvert and reverse some of the hierarchical binary oppositions (including those implicating sex and gender) prevailing in the early feminist thought, these studies questioned the overconfident distinction of the earlier decade between sex and gender identities.

These theoretical questions are taking place in the context of the changed socio-economic and political realities. The deification of free market economies since the 1990s has eroded the regulatory powers of the state; it has also undermined the notions of a welfare state, resulting in the whittling down of the social sector spending. The women's movement is thus confronted, on the one hand, with the overwhelming poverty of local communities, undermining of people's livelihood rights and the destruction of the environment; and on the other, with the rising conservatism and backlash against women. Grappling with these diverse factors, feminist politics is in flux: past strategies aimed at the state are ineffective, as an unresponsive state no longer maintains the fiction of fairness and justice. Additionally, such right-wing ideologies have insidiously permeated educational institutions, policies and ideologies. Apart from undermining the secular fabric of the country, the outreach of right-wing ideologies has serious implications for women's studies as a discipline. Given that the discipline is interdisciplinary and draws its theories from many sources, how do we ensure that it remains secular and does not succumb to right-wing propaganda? The resolution of this question is not as easy as it appears – neither strategically nor theoretically. The strategic difficulty of spear-heading a homogenous feminist position comes about because women from diverse political affiliations have entered the bandwagon of women's studies and are divided by their class/caste/religious identities. Theoretically, feminist commitment to a secular and progressive ideology aimed at establishing women's equality is weakened by its recognition of a relativist position of truth. If no truth is non-negotiable, how can we claim the falsity of non-secular ideologies? Today, they are confronted with ideological fragmentation and the interpolation of identity politics. If women are not a homogenous group, is there no possibility of coming together. How do we accommodate differences so that there is also a possibility of solidarity among women?

The growth of religious fundamentalism can be seen as a response to globalization. Confronted with the rapid changes in society, people are turning towards religion and other ethnic identities for solace and support. Patriarchal in its essence, these fundamentalist discourses target women. The failure of the women's movement to effectively address this issue has fragmented the movement. While it was easy to condemn religious bigotry, there is this question of feminist response to spirituality and the need for cultural roots for children. Both these issues are subtly eroding feminist radicalism.

To begin with, feminist response to spirituality becomes extremely problematic because, on the one hand, patriarchal religions tend to espouse misogynist values and, on the other, religions also provide women with the necessary socio-cultural spaces. While religions encapsulate some of the highest aspirations of humanity and have liberating potential, it cannot be denied that these seemingly liberating trends are ideas that subvert the political challenge of feminism. Representing a deeply individualistic vision of transformation, religions see liberation as an introverted process and in the final analysis uphold the economic and political status quo. And yet would it be possible to deny human quest for spirituality? Would it be possible to visualize a feminist utopia without ascribing to and defining feminist ethics? And can the ethics arising out of feminist action gain wide acceptance without faith in some form of spirituality?

Could these trends that subvert feminist politics be seen as a backlash arising out of the current trends of economic liberalization and privatization? Apart from undermining the economic basis of realizing gender equality by pushing women into the unorganized sector, these trends are deflecting attention from the failures of the state to create a just social order by targeting women.

The Implications of the Growing Divide between Theory and Praxis

Women's studies is challenged by many forces that threaten its disciplinary grids and political visions. Apart from the subtle erosion of its disciplinary and ideological boundaries by the onslaught of identity politics and right-wing ideologies, there is a subtle process of patriarchal backlash confronting the discipline. One never knows whether the current preference for the use of nomenclature 'gender studies' instead of 'women's studies' is appropriate. Does the term 'gender studies' broadens the scope of the discipline to include a critical understanding of the ways in which men's identities are also structured or does it in someway undermine the existing disciplinary grids? Recognizing the politics of knowledge generation, women's studies scholars questioned the notion of objectivity of truth. They argued that mainstream disciplines developed male perspectives of reality. Women's studies was seen as the only intellectual space for women's experiences and knowledge. Therefore, does the seemingly objective approach suggested in the term 'gender studies' make invisible the privileges that masculinity confers on men over women?

Again, much of women's studies scholarship is determined by the availability of funds. Given that funding agencies (both national and international) are different faces of patriarchy, could this dependency undermine feminist radicalism? This fear of co-optation arises from the ways in which funding agencies and development bodies have appropriated the feminist language. But somewhere along the process, the stir for women's equality is forgotten. Therefore, can the call for women's empowerment, given by development agencies, change the prevailing gender equation or does it merely lead limit itself to women's upliftment? Encoded in the concept of equality is the call for structural changes in the prevailing social order, while the concept of empowerment, on the other hand, speaks of enabling women to fight for their rights. Does this mean that women's legitimate rights as citizens will not be given to them unequivocally and without a struggle? If, in keeping with the promises of the Constitution, the principle of women's equality was non-negotiable, then surely it would be simpler for the state to change the prevailing structures of inequalities by enforceable legislations than to expect women to expend their energies struggling for minimum rights and entitlements.

Entrenched in the university system, women's studies scholarship has given rise to hierarchies among scholars. These scholars face contradictory pulls. They are expected to produce high quality research and, at the same time, are expected to bring about social change through activism and extension activities. The current expectations from women's studies centres and cells are not easy to fulfil in an environment that is bogged down with bureaucratic tangles and non-availability of funds. Therefore, how effectively will women's studies centres/cells fulfil their obligations to the women's movement? Further, how will women's studies scholarship fulfil its role and strengthen the feminist action? Increasingly influenced by postmodern thought, the current women's studies scholarship has questioned the previously held definitions of power/powerless, sexuality and fixed gender identities. The challenge to 'grand' theories has developed a rich understanding of the heterogeneity of human experiences. Nonetheless, the fear is, whether this legitimate critiquing of the shortfalls of the theories of the 1970s undermined the political vision of feminism's original project? Has the relativist and experiential basis of knowledge undermine the goal of accurate and systematic knowledge? And, has the focus on historical heterogeneity obscured the traditional male privilege in the construction of knowledge? Furthermore, can feminist politics survive the theoretical onslaught on the assumption of the absence of a fixed female identity? And, without a shared vision of political change, can the movement oppose the current backlash against women? Thus, by failing to acknowledge the legacy of the earlier feminist struggles, are the feminists of the present generation doomed to reinvent their battles? And, how far has women's studies programmes fulfilled their role as the repository of women's knowledge?

References

Agarwal, Nisha et al. (2002) Women's Studies Programmes in the Humanities and Social Sciences Departments of SNDT Women's University, Tata Insitute of Social Sciences and the University of Mumbai, Mumbai: Research Centre for Women's Studies.

Barrett, Michele and Anne Philips (eds) (1992) 'Introduction', in *Destabilizing Theory: Contemporary Feminist Debates*, Cambridge: Polity Press, Reprint 1993, pp. 1–9.

Farnham, Christie (ed.) (1987) 'Introduction: Same or Different?', in *Impact of Feminist Research in the Academy*, Bloomington: Indiana University Press, pp. 1–11.

Fraser, Arvonne S. (1987) *The UN Decade for Women: Documents and Dialogue*, London: Westview Press, pp. 1–68.

Lamphere, Louise (1987) 'Feminism and Anthropology: The Struggle to Reshape Our Thinking about Gender', in Christie Farnham (ed.), *Impact of Feminist Research in the Academy*, Bloomington: Indiana University Press, pp. 11–35.

Nicholson, Linda J. (ed.) (1990) 'Introduction', in *Feminism and Postmodernism*, New York: Routledge, pp. 1–16.

Poonacha, Veena (1999) *Understanding Women's Studies*, Contributions to Women's Studies Series 11, Mumbai: Research Centre for Women's Studies.

3

Girl Child in India

Changing Perceptions

Vibha Chaturvedi and Nilima Srivastava

Women's Studies and Development Centre undertook a research study by involving six Women's Studies Centre from North India (Delhi, Kurukshetra, Jaipur, Shimla, Jammu and Yamuna Nagar) on 'Attitudinal Difference towards Girl Child in Selected Districts of North India'. This chapter is based on the recommendations and suggestions that have come from all the institutions involved in the research.

This research has thrown up some interesting and significant insights on the status of the girl child in North India. Some of its findings such as less preference for girl child by parents or greater chance of the girl child facing withdrawal from education or health facilities in the event of a choice between the boy and the girl child, confirm to findings of already existing studies. However, in most cases, it was difficult to create common patterns across the areas of study. The data showed a diffused spread of choices with respect to education and health of the girl child and differing perceptions about the status of the girl child among the girls themselves as well as their parents. Although the rural and urban areas also do not show a clear pattern with respect to different indices about the girl child's status, on certain variables, greater vulnerability of the girl child in urban setting is visible.

When regional trends are considered, girls are found most unwanted by parents in general and maternal grandparents specially, from Delhi and Jammu in particular, with higher percentages from urban areas in this regard. Girls from Kurukshetra feel most unhappy about being born as a girl in their family. Difference in rearing between boys and girls in the family is felt most by the girls from Jaipur followed by girls from Shimla. School drop out cases among girls from urban areas show apathy towards going back to school system because they no longer feel motivated to study, as most strongly stated by girls from Delhi while the drop out cases from rural sample point out distance to school as the main cause, as stated in largest percentages by girls from rural Jaipur.

The recent concern for gender equity and equality is based on a wide gap in the status of men and women in society. In Indian society also, girls and women face discrimination in all spheres. They are given secondary status in the family than the boys and other male members. When a girl sees her mother looking after the household chores, like cleaning, washing, cooking, baby care, etc., and deprives herself of comforts of life, she also imbibes these notions. Girls also observe the modesty and submissiveness of their mothers in the family environment. The institution of marriage further confirms the low status of the girl when she has to accept the subservient standing in the family hierarchy and poorer allocation of resources to her. Persisting gender inequalities, existing cultural beliefs and practices permeate into almost every aspect of the growing girl's socio-cultural milieu and even her own sense of judgement. The family value system does not provide for any revolt or liberation. Thus, gender disparity replicates itself from generation to generation, violating the rights of a girl child and impeding her full development.

With the awakening of concern for human rights and lobbying by women activists, efforts are being made by the governments of various countries and other international bodies to ameliorate the condition of the girl child in society. Every instrument created for women has a special focus on the girl child highlighting the severity of the action required.

Indian society displays a contradiction in handling women in its fold – on one hand women are put on a pedestal and on the other hand we find declining sex ratio, more alarmingly amongst the lower age group of 0–6 years, which a pointer towards the violation of the right to their existence. Severity of the situation has been taken note of by the Indian government and over a period of time special corrective measures have been taken.

Despite various measures initiated by the government through various programmes and policies in providing health, nutritional and educational inputs to girls, their position is not likely to change unless social bias against girls, which is deep-rooted in our society, is removed through social education. Efforts are needed to mitigate age-old beliefs and practices that lower the status of girls by way of their re-socialization in society.

It is against this backdrop that a research project to study the status of girl child in North India was undertaken on the recommendation of the Advisory Committee of the Women Studies Development Centre (WSDC) of University of Delhi, focusing on the two objectives of National Policy for the Empowerment of Women (2001), viz., (i) assessing changing societal attitude and community practices by active involvement of both men and women; and (ii) elimination of discrimination and all forms of violence against girls and women. Four Women's Studies Centres in other universities and an NGO also came forward to join hands with WSDC in this endeavour.

Based on the findings of the study, the following key recommendations can be suggested to lessen the prevalent gender discrimination in our society:

1. *Creating mass awareness:* The study shows that out of 1,200 respondents contacted for data collection, more than half do not know about the prevalence of low sex ratio in the country. The percentage is even lower when the query relates to abysmal situation in the national capital Delhi.

   This is in spite of the efforts to tap media for creating awareness. Mothers of the sample are found to be ignorant in largest percentages. Advertisements and programmes on radio,

TV and hoardings showing 'Save the Girl Child' were seen during data collection but the low percentage of knowledgeable respondents points to the fact that the strategy remains largely ineffective. Affected sections of society, therefore, needs to be properly targeted for the message to sink in.

Advocacy for valuing girl children is a requirement for success and relates to intervention through community involvement and participation. Thus, gender sensitization of family and community is urgently required.

For creating awareness the suggested methods are:

(a) *Hand-holding with bodies of local governance:* Panchayats and Municipal Corporations to be involved in sensitizing the community about the fallouts of discrimination against the girl child by employing situation-based intervention. Their role can be to highlight and reward girl achievers of their constituency.

(b) *Media:* Media, especially TV, is a very forceful tool to create awareness and bring about change in attitudes of people on a large scale through innovative programming, and spreading the message of protecting the girl child. It can play a vital role by projecting positive images of women and girls in their programmes and writings. Media can highlight the repercussions of discriminating against the women and how it affects men as well. Instead of highlighting female sexuality, media should portray women as socially and economically productive citizens of the country. It should also depict women as achievers in their own right and showcase successful women as role models.

2. *Change in socialization process:* The field data clearly suggests that in spite of change in attitude towards both boys and girls, socialization process is still entrapped in the age-old ideals and stereotypes based on patriarchal values. For instance, we do find change in attitude regarding the desired qualities in girls and boys that are common to both (hardworking, intelligent, obedient, etc.), but the desired skills for girls and boys still remain widely diverse. Girls are expected to be deft in household chores like cooking, sweeping and washing, while boys are expected be able to handle tough situations, possess

good communication skills, taking up responsibilities that require treading out of the four walls of the house and also good in sports. Thus, the 'feminine' and 'masculine' constructs are conforming to the patriarchal mindset. Data does point towards seeds of change where a handful of respondents have desired boys to be lending help in carrying out household responsibilities but that is more of an exception than the rule.

Sustained efforts to address stereotypical socialization patterns through education, both at school and higher education system, political leadership, religious leaders and celebrities and media can be instrumental in promoting values that do not replicate age-old socialization practices. All segments of society should work towards promoting equal opportunities with respect to educational endowments, health and nutrition, physical and emotional needs and harnessing professional aspirations in both boys and girls.

3. *Democratization of institutions in society leading to women's participation in decision-making:* Girls in negligible percentages are found to be part of decision-making. Democratization should start from the institution of family. More than 80 per cent of the girls admit that the father or the mother is the sole decision-making body. Joint decisions are prevalent only in small percentage of families and that too in urban settings. Although signs of change are evident from the data but these are far from satisfactory. Girls' participation in decision-making within family as well as about their lives need to be encouraged.

   Institutions that work in tandem with community people like Resident Welfare Associations, Panchayats, Municipal Corporations, etc., should be made to play more pro-active role in bringing about change in the outlook of people. Other institutions operative in society, viz., bureaucracy, political system, judiciary, police all should be made more transparent and accountable vis-à-vis gender concerns.

   Socio-religious, political, economic and other systems that in totality effect socialization process should lead by example in functioning in a more democratic way, involving greater participation of women, and facilitating them to move up to higher decision-making positions.

4. *Gender-sensitive education system:* Education system, both at school and higher levels, should promote gender sensitivity amongst students and the teaching community. It is crucial to eliminate gender bias from the contents of textbooks but it is equally important to transect the curriculum by the teachers in a gender-neutral manner. Rights of girl child and legal literacy should be part of curriculum for both boys and girls. With enhanced self-esteem, girls will value themselves and, therefore, remain open to acquire educational skills eventually leading to their empowerment and exercising constitutionally guaranteed rights that the study has pointed out, are not being put into effect.
5. *Capacitated schooling for girls:* The study shows that the most of the girls who have dropped out of schools want to get back to studies. Major reasons are parental neglect, household responsibilities and no teaching in school. These need to be addressed. Well-provided infrastructure, amiable school environment, innovative school timings, material support for education of girls and vocation or skill-based education coupled with employment will all be instrumental in enhancing education to girls. Linking open school system to school drop outs, making curriculum relevant with emphasis on life skill education, and making school education accessible and useful for the girls who had to drop out will go long a way in retaining girls in formal education system.

   As evident from the data, most of the girls dropped out between 6th and 8th class. Opening of more schools at middle and higher secondary level and ensuring 100 per cent enrolment by involving community groups and community leaders will help in overcoming the barrier of lower retention of girls in middle and secondary classes.

   The study further points out that in urban settings especially, girls take care of their younger siblings and shoulder other household responsibilities leading to their exclusion from formal schooling. Provision of adequate child care support, especially for low socio-economic strata, will ensure continuation of education of girls.

   Distance to school and no teaching in school have also been cited as reasons by girls, more by girls from rural settings, for not being able to continue their studies. This should be addressed by opening new schools and providing transportation to school. Administration needs to ensure that teaching is regularly undertaken in schools. Lack of human resources and infrastructural support should be high on mind when addressing the issue of low educational endowments by girls. Strengthening of interlinkages between various government agencies and involvement of community leaders will help in overcoming the problem of low enrolment and retention of girls in school. Remedial classes and bridge courses will help girls to make up for their lost years of schooling.

Thus, strategies for increasing participation of girls in school should include a wide range of interventions at various levels, viz., community, family and the girl child herself.

As the data clearly show that the society is open to the idea of economic independence of girls. Education should be linked with vocational training in schools so that girls can make use of that learning later in life for being economically independent.

6. *Dissemination of government programmes and schemes:* Large percentages of mothers and fathers too do not know about the programmes and schemes for girls that the central and state governments have initiated. A very small percentage of parents was found to have actually made use of these provisions, making implementation of the schemes ineffective. It is found that the parents face several difficulties to access these. Thus, the most urgent need is to make the process of obtaining benefits of the existing programmes and schemes for the girl child more people-friendly.

   Moreover, wider publicity of government schemes and programmes among people is extremely important so that people can benefit from what evolve at the planning and policy level.

7. *Bhagidaari on the issue of girl child:* Various positive indications show that the society is open to changing its attitude towards girls. Initiation of concept of 'Bhagidaari' with respect to the issue of girl child will also ensure involvement of common people and seriousness of the government in mitigating discriminatory practices against the girls and women.

Conclusion

For indicators of changed status, it is found that admired qualities that are advocated for the girls and boys are roughly the same. The need to be educated is strongly recommended for both boys and girls. Enrolment and attendance of girls in schools are high and almost the same as that of the boys. Rewards and punishment for children are also the same irrespective of the gender. In fact, 'no reward' category has higher percentages for girls. Economic independence of girls is expressed to be essential by both the parents and the girls themselves. Parents say that there is improvement in the status of girls in society from what it used to be when they were small.

A question then arises: Does the subordination of women continue to be as strongly rooted as before or can one notice changes in this regard? Based on the girls child project, one can say that girls continue to remain in a subordinate position to boys. This is evident in their various educational, health and other socio-cultural indices within the family and the benefits that they receive vis-à-vis their brothers often in a more subtle way. However, the study also shows that a fair degree of change is evident in the position of the girl child in the family based on these very criteria, when compared to the past.

Part II

Expanding Horizon: Touching Multiple Concerns

4

Women, Literature and Culture in India

Multiple Perspectives

Malashri Lal

> We are talking of women writers who are writing with a definite perspective – on some democratic values, women's rights, against fundamentalism et al. We are guided by certain principles. And those women who respect these values can come together. They may have differences among themselves – how they write, in terms of language, caste. But those can be overcome. The idea is to form a broader base.
>
> —Volga

Gender issues can, and should, cut across class and language differences in order to lead towards feminist frames for Indian literature. The 'oppositional aesthetics' that may perceived between, say, Indian writing in English on the one hand and orality/literature from marginalized communities, on the other, is an artificial one, because at the core of both is the awareness of woman's disadvantageous condition within patriarchy. It is possible to incorporate the aesthetics of both within the larger need for a coalition politics in feminist theory.

Mulitilingual and Multicultural Contexts

In working towards a formulation of Indian feminism, one runs into several obstacles. Quite evidently there can be no monolithic concept of literary feminism in a country with such a diverse range of languages and dialects. At the Neemrana festival of Indian literature, sponsored by the Indian Council for Cultural Relations (ICCR), the media played upon a so-called divide between English and the regional languages. Actually there was considerable debate among the writers of 'bhasha' literature – as the edited recordings demonstrate. U.R. Ananthamurthy makes a distinction between a 'house language' (*mannimatur*) (84), 'office language' and 'street language,' Paul Zacharia speaks of the metropolis and the village, and Srilal Shukla of the 'many Hindis' (82). Those who write in English had their own declarations of divisions. The diaspora being an obvious category which Khushwant Singh labelled as 'five star exile' (69), others such as Farukh Dhondy countered by speaking of the angst and anxieties of alienation. V.S. Naipaul, the star of the show, and certainly a trial blazer in socio-critical fiction, declared that a creative writer belongs nowhere and everywhere. Was gender a category for any of them? Marginally so. Nabanita Deb Sen said as much (19). The intersection of gender and nation takes the debates over English and regional languages to yet another plane. Such scenarios are symptomatic of the troubles that beset thinking on Indian feminism, and yet I believe we must persevere lest the term 'feminism' gets buried under the weight of many other isms, and gender issues get subsumed under supposedly 'larger concerns' of postcolonialism and nation–state agendas.

I place in this paper into what I consider as some directions towards a feminist theory for India, which must have cross-cutting themes and contexts. Within my identification of significant issues, I will suggest literary examples from English and several other Indian languages, though I have neither the time nor the linguistic capability to examine all these in detail in the current paper.

The Notion of Home

At the beginning of the last century, Rabindranath Tagore's novel made popular the phrase '*Ghare Baire*' (*The Home and the World*) which contained the famous line, 'In trying to manufacture a helpmate, we spoil a wife' (*The Home and the World*, trans. Surendranath Tagore and revised by Rabindranath Tagore, London: Macmillan, 1919, rpt. 1961: 272). Towards the end of the century, Salman Rushdie's concept of 'imaginary homelands' pushed the geographical and political space into the cartography of the mind. With the dawn of the new millennium and the advent of globalization, the term 'multilocality' has gained currency. Today, most of us can probably claim more than one named territory as 'home,' and claim it in more than one language, bringing into play a complex matrix of references by which we attempt to define our 'identity'. The opening chapter of Amartya Sen's book, *Identity and Violence*, draws notice to the fragments and provisional attachments that are perpetually shifting in an individual: 'In our normal lives, we see ourselves as members of a variety of groups – we belong to all of them. A person's citizenship, residence, geographic origin, gender, class, politics, profession, employment, food habits, sports interests, taste in music, social commitments, etc., make us members of a variety of groups' (p. 5).

We could also turn to literary critic Chandra Talpade Mohanty's formulation in which being 'at home' refers to 'the familiar, safe, protected boundaries' whereas 'not being home' is a matter of realizing that home was an 'illusion' of coherence. Through this critical shift from physical location to psychic interpretation we have bridged the gap between subjectivity and agency. Further, we succeed in wrenching from the brick-and-mortar definition of home the possibility of a metaphysical home that clings to the person who sets out.

To what extent does women's writing address this issue of home? A case in point could be Anita Desai's *Clear Light of Day* (1980) which prefigures many feminist avowals which came into prominence in later decades. A novel spanning the partition years in Delhi, it works through the metaphor of Bim's crumbling ancestral home to reconfigure the fragments of the nation, the family and the individual. A single, self-supporting college teacher, Bim's knowledge of history produces a wry commentary upon the factious developments that claim the nation's freedom even as circumstances bind people to fetters of memory and lost communities. But Bim's singleness has little in common with concepts such as the 'unitary woman' of Margaret Atwood or the self-reflexivity of Doris Lessing's *Martha Quest*.

Towards the middle of *Clear Light of Day*, Bim asserts her choices as being pro-family and in adherence with social responsibility: 'I won't marry,' she added, very firmly ... 'I won't,' repeated Bim, adding, 'I shall never leave Baba and Raja and Mira-*masi* .... I shall work – I shall do things,' she went on, 'I shall earn my own living – and look after Mira-*masi* and Baba and – and be independent' (140). Such declaration of solidarity with the less capable members of the extended family speaks for the values of the 'great Indian middle class' that Pavan Verma has analysed with acumen. Bim is not a figure of martyrdom but a person who negotiates her place in the kinship net. In such 'compromise', which does not hold a negative image in India, traditions of the past attempt to conjoin with the promise of the future, despite struggles and tensions.

To my mind, Anita Desai's use of English and the location of her novel in the educated middle class of the country places no limitations on her enquiries into women's identities and the notion of 'belongingness'. From the political milieu of partition to the personal spaces, the tone of displaced identity is retained in many languages. Given the social practice of 'kanyadaan' and attendant rituals of the transference of a girl from a natal to a marital home, stories abound about the process. Several examples of women's poetry demonstrate a desire for 'reterritorialization' cultural space, create home as space of openness and creativity.

The protagonist of Anamika's poem 'Without a Place' is taught homelessness from her childhood:

> When hair, women and nails
> fall from their place
> they remain nowhere
> So our Sanskrit teacher
> would analyse a verse
> and panic would freeze
> us girls
> in our places.
>
> Place? What is a place?
> This we had learned
> In our very first class!
>
> We remembered every moment
> of our first classes

Ram, go to school!
Radha, cook a meal!
Ram, come, have a sugar-cake!
Radha, sweep the house!
Your brother will sleep now,
go and make his bed!
Wonderful! A new home!
Ram, look, this is your room!'
'And mine?'
'Silly girl,
Girls are air, sunshine, earth,
they don't have a home!'
Those who have no home
what place can they have? ...

The Autobiographical Impulse

According to Urvashi Butalia, 'Women's autobiographies, memoirs, first person narratives have become an important genre of writing and publishing in recent times. Many such accounts have existed for years, but are only now being published, or translated, while there are others that are being reissued because of the renewed interest in these writings as presenting an alternative view of history ... . Virtually all autobiographical accounts by women describe how difficult they find the act of writing. This isn't something specific to women of course, for writing may be difficult for anyone, but in many ways, it is symptomatic of the condition of women. Leisure and the space to write are difficult to find in the daily grind of life, and if these spaces are available, then the act of writing itself is derided – for after all, women are often asked, what will you write? WHY do you want to write? ... . Rashsundari Debi taught herself to read and write in secret – inspired by watching her husband read, this young wife turned every available space to advantage in her project to read and write. The result was her life story, Amar Jiban, recently translated into English (*Words to Win: The Making of Amar Jiban, a Modern Autobiography* by Tanika Sarkar, New Delhi: Kali for Women, 2000). Binodini Dasi, well-known actress on the Bengali stage in the early twentieth century, wrote two autobiographical accounts, *Amar Katha* and *Amar Abinetri Jiban* (translated into English by Rimli Bhattacharya), the latter describing her long relationship with Bengali theatre. Not only was Binodini's work and career exceptional, but she herself was an unusual woman, but much of the time, as Rimli Bhattacharya points out, her insights into theatre history are relegated to the footnotes of history, rather than forming its substance. Pandita Ramabai, so central to questioning Brahminical patriarchy in Maharashtra, suffered the same fate and it is in her carefully written accounts of high caste Hindu women that we begin to see some insights into what she had to tackle.'

Butalia continues with the opinion: And these small acts of heroism, significant though they are, are available only to those women who have the luxury of education, and who can write. For others, it is difficult to find both words and spaces. Thankfully, because there now exists a hospitable environment in which women can and do actually write, and their writings are received well, and read, this acts as an encouragement to others who may wish to write but do not have the means to. In recent years, some effort has been put into recording the stories of women on the margins of society, who have been unable to take up the pen, but who do have the words. The story of Viramma, a Tamil Dalit woman, recorded and told by Jean Luc and Josiane Racine (*Viramma*), stands out as an important example. The story of Baby Haldar, a housemaid compelled into servitude (Zubaan), is a prominent success in this genre.

Autobiography can be thinly disguised as fiction. To Bama, autobiography, as in *Karukku*, is imaginative narrative, orality and myth fused into a literary document. It frightened her father about reprisals from an angered male dominated community, but she felt liberated from the constrictions of silence. Brute force and violence are terrible tools of control on women. How different as a literary expression is this from Kamala Das' 'My Story'? The point is about a female experience if marginalization and neglect, violence to the body and the intellect, the denial of creative avenues and the story of oppression. I refer you the epigraph of this paper which stresses the need for women's solidarity.

Writing the Body: Women and Violence

Taking a leaf from Althuser's theories of ISA, the family in India may often be shown as an oppressive state structure with authority figures dominating over personal choice. Arundhati Roy refuses to be called a 'writer-activist', saying that the term reminds her of a 'sofa-bed'. Yet hybridity is the key to her literary performance no matter in which genre. She writes about families with equal concern for the displaced people in the Narmada valley or the Kerala of her novel *The God of Small Things*. Surely one can decipher common ground in the subjects that the Dalit writers are concerned with: psychic and physical control, poverty, denial of rights, violence, caste-based humiliations. All of these see the individual within the real and imagined corpus of society, history, myth and belief systems specific to a location in India.

Arundhati Roy's novel drives home the point that even in the contemporary scenario the Indian dependence on the familial and societal systems is obvious. *The God of Small Things* is a novel about the intersection of caste and gender. In a curious inversion of the usual hegemonic pattern, here it is Velutha, the physically strong man who is oppressed by the so-called weaker but economically powerful women. Caste intervenes in the hierarchies of patriarchy – a uniquely Indian condition. A male from an 'untouchable' caste is vulnerable to individual, and even more so, institutional authority which is ranged against him through traditional causalities.

In the final chapters of *The God of Small Things* there is the account of unspeakable horrors foisted upon Velutha's broken body. The report against him had been lodged by Baby Kochamma, an upper caste woman, to avenge the transgression that had led to the intimacy of Velutha and Ammu. The police heeded the command of the persons in power. Yet, there is another dimension. The brutality with which the police batter the dark man is not a simple call of duty but the expression of class hatred at the dare of Velutha's physical act with an upper class woman. Embedded in Roy's gut wrenching description is also the suggestion of the policemen's male envy and the interpretations of masculinity.

Its about impermissible love across the caste barriers. On the subject of the body, mention may be made of several stories written by Mahasweta Devi, but specially pertinent here is the collection called *Outcast*. In the experiences of Douli, a *dusad* girl made pregnant and discarded by a Brahmin man, and her subsequent suffering in the hands of men of her own and that of other castes, in fact, in the curses heaped upon her by her own mother, the foundational view of a woman's body as sexual object is foregrounded. The

French feminist perspective of the woman's body as a sexual counter in man-woman relationships will not operate in the Indian context. Once again, society plays up collectively to interpret and direct the woman's sexual expression, it is not by individual choice that she grants access to her private self.

Family, society, violence and caste is a combination particular to the literature of India. Mahasweta Devi in her essay on 'The Chain of Untouchability' describes her visit to the *domtoli* in Daltongunj in Bihar: 'The ostracized existence of the *domtoli* reveals the pulse of the place. Daltongunj is a small town and the social injustices go on openly there, and no one is concerned.' Giving accounts of large-scale embezzlement of public funds, neglect of minimal wage laws, common practice of trafficking in women, grinding and degrading poverty, the misuse of the democratic vote, Mahasweta Devi concludes ironically, 'Dr Ambedkar's birthday celebration takes place somewhere, official institutions for the upliftment of harijan's exist, but the untouchables are left untouched' (*Dust on the Road: The Activist Writings of Mahasweta Devi*, edited by Maitreyi Ghatak, Calcutta: Seagull, 2000: 190).

Orality and Literature

India's rich and varied oral literature must find mention in any framing of theoretical principles. Here, the kinship with some African countries may be useful. Aime Cesaire's term *Negritude* in the 1930s and Franz Fanon's concept of *Black Skin, White Masks* (1996) sought to recover and define black cultural values and succeeded in separating the critical discourse in Africa from that of the colonizing countries. It is the orality and particular ways of recording social history that made the difference. In India too such an exercise is called for.

Oral literature in much of our country is demonstrative of group aesthetics. It is flexible and adaptable to the immediate circumstances, and astute raconteurs will cleverly play upon the mood of the audience. From my own experience and upbringing in Rajasthan, I wish to comment of the pictorial scroll of *Pabuji ka phar* as an example of woman's position in this collective. Pabuji is a folk hero who agrees to marry in a distant land but also pledges that he will always save the cows of his own territory from any invaders.

While he is sitting at the *mandap,* news comes that attackers are pilfering his village. Pabuji abandons his incomplete wedding ceremony to go immediately to the rescue of the cattle. Like all folk narratives, there is magic and moral dilemma, digressions and improvisations. Its interesting to note that the directing figures in this folk narrative are women though the hero is a man.

The point is that the performance of Pabuji has changed with the induction of women-oriented NGOs in Rajasthan and the state patronage given to the performing arts. The women characters have become far more prominent in recent renditions so much so that the power of determining Pabuji's destiny is that of the woman Charan. The story telling too is no longer done only by the male Bhopas but his wife and children have a substantial role. The commentary has also taken up the contemporary rhetoric about educating the girl child and respecting nature and the environment.

New story telling has also become an instrument for social change in Rajasthan. There is a wonderful vignette about a land tilling couple. Sethji traditionally does not allow his wife to labour on the farm but is getting old and tired. Sethani cooks his lunch and rushes with it everyday to the farm. One day the Sethani asks to reverse roles, and the Seth readily agrees thinking let her find out what a tough life he has. He stays at home; cooks labouriously, gets late, and rushes to the farm with her lunch. At seeing him, the Sethani bursts into laughter. In his haste Sethji had forgotten to wear his *dhoti*.

There are many lessons for community learning on the new roles for women in the examples I have cited. Perhaps we should note that while the old stories are told afresh, and new ones added to the folk idiom, instead of positioning hostility between genders, the attempt is to show understanding and humour.

Revisiting Mythology

I will now turn to the wonderful and high achievement of women's writing in India which calls for more assiduous understanding. Indian feminism has succeeded in creating a unique niche in reworking images from mythology and legend. The proliferation of tales about Draupadi, Sita, Meera, Radha and Shakuntala, and the deliberate encompassing of scripted as well as oral traditions speaks for the energy in the field. Shashi Deshpande's recent collection, *The Stone Women*, has the author exploring the silence of many women in the *Mahabharata*. This could be a method for decoding the placement of women in customary narratives, but need not be limited to only Indian texts. Githa Hariharan inverts the Scherezade story to great effect in the novel *When Dreams Travel* and Suniti Namjoshi reworks versions of fairy tales in *Feminist Fables*. Unlike the West, we have living mythologies, the line between the secular, the spiritual and the societal remains blurred in a promising liminality.

How the strategy works can be illustrated by Shashi Deshpande's telling of Draupadi's tale in a direct address to Krishna: 'How can you, who can be with two women, with ten, with twenty, even a hundred women and satisfy them all with the bottomless ocean of love you have in you – how can you imagine the hungers of a woman's heart? Hungers that for me are never satisfied? I am Yudhishthira's Queen not his beloved .... And Bhima treats me like a precious, fragile flower he is afraid to pluck ... and Nakul and Sahadev are only boys. But Arjuna .... If any woman was deceived in a man, I was in you, Arjuna' (Shashi Deshpande, *The Stone Women*, Calcutta: The Writers Workshop, 2000: 31–32).

The problems of the polyandrous marriage to five brothers are stated in Draupadi's frank appraisal of an unreciprocated passion for Arjuna. In such a version of mythology the greatest war heroes are shown up for their personal limitations, and quite openly, through the words of Draupadi, even the eternal God Krishna is accused of philandering in a way which disregards the affections of any individual woman.

Other examples of retelling the story of Draupadi are the well known – one by Mahasweta Devi and the less discussed one of Surendra Verma's play.

Men in Feminism

Here I would add a corollary that men writers have also reworked mythology to give the traditionally silenced woman a voice and presence. Bhisham Sahni's *Madhavi* for example largely stays with the original narrative of how Madhavi's father gifted her to Galav so he could find 800 special white horses to give as Gurudakshina to

Vishawamitra. Galav used Madhavi's exquisite capacity to bear royal sons and to turn virginal after each 'marriage' in order to gather the horses. Sahani's play grants Madhavi a powerful rhetoric of attack on patriarchy, literally her father's wish and her keeper's command that makes material use of her body and denies her any psychological or emotional bonds. In a telling episode towards the end of the play, Sahani uses the 'beauty myth' too in showing Madhavi looking old and dishevelled and non-virginal, and Galav trying to avoid a possible marriage with her. There is both mockery of the male pretences and also dark humour on the subject of fragile masculinity.

Men in feminism in India is a subject of worthy enquiry where one can list strong women-centred texts by Bankim Chandra, Rabindranath Tagore, Sarat Chandra, Tarashankar Bandopadhyay and many others in Bengal, and I am sure in other languages of the country as well. Premchand, certainly. My favourite example here is *Streer Patra* (A Wife's Letter), where Tagore writes in a feminine first person narrative. The letter written by a wife, Mrinal, to her revered husband, addressed carefully to 'His Lotus Feet' recapitulates the many years in which she has remained constricted within patriarchal norms and her existence has not even been noticed by the family so long as she has subscribed to its age old rules. She had yearnings to read and write, and could not, she wished to travel and see the world, this was not to be expressed, she longed for company and conversation that would feed her hungry intellect, such was not a available. When she befriended an impoverished orphan girl, she found a social cause and personal fulfilment, a companion, a disciple and follower. But this relationship too was disallowed after a point because the family decided that the child should marry an insane and much older man. The girl-woman caught between the dependence on the family and the enlightened world view opened to her by Mrinal, falls into despair and commits suicide. Mrinal realizes the sham of the family system and the pretences of patronage. Seeing not much difference between Bindu and herself as women who have no freedom, she inscribes this long letter and signs herself away from her husband, his family and, in fact, a pretentious society.

In Hindi, using a postmodern narrative technique, Rajendra Yadav begins his story: 'Where Lakshmi is Imprisoned' with the words, 'Wait a minute, this story is not about Vishnu's wife Lakshmi but about a girl who wanted to get out of her prison' (*Anthology of Hindi Stories*, compiled by Bhisham Sahni, New Delhi: Sahitya Akademi, 1993: 134–59). The clever word play shows the pretense of worshipping woman as goddess but keeping the real woman confined and controlled. This happens to be a prevailing trope in many discussions of feminism in India and the deification of goddesses almost offered as an excuse for ignoring real-life conditions. Yadav along with several other sympathizer of feminism expose such fallacies in the traditionalist argument that hides a long history of neglect of women in India.

Conclusion

Censorship and self-censorship are factors that women's writing has had to contend with. In the words of Nabanita Deb Sen: 'It is not in the process of literary imagination but in the expression of our literary imagination that we are limited and differ from men … . Not because we lack literary imagination but because we lack social sanction and the courage to defy it' (*Just Between Us*, edited by Ammu Joseph and others, New Delhi: Woman Unlimited, 2004: 19). Feminist literary theory for India will have to take numerous factors into account of which I have tried to list my priorities. Patriarchy has created hierarchies of power within which men and women are equally caught. Whether it is in the grid of the family, community, ethnic and/or caste configurations, or the economic matrix of poverty, oppression and exploitation, individual will and self-directed action has not recorded to have yielded significant gain for rectifying the disadvantaged position of woman. Collectivism in action is the strategy that I would advocate for feminism in India. Read Bama's *Sangati*, a book about a community's identity, not about the single self. See Krishna Sobti's interviews on how women can change their lives. Feminist theory is a body of knowledge that gives the analytical capacity to those who wish to understand the inequities. Some may bridge the traditional gap between academia and activism and wish to help in correcting those inequities if possible. Literature is a powerful tool for social change for it reflects upon social reality and allows imaginative transference to enlarge the areas of sympathy and understanding. Literature will also need to align with other subject disciplines to evolve viable theories of feminism.

Among those who practise feminist theory, this will not be a surprise. But I wish to reach out to all those who seek an indigenization of feminist theoretical premises so that they match the socio-political world that literature depicts.

Finally, I would say that the divide between English and bhasha in contemporary India is entirely artificial and non-operational for the feminist discourse. There are specific locales and *contexts* which should *not* be interpreted and differing *concepts*. The gain for feminism in literature here would be in recognizing the multilingual resources, in acknowledging the multi-layered social and economic conditions of women, and moving on to map common ground through *cross-cutting concepts*. My paper has tried to identify directions for a feminist theory framework for India. Responses from scholars and writers would stimulate further thinking.

5

Women in India

Terror and Trauma in the Sacred Space

Sanjukta Dasgupta

This chapter deals with the sacred space inside the home. Two concerns of women's subjugation have been examined to locate women's position in home. The first issue is unpaid domestic labour by women and the second is the dowry demand. The discussion on unpaid domestic labour by women indicates that now this work has been romanticised as love of a woman towards her family. The issue of dowry indicates that it may take various forms and sometimes it can be in the form of preferable employment of women like school teaching, which allows them to participate in both paid labour and unpaid labour effectively.

I

Labour of Love: Housewives' Unpaid Domestic Work[1]

Recently, Krishna Tirath, Minister of State for Women and Child Development, Government of India's suggestion that parliament should consider the proposal of making it mandatory for husbands to pay housewives for domestic work raised quite a storm in conservative and tradition-bound Indian society.

Tirath advocated that husbands must pay a portion of their salaries to their full-time housewives for the domestic work done by them. After all one cannot ignore the fact that housewives are not just married to their respective husbands but are also tied in wedlock to the marital houses as well. In Bengali culture a just married young wife is often sensitized that her so-called wayward manners that were so long a part of her life must be surrendered as she has now transformed into not just a wife but is also delegated the onerous task of behaving like a *'barir bou'*, a housewife, implying that she would have to re-invent herself as a desirable wife in her marital home. This role invariably implies that the wife as a member of the marital home is expected to be obedient, dutiful, hardworking and preferably will speak, of course deferentially, only when spoken to. The role of husbands in such situations is very complex, this can be sadistic, pathetic, helpless or violent, but that is a different subject and not germane to the issue to be discussed here.

Economists cite both economic and social gains, if the house work done by married women becomes paid work, that is, if it becomes mandatory for husbands to pay their wives for their 24×7 domestic work. Domestic work, performed by married women, has been romanticized for centuries as unconditional, sacred labour of love. The more a woman performs in the domestic domain without claiming anything, the more she will be iconized as the ideal woman, the domestic Lakshmi, the mystical angel in the house.

The naysayers, who extol the merits of the sacred domestic space and women's excruciating labour of love, feel that the state should not intervene in this area as it violates the hallowed space of family dynamics and some even suggest that the state that should create more job opportunities for women, instead of coercing husbands to pay their wives. All this discourse however suggests that the traditional binaries remain intact. Women's roles remain entrenched within the domestic space and men's roles are about performance in the public space, as a result, this stereotyping of gender roles consolidates the binaries even in the globalized 21st century. A more gender-neutral approach can be suggested here. If husbands opt for full-time domestic work, their wage-earning wives can pay them for home management. This would ensure gender justice a level playing field and gender equality within the patriarchal family system. This may be an exciting target to strive for, even if it takes a thousand years to succeed.

It is common knowledge that the celebrated British novelist Virginia Woolf had seriously upset the British phallocratic society by asking such questions as 'why do men drink wine and women water' or 'is the work of a mother, of a wife, of a daughter, worth nothing to the nation in solid cash' and had made the educated, cultured male British decision-makers fume when she stated in her categorical one-liner, 'Husband and wife are not only one flesh; they are one purse' (TG 54). Woolf obviously was emphasizing the need for systemic transformation.

We find that Woolf's statements and rhetorical queries link women's marginalization to patriarchy, poverty and, in a more extended sense, to race, location and culture. In two of her explosive non-fictional texts *A Room of One's Own* (1929) and *Three Guineas* (1938), often regarded as two powerful feminist manifestos of the twentieth century, Virginia Woolf underscored that a woman could be liberated only when adult women were adequately educated and trained in professional skills. Such education would enable her to have an independent income thereby empowering her to have an identity and as a result she would be able to live her life on her own terms. All this is easier said than done, as we are aware of the domestic entrapment of women harnessed in a relentless environment of permission and control. So even if women are part of the workforce and are able to earn their living, the salary cheque has often to be surrendered to the male family members such as husband, father or even uncle or brother depending on circumstances.

Economic, social and emotional dependence of adult women on male authority have fortified patriarchal norms that vary from social conditioning, threats of ostracism to emotional blackmail that fractures women's sense of self-esteem. The end result is that women who engage in remunerative work find that there is no relaxation in their responsibilities as caregivers, cooks, nannies, basic educators of minor children, that is, chores that are integral to overall home management and therefore women, as wives and mothers, are seduced into accepting multi-tasking as their way of life. These roles of superwife and supermother are glorified with widely canvassed ideologies of the mythic Shakti, creating a mystique that narcotizes women and such social conditioning makes them accept the dual roles as wage earner in the public domain, and as unpaid labour within the domestic space that involves home management, kitchen work, bearing and rearing of children, care for elderly family members and attending to the needs of the helpless husbands. Women's compulsory roles in production (unpaid domestic labour) and reproduction (childbirth) create a mesmeric mystique that blinkers women into accepting their roles as unpaid labour. The Human Development Report of UNDP documents that while 67 per cent of the world's work is done by women, only 10 per cent of global income is earned by women and mere 1 per cent of global property is owned by women.

Interestingly, key research findings initiated by WSAF & Health Bridge titled, 'Women's Economic Contribution through Their Unpaid Work: The Case in India' (2009) include the following:

(a) woman typically work 16 hours per day on both paid and unpaid labour;
(b) most women have no leisure time;
(c) women bear the greatest responsibility for household chores, including many tasks related to income generation;
(d) most women, even if they have a servant, do their own cooking;
(e) women generally assume full responsibility for tutoring and helping children with school work;
(f) rural women perform a wider variety of tasks than do urban women;
(g) while both men and women recognize that women's household activities constitute important work, they fail to grasp the extent of its economic value; and
(h) the value of unpaid household work performed by women throughout India is upwards of ₹ 612.8 billion.

We have seen that the incisive text of Virginia Woolf's *Three Guineas*, apart from being an anti-war, anti-fascist text, is also a diatribe against gender injustice, oppression and exploitation of women, women's unpaid domestic labour and romantic notions of feminine roles of women as caregivers and glorified mothers. In India, the move to introduce the legislation in parliament may have strange results, as women who challenge men in the public domain and complain about glass ceilings may be told to return to where they truly belong, the home, and more so, now that they would be paid for house work. Perhaps anticipating such distortions of the intended purpose, Virginia Woolf had quoted the following from the *Daily*

Telegraph, 22 January 1936: '… if men were doing the work that thousands of young women are now doing the men would be able to keep those same women in decent homes. Homes are the real places of the women … . It is time the Government insisted upon employers giving work to more men, this enabling them to marry women they cannot now approach' (TG 51).

This is the implied risk, women may be advised to work at home and leave the job market for men as the woman's world is her family, her husband, her children and her home. Besides, Woolf raises another pertinent question about distribution and utilization of the husband's half salary that may be legally and even spiritually surrendered to the wife. Woolf asks whether the wife will have similar freedom to use the money in any way she likes after meeting the common household utility bills, as her husband does. That is, can she spend the money on wine, cigars, clubs, sports, race course or would she be expected to be satisfied as she had secured boarding, lodging, clothes and petty pocket money?

I will conclude by citing two more quotes from *Three Guineas* published in 1938 which probably addresses issues that will be debated in our parliament in 2012. So Woolf refers to the paid work of archbishops, army captains, policemen and postmen and observes, '… but wives and mothers and daughters who work all day and every day, without whose work the State would collapse and fall to pieces, without whose work your sons, Sir, would cease to exist, are paid nothing whatever. Can it be possible? …' (TG 54).

Finally, claiming that women's work at home, as housewives, should be remunerative work, Woolf however urges the necessity to consider whether wives will be given the freedom to spend the surplus money as freely as their husbands in hobbies and pastimes, or will they be called up at the end of each month to account for each coin spent, that is, they may be well asked: have they spent the surplus money on family needs or did they indulge in private pleasures? The threats and demands of accountability and transparency may even make wives decline the generous offer of payment for what after all are unquestioned wifely duties, as tradition and societal norms had trained them into accepting as a matter of faith. As marriage plans are made, it would-be considered a combustible question if a would-be housewife asked what sort of daily domestic chores she was expected to do and the total time involved per day and the rates offered per job, whether she could expect work sharing at home, public holidays according to the calendar, earned leave, medical leave or leave encashment? After all Woolf succinctly sums up, 'It stands to reason that if the wife has a spiritual right to half her husband's income because her own work as his wife is unpaid, then she must have as much money to spend upon such causes as appeal to her as he has' (TG 55).

All this may make us wonder whether it's a Hobson's choice, as Woolf reasons. Marriage is a profession, because it is an unpaid profession, and because the spiritual share of half the husband's salary is not, facts seem to show, an actual share (TG 58).

Virginia Woolf wrote *Three Guineas* in 1938 addressing mainland Britain; India of course was a British colony then. More than 65 years later in post-colonial India we are addressing similar issues, with an awareness of the sameness and difference that define developed and developing locations, with its specific socio-economic and cultural parameters. But are we ready? Wives as unpaid domestic workers are powerless in comparison to the paid domestic workers in the unorganized sector. In fact, a newspaper survey recently revealed that many married women, both housewives and professional married women, regarded their domestic maids as empowered, supportive and dependable Durgas. Wives as full-time homemakers and married professional women declared that in the absence of the support of their paid domestic workers they would find it very difficult to pursue their preferred chores and professions, even for a single day. A simple solution therefore is not easy when the culturally sensitive issues are married women's unpaid work at home and the need to make husbands pay their wives for domestic work.

II
Defeating Dowry: Some Reflections[2]

Dowry deaths stigmatize our self-appreciation that we are a progressive society. Recently, the pitiful suicide by a councellor in Delhi due to dowry harassment perpetrated by her marital family members puts the nation to shame (*Times of India*, 9 November 2012: 12). Moreover, what is a matter of alarm is that the husband of the councellor is a school teacher, and we have this rooted notion that teachers are the liberated thinkers who can lead young minds to an inclusive understanding of both the home and the world.

In our MA English *Gender and Literature* classes we read the texts of Kate Millet, Gayatri Chakravarty Spivak, Simone de Beauvoir and Virginia Woolf among several others. We explain to the students how some of these writers emphasize the need for financial independence for adult women – a most effective way to free women from the rigours of patriarchy. Our students industriously jot down the points discussed in their notebooks. In their examination answers they faithfully reiterate and critique the arguments of the mostly 20th century Western feminists.

In their own personal lives, however, marriage emerges as the institution that excites challenges and humiliates our girl students. Some fall in love and marry, some are married off, some wait to be married, some have parents obsessed with the desire to arrange an auspicious (*shuvo*) marriage, some go through excruciating trauma, verbal, psychic or physical violence in the process of being married or remaining married while some get divorced.

A few years back, a student of mine came to visit me. She had both an MA and BEd. degrees – the ideal combination for a career as a schoolteacher. She came to invite me to her wedding. I was obviously very happy and congratulated her. I knew her parents had been trying for years to arrange a match for her, but without much success. But now her parents had arranged her marriage with a bank official. As my student was leaving, she turned round from near the door and said, 'Actually, it's my recent permanent job in this school, Ma'am. Suddenly I seem to have become very attractive for prospective suitable boys'.

I was aware of my student's caustic wit but this one-liner was much more ballistic than a Parthian shot. I was aghast. After all, the humankind cannot bear very much reality, as someone said.

Also, my close association with the Women's Studies Research Centre led to our startling discovery during a project on dowry deaths, that after Tagore's '*Dena Paona*' very few powerful narratives had been written about the menace of the dowry system. Not even Bengali women writers seem to have paid serious and sustained attention to this social evil. I asked a Bengali woman writer about the possible reason for this elision if not total silence. She said, the urban Bengali educated middle class had de-recognized the existence of the dowry system now. It just didn't exist. The giving of expensive gifts from the bride's family and gracious acceptance of the same by the groom's family, had now become socially internalized as an integral part of the rituals and customs of a typical Hindu marriage. It was as expected a custom as the ritual of applying *sindoor* by the groom in the middle parting of the bride's hair.

Very recently, I asked a married student with a school job about the prevalence of dowry, wife beating and other acts of *mild* domestic violence in her immediate social circle.

'Oh no, Ma'am, it's all changed now', she said. My look of surprise made my student explain at some length, 'Thanks to the School Service Commission, the grooms' families now look out for graduate brides and many insist that the brides have to clear the SSC written test and interview and get a school job. The first priority of course is a schoolteacher bride. After all teaching is a noble profession and hence doubly contributes to family prestige. As a matter of fact, the husband and in-laws become irritated if the bride is unable to clear the SSC eligibility test for securing a permanent job as assistant teacher. 'What a dunderhead of a bride we have got' they have been known to lament. *After all, Ma'am its dowry every month, incremental dowry, till the bride retires* – approximately for the next thirty years, followed by pension, provident fund and gratuity. Even unmarried girls with teaching jobs are looked upon as life insurance and hence pampered by their ageing parents who hope silently that their daughters will shun marriage. It's a much better life for the average educated Bengali woman now even in the suburban and rural districts ...'

Dowry demands, dowry deaths, women in remunerative work, unpaid domestic labour are all interlinked issues that need to be addressed in the 21st century with sincerity and seriousness by decision-makers at all levels, from the home to the parliament.

Notes

1. This is a revised version of an article published as 'Role Call' in *The Statesman*, 6 November 2012.
2. This is a revised version of an article published in *The Statesman*, 26 June 2007.

Reference

Woolf, Virginia (1966) *Three Guineas*, New York: Harcourt, Brace & Co.

6

Ethnography of Gender Among North Indian Muslims

Zarina Bhatty

The common approach to study Muslim women in India has been to examine women's status in the Quran and the Hadis (the utterances and actions of Prophet Mohammad) rather than to study their actual life situations. This approach has been full of pitfalls.

In the first instance, to delineate women's status from the Quran and Hadis suffers from the confusion over the interpretation of the two texts. There is no final authority whose interpretation can be accepted by all Muslims. As in other parts of the world, Indian Muslims are also divided into two major sects, viz., the *Sunnis,* who are in a greater majority, and the *Shias.* These are further divided into smaller sects like the Bohras, the Khojas, the Ismalilies, the Memons and the Moplahs of South India. These sects are collectively known as 'Nau Muslims' (more recent converts). Each of these sects presents its own interpretation, and justifies it on its understanding of the holy Quran. Based on these different interpretations, four systems of jurisprudence emerged, each claiming to have drawn from the Quran and the Hadis, which were compiled two hundred years after Prophet Mohammad's passing away *(Mernici)*. However, it may be noted that all interpretations of Quran have been greatly influenced by the socio-economic, cultural and political situations in respective countries, including India. Therefore, Indian Muslims are not a monolithic community and even their religious practices show regional variations and it is erroneous to represent them by a uniform Islamic image. Although no recognized feminist interpretation of the holy texts has emerged in the subcontinent, in recent years a few Muslim scholars – women and men – like Hussain (2000), Ahmed (1992) and Engineer (2001), have dared to interpret the Quran with a feminist perspective also. And discourses on Indian women's status in Islam have been taking place.

Islam has shown a great deal of flexibility in absolving local traditions in India and, likewise, in the neighbouring countries. Muslims in Lakshadweep and in the islands of Maldives have, for example, adopted Islam for dealing with kinship and marriage in different ways (Dube, Bhatty). In the islands of Lakshadweep, matriarchy is practised, although most Muslim societies are patriarchal. In the exclusively Muslim society of Maldives, divorce and remarriage have been regulated according to their own norms. The Maldivians have modified the triple *talaq* by allowing *talaq* (divorce) by only two utterances of 'I *talaq* you', instead of three such utterances (known as triple-divorce formula), which is the Islamic requirement, only after which divorce becomes irrevocable, Maldivian deviation gives a choice to woman thus divorced to marry another person or remarry the previous husband without her going through another marriage and its consummation, thus avoiding *Halala*, in Islamic legal requirement. This legal requirement was modified in Pakistan also though in a different manner, when President Zia-ul Haq introduced modifications in Muslim Personal Law. As the law now operates in Pakistan, a husband can divorce a wife by saying 'I divorce you' three times yet remarry the same woman twice again without her going through *Halala*, and only if the divorce happens third time then it becomes irrevocable and *Halala* is imposed upon her (Balchin, 1994). In India *Halala* is imposed even after the first divorce by the triple-divorce formula.

Among Indian Muslims, Islamic injunctions have been considerably diluted by the socio-economic, cultural and political structure of the wider Indian society. In India, the Little Tradition of local culture has often overruled the Great Tradition of Islam (Singer, 1959). Indian Muslims could not escape from accepting Indian cultural traditions and its social structure, and adopted many Hindu customs and rituals in their daily life. For example, despite claims of Islamic concept of *Masawat* (social equality) by Muslim orthodoxy, Indian Muslim society has been hierarchical and practices a caste system analogous to Hindu caste system. Muslim community in India is sharply divided between the Ashrafs and Kameens, (the non-Ashraf, occupational castes). Ashrafs also discriminate between themselves and the Nau Muslims, whom they consider to be inferior. The Nau Muslims fall between the Ashrafs and the Kameens on the ladder of Muslim social hierarchy.

The Nau Muslims, like the Kameens (occupational castes), have retained many of the social customs. Some of them have even retained their pro-conversion surnames, like the Meos of Haryana and Rajasthan, who are proud of their Rajput heritage, and the Patels, the Desais and the Shahs of Gujarat. Muslim women too, like their Hindu counterparts, have occupied a position of subservience to men both in the family and the society.

Thus, there has existed from the beginning a confusion between the religious precepts and the existing social reality, which has continued to the present day, blurring the understanding of Indian Muslim community, particularly the status of women. Indian feminist scholars and activists too have been caught in this perplexity and have also been hesitant in addressing Muslim women's issues for fear of not only hurting their religious sentiments but also interfering in their religion and culture. As a result, in India, the task of studying Muslim women's status has been confined mainly to Indian Muslim scholars. This trend is evident among the social scientists too. Very little scholarly research conducted by Indian scholars, other than Muslims, is available on Indian Muslim community. Therefore studies on gender among Indian Muslims are few and far between. However, it is encouraging to note that this barrier seems to be lifting now and feminist scholars, other than Muslims, like Chhachi, Dube, Madan and Menon among others, have begun to study Muslim women in the context of their existing socio-economic environment. A number of foreign scholars have also contributed to the understanding of

Muslim women's status in Indian society, notable among them are Jeffereys, G. Minault, Jacobson, Papanek and B. Metcalf.

In India discourses on Muslim women's status started during the British period, when under the British cultural dominance, Indian Muslim intelligentsia perceived their identity being threatened. Therefore, in order to safeguard their cultural identity, they initiated a process of self-examination which led to a greater awareness of the backwardness of their community. Lack of education among Muslim women was identified as the most important reason for this backwardness. Thus, the closing years of the 19th century and early 20th century saw the upper class Muslim men promoting western education for boys and men, and reading and writing skills in the vernacular along with a knowledge of Quran for their wives and daughters. In this way, women of the upper classes were exposed to some limited knowledge of the world around them, so that they could play their role as wives and mothers more efficiently in the changing times, but all within the confines of domesticity. Muslim social reformers encouraged women's education by opening schools for girls, where education 'suitable for girls of respectable families' was provided. Girls coming to these schools wore *burqa* (a garment which covers a woman from head to toe, with two little holes on the top to enable vision) – a garment peculiar to India and Pakistan, and not found in other Islamic countries. These schools, exclusively for girls, provided education in domestic science, humanities and elementary knowledge of Islam. This was no doubt a departure from the practice whereby Muslim girls were only schooled at home in reading and writing in Urdu and were taught to read Quran in Arabic without any knowledge of Arabic language. But reformist movements of this kind as well as discourses which took place in the late 19th and early 20th century were confined to the upper classes only and the conditions of the lower caste masses of Indian Muslim women were totally ignored. These reformers, while exposing the superstitions and deviations from Islamic teachings in everyday life of Muslims neither addressed Indian social customs such as practice of caste system which had become rooted in the Indian Muslim society, nor did they refer to the glaring legal and social gender inequalities, which were contrary to the professed Islamic principles of *Masawat* (equality). These reformist endeavours have been documented and commented upon by Indian and foreign scholars like B. Metcalf, S. Lateef, G. Minault, Z. Bhatty and Q. Hyder among others. They share the view that the reformers placed women in a situation that made them a vehicle for achieving men's aspirations rather than their own.

Social scientists have defined 'status' in different ways. The term is full of ambiguities. Generally, the term refers to the 'positioning' of a person or a group in relationship to the other similar entity in a hierarchical social system. Therefore, for understanding women's status in Indian Muslim society, who in this hierarchical social structure are placed lower to men within their own caste and sub-caste, it becomes inevitable to compare their status with men's status. Thus, gender equality has been a central theme in women's discourse. I find the principle of reciprocity, advocated by P. Mukherjee (1988), pertinent and useful in determining the status of a person or a group of persons, in relation to 'the other' which, in the case of women's status, invariably refers to men's status in Indian family and society. Status also depends on the privileges – personal and legal – enjoyed by a person, or a group of persons, belonging to a gender or class, and it is indicated by the amount of freedom and the extent of restrictions placed on a person or a group for self-realization. No less important a parameter determining the status of men and women is the complementarity of rights and duties towards each other. The status of Indian Muslim women has been and continues to be inferior to Indian Muslim men on all these counts.

Despite a vigorous feminist movement and a number of legislative measures to reduce gender inequalities, not only men enjoy more privileges and freedom for self-realization but society has also placed fewer restrictions on them to shape a future for themselves, which is not the case with Muslim women. There is very little reciprocity or mutuality in the relationship between men and women, whether it is between husband and wife or sisters and brothers. The status of Muslim women in the light of the above parameters is rooted in highly structured gender and caste discriminative institutions (here I have deliberately avoided the term 'Islamic', because these institutions are shaped more on the indigenous economic and socio-cultural basis than purely Islamic) of patriarchy and feudalism. Patriarchal culture dictates that a woman lives her entire life in subservience to male authority, and her circumscribed existence finds expression in innumerable social customs and rituals. The performance of these rituals at life cycle events to be discussed later in this paper has been an important device to reinforce unequal gender relationship among Indian Muslims.

In the early years of Muslim reform movement, poetry and novels were written specifically for women to project ideal Muslim womanhood and poets like Altaf Hussain Hali lauded women's role as 'mothers, sisters and daughters' and writers like Nazeer Ahmed, Maulana Ashraf Ali Thanvi and others wrote both poetry and prose to portray an 'ideal' Muslim woman. In these works she was presented as literate, good in home management, and rearing children, discarded superstitions, was pious, and obedient to her husband and well versed in religious teachings and presented herself as a model to her daughters. These books were given as a part of a girl's dowry as it was considered essential for every 'respectable' girl to be conversant with. A woman enhanced her husband and his family's *izzat* by conducting herself in a honourable manner, while men decided what was honourable for women. This highly patriarchal and feudal approach to women's liberation resulted in at best maintaining a status quo regarding Muslim women's status socially and legally. It did not liberate them nor lead them towards gender equality.

In a highly patriarchal Indian society the paternity of the offspring is of paramount importance, especially among the upper classes, in which the title and property are passed on from father to the legitimate male offspring. This required that a woman's conduct be guarded closely and thus the practice of *purdah* (seclusion) came into vogue. The responsibility of bringing up daughters, according to the rigid patriarchal code, was ironically placed on women themselves. All patriarchies are based on subservience of women, but for a Muslim woman subservience to man is doubly justified – by the concept of *izzat* and by the Islamic precept of 'obedience' of woman to man. Islam instructs that a wife be 'obedient' to the husband, obedience required that a woman 'respects' her husband. This is expressed in a number of ways. One of these being the practice of avoiding uttering the husband's name; therefore, a wife was forbidden to address her husband by his name and would address him by calling him so and so's brother or her child's father after she had a child. Sometimes it will lead to funny results, like if a piece of furniture or any other item of use was called by a term which has any similarity to the name it was not called by its proper name but a different name was coined for that item.

In Indian Muslim community, the consciousness of gender arose from the very time of conception, when a pregnant woman was generally referred to as carrying a '*bachcha*' (baby boy), the term '*bachchi*' (baby girl) was never used. Even these days one never refers to a pregnant woman as carrying a '*bachchi*'. A host of superstitions have been associated with conceiving a son: sons are conceived in moonlit nights while daughters are conceived in dark nights; a son is to be born if the expectant mother sleeps on her right side during pregnancy since right is preferred to the left; a son is indicated if a pregnant woman has craving for sweets as sweets convey joy; and many other similar superstitions. The birth of a child continues to be received in a distinctly different manner depending on whether it is a girl or a boy. A girl baby is declared with complete silence in the delivery room while the boy baby is declared with joyful shouts of '*Larka Hai*' (It's a boy). Meer Hasan Ali, an English woman married to a U.P. Muslim in the first decade of the last century, records the attitude of Muslim families towards the birth of a baby girl thus: 'It is generally to be observed in a Mussalman family even at this day that the birth of a girl produces a temporary gloom whilst the birth of a boy gives rise to a festival in the *zananah*. Some are wicked enough to say that it is more honourable to have a son' (Ali, 1917: 186).

The preference for sons has continued to the present times. Change in this respect has been so slow, even among the educated in urban areas, that when I gave birth to my third (daughter, a complete hush took place in the delivery room. Despite my repeated queries about the sex of the child (there were no ultra-sound devices those days) no one told me that it was a girl child. When I was to be transferred to the ward from the delivery room, the doctor came up to me, pressed my hand sympathetically and in a gloomy tone informed me that I had given birth to a third daughter. When I retorted angrily and said, 'so what? I have not given birth to a monster, it is a human child'. She was very surprised and tried to explain to me that most women cry and are afraid to take their baby girl home for fear of being unwelcome. That was her reason for 'breaking the news' to me with caution.

Gender discriminative practices extended even to breast-feeding. A mother, among the Muslims of the Oudh region of Uttar Pradesh, was instructed to breast-feed the male baby for two years and three months, but a girl baby for one year and nine months only. It was erroneously asserted that this was a Quranic instruction. This practice was followed even in the semi-educated upper and middle class Muslim families. I remember my mother fed our brothers six months longer than she did us daughters. There has been a change in this regard with more scientific information being available on breastfeeding, but this is confined to the educated elite only. Among the uneducated rural families such discriminative practices continue to be followed even today.

Gender inequality among Indian Muslims is expressed and periodically reaffirmed through life cycle rituals and ceremonies. Although strongly disapproved by Islam, rituals play an important part in everyday life of Indian Muslims and reaffirm and strengthen gender discrimination prevailing among Indian Muslims. Right from the birth, ceremonies that follow differentiate between a baby girl and a baby boy. The birth of a boy was celebrated with rejoicing and that of a girl without any particular pomp and show. According to custom, on the sixth day after the birth of a child, elaborate ceremony called *chhatti* was performed, when the new mother was given a ritual bath and usually the *aqiqa* (the naming ceremony) also took place on the same day. A feast was given and two goats were sacrificed if it was a baby boy and only one if it was a baby girl. Among the Muslims, *aqiqa* has religious connotation and, therefore, the practice of sacrificing two goats for a baby boy and one for a baby girl continues to this day, even among the most educated urban elite. A newborn child's father's sisters were given gifts, called *neg,* in cash or kind. Folk songs reflect the desire of sisters for their brother to have sons so that they could ask for *kangans* (expensive gold bracelets). In the case of a baby girl not only that celebrations were considerably toned down, inexpensive gifts were given as *neg,* and the bargaining power of sisters for more expensive gifts was markedly reduced. Similar discrimination was made in making payments to the *praja (Kameens)*, i.e., the serving castes, bound in the traditional *jajmani* relationship to the Ashrafs. These castes had prescribed roles to play, under the *jajmani* system, e.g., the Nai's (barber) wife helped the new mother with her ritual bath and massaged her body after the baby's delivery and was compensated for her services both in cash and kind. She was entitled to the clothes that the new mother was wearing during the first six days after the child was born. The barber who shaved the baby's hair at *aqiqa* (as the hair that a baby is born with was regarded to be impure) was also rewarded for in cash and kind. He was given the silver container in which sandalwood paste was kept, to be put on baby's shaved head as a good omen. Traditionally, the barber also performed the circumcision of a male child, for which he was rewarded so that he too stood to gain more at the birth of a baby boy than that of the birth of a baby girl. In villages where deliveries are not handled by qualified doctors the barbers still perform the circumcision. The status of the daughter-in-law, in her conjugal family, also changed for the better if she delivered a boy baby. 'She could put her head up in the susral' (conjugal home) used to be the usual refrain.

Gender relations in Muslim society have been structured around woman's sexuality, and the concept of *izzat* has been closely related to it. There is a duality in society's attitude towards a woman's sexuality. On the one hand, it curbs a woman's sexuality and, on the other, it enhances it for consumption of men. Thus, a woman is regarded to be an object for man's sexuality, and her own sexuality is subservient to man's. The absence of reciprocity in this sphere is also evident from the approval of polygamy and institutionalization of prostitution: while for a woman extra-marital sex is most severely condemned, among men it was condoned and, thus, double standards of sexual morality prevailed.

The onset of puberty was the most crucial time for a girl. A girl's physical development was watched closely, as this signified her marriage ability and with it her reproductive potential. Woman's body from puberty onwards became the most guarded site for securing a family's *izzat*, as nothing could hurt a family's *izzat* more than a daughter losing her virginity before marriage. The realization of dangers inherent in her body were brought to the girl's consciousness very early in life. Even before a girl reached physical maturity she was trained in keeping a low profile and was not allowed to mix with boys and the inside and outside domains of her activities were strictly demarcated.

Marriage of a daughter, with virginity intact, was the most important duty of parents, who must 'hand her over to her rightful owner'. A man's desire to have a 'virgin' wife has been so strong that even today they prefer to have virgin wives. Daughters have been referred to as *Paraya Dhan* (some one else's wealth) and daughter's own parents were regarded as only the custodians of that *dhan* (wealth). To safeguard virginity, girls were made to feel 'ashamed' of their bodies and their sexual functions, and were instructed to hide any manifestation of their having arrived at puberty. At the slightest sign of her sprouting breasts, a girl was instructed to cover the upper part of her body properly. Unmarried girls were not allowed to wear brassieres as these could enhance the breasts and were instructed to deal with the menstruation secretly. Unlike other parts of India, onset of menstruation among UP Muslims was not celebrated; on the contrary, it was concealed. A Muslim woman during her periods was and continues to be regarded impure. She should not say her *Namaz* (daily prayer), nor touch the holy book Quran, nor enter any place of worship. She should not fast during the month of *Ramazan* on days she is menstruating. The concept of' 'sharam', after reaching puberty, permeated every movement of a girl's life. There was shame in walking fast, in talking loudly, in having a good appetite, in the manner of covering body, in talking about sex, and even having knowledge about sex. All this was regarded as 'shameful' for girls. For this reason unmarried girls were not informed about sex, until just before the wedding. Usually young girls learnt about sex from a young *Bhabhi* (brother's wife) or just picked up patchy knowledge to satisfy their natural curiosity. A day before the wedding a senior woman of the family briefed her on what to expect on the nuptial night, and was instructed to conceal from her husband any knowledge of sex that she might have had, lest he may regard her of bad character.

Gender inequalities in spheres other than familial, like economic and political, also rest on the regulation of a woman's sexuality and her submission to the male authority. Institution of *purdah* and her confinement to the inner domain of the household has been designed to restrict her movements and to eliminate the possibility of her interacting with men outside the household. In fact, even inside the household, she was required to observe *purdah* with men who were in the permitted marriageable category, such as mate cousins.

The concept of *izzat* (honour) is inimical to a woman's status as it restricts her access to education and employment and keeps her away from public life. Restrictions on her mobility to keep her away from productive activities reinforce her dependence on men. Keeping women away from participating in economic activities was legitimized among the Shareefs (upper castes) on the basis of *izzat*, because any exposure with the outside world and any interaction with men beyond the prescribed category threatened the family *izzat*. It may be noted that the association of *izzat* with women's physical mobility has been so strong in Muslim society that even now, when middle and upper class women are acquiring education and are entering employment, their participation in public life has remained limited.

Interestingly, after India's partition, many young men migrated to Pakistan in search of better career opportunities, while their families, specially those belonging to the landed gentry, remained in India for fear of losing their land and property. This for a while created a gender gap whereby young girls of marriageable age did not find suitable men to marry within their caste and community. By force of circumstances many of them remained unmarried and were willy-nilly allowed to take up jobs. In the wake of communal riots that followed India's independence a number of them gave up wearing *burqa* for fear of being recognized as Muslims. This initiated a process that, to a large extent, diluted the concept of *izzat* attached with woman's appearance in public. Currently, however, fundamentalist forces seem to be reversing this process and insisting on *purdah* for Muslim women as an assertion of Muslim identity. Even lower classes are adopting *burqa*.

The Kameens (occupational castes) were not regarded as *izzatdar* (having *izzat*). Among them sharp demarcation between the private and the public did not exist as it did among the Asharafs, because all Kameen women could not stay away from economic activities. Women of the Kameen castes also have a hierarchy among themselves, so that the relatively higher castes amongst them, like Manihars (bangle sellers), Nais (barbers) and Mirasis (professional singers) assume a superior status. The higher status of these castes is derived from the fact that their women serve only the women of Ashraf households and do not interact with men in performing their professional duties. Those who belong to the lower castes among the Kameens, by virtue of their poverty, have to work as labourers in farms or elsewhere and cannot avoid interaction with men and hence do not claim to have *izzat*. On account of their regular contact with men the moral character of women in these castes is often suspect.

The desire of lower castes to acquire some semblance or *izzat* is expressed through withdrawal of women from economic activities as soon as the family's economic status enhances. This process of emulating upper caste practices in order to raise one's caste status is very similar to the process of 'sanskritization' as M.N. Srinivas has described it for the Hindu castes. I also observed this phenomenon in Kasauli, predominantly a Muslim village in UP, where I conducted my field research.

A young man from a Mirasi caste (professional singers) in Kasauli, who studied up to High School, acquired a job in the nearby town as a bus conductor. He was engaged to marry a girl from his own caste within Kasauli. According to the *jajmani* custom women from the Mirasi caste were required to sing at auspicious occasions, such as births and marriages, at the Ashraf houses. The young man on the basis of his education and economic status aspired for a better social status than that of the other members of his caste. He therefore expressed his displeasure at his fiancee singing at Ashraf households and threatened to break the engagement if she continued to do so, as it would be against his newly acquired *izzat*. He was obviously aspiring to improve his caste status. This created a problem for the girl's family as they were traditionally bound and economically dependent on the Ashrafs. Finally, a compromise was worked out whereby his fiancee could sing film songs in Ashraf households but not the traditional folk songs. This shift in the fiancee's song menu was considered as an upward deviation from the traditional role of the Mirasi caste, whose singing was restricted to only folk songs appropriate to the occasions. In addition the young man also made it very clear that after marriage his wife will not follow the profession at all. She was also advised to wear *burqa* and observe *purdah* to emulate Ashraf women. The Manihar caste also went through the same experience, when the men of a particular Manihar family got into the business of providing film music at weddings and made good money. They stopped their women from going out vending bangles and put them behind *purdah*. The women lost their freedom of movement and the economic independence that they earlier had from vending bangles.

Among all sections of Muslim community girls were married soon after reaching puberty. Early marriage was considered desirable not only for the fear of the girls losing her virginity but was also important because through marriage a girl came to be recognized as a woman and thereby acquired a social status, which was derived from her husband's status in society. For this reason hypergamous marriages were preferred among the Indian Muslims, as the offspring's status was mainly determined by father's caste. A woman's marital status was expressed verbally by calling her a *suhagan* and granting her adult privileges, such as entitlement for a separate invitation at festive occasions and the right to reciprocate by giving separate gifts. She was permitted after marriage to wear flowers and adorn herself to her heart's content. Unlike in African societies where initiation ceremonies take place to signify a person's entry into adulthood (la fontaines), among Indian Muslims, a woman is initiated into her marital status and this is expressed through a host of rituals and ceremonies, not reciprocated for men. To emphasize the difference in a girl's social status after marriage, unmarried girls in UP were traditionally not allowed to wear flowers and were required to dress simply. Certain items of jewellery, like a nose ring, were also not allowed to be worn by unmarried girls as these symbolized the status of a *suhagan*.

Just as marriage bestowed certain personal privileges on a woman, which were derived from the fact of having a husband, a woman also lost these privileges as soon as her husband expired. Although personal restrictions on Muslim widows were not as stringent as those placed on Hindu widows, Muslim widows were nevertheless subjected to many personal deprivations. For example, they were not allowed to wear bangles or any other jewellery, or adorn themselves with flowers or perfume, and could wear only simple white clothes. Irrespective of age, these restrictions separated unmarried girls and widows from married women. A sixteen-year-old married girl would be regarded as a *suhagan* and could enjoy the privileges of a married woman, while an unmarried twenty-year-old would be referred to as a 'girl' and would be deprived of the arsenal privileges accorded to a married woman. No restrictions were placed on widowers. Orthodox Muslims rightly argue that Islam does not prescribe any restrictions on widows, except to remain pious. In fact, Islam not only allows widow remarriage but explicitly provides for it. But, contrary to provisions in

Islam, widow remarriage was socially disapproved and seldom took place. My own grandmother had become a widow in her teens, after being married only for one and a half years, when my father was only six months old, but she was never remarried. She lived the life of a widow with all the prescribed restrictions for the rest of her life. I have vivid memories of her wearing only white clothes and instructing us not to wear white clothes as it signified widowhood.

As stated above, a married woman did acquire a derived status of an adult by virtue of being married and acquiring certain rights in her conjugal home, like the right to residence and maintenance, but the most crucial right to property has been circumscribed by gender inequitable practices among Indian Muslims. Legally, a Muslim woman is entitled to only half of her brother's entitlement in her parents' property, and only one-eighth of her husband's property, while her husband is entitled to one-fourth of his wife's property. During the British rule, the customary law of inheritance prevailed over the Islamic and on that basis a Muslim woman, like her Hindu counterpart, could be deprived of inheritance in her parental property. Until now, a Muslim woman is deprived of her share in agriculture land. The marriage between paternal first cousins, preferred among North Indian Muslims, has been one of the mechanisms to circumvent the legal provision of female inheritance.

Conjugal rights and obligations between couples are similarly uneven. Custom places many more obligations on the wife than rights, while husband enjoys more rights than obligations. The most important right that a husband possesses is the right to marry up to four wives and to divorce a wife verbally and unilaterally without assigning a reason. He is not even required to pay maintenance after divorcing his wife at will, except for the period of *iddat*, which is three months and ten days. This provision is made to establish paternity of the child, in case she was pregnant at the time of divorce. Rights are not reciprocally accorded to the wife neither in law nor by religion and custom.

A wife changes her residence, her name, her allegiances, her entire self to the service of her husband and to his lineage. She devotes to him her body, her reproductive potential, her skills – domestic and professional. No such obligations are reciprocated by the husband, who neither changes his residence, nor his name, nor commits to the wife his fidelity, for men visiting prostitutes or keeping concubines has been culturally accepted so is bigamy and polygamy.

The strong patrilineal bias and patrilocal residence among Indian Muslims is expressed through many customs and marriage rituals. Marriage ritual among North Indian Muslims signify a girl's transfer from her natal home to the conjugal home, breaking ties with the former and building with the latter. She is thus put through an intermediary stage what Van Gennep calls a 'liminal' stage, where she is neither 'in' nor 'out'. This stage is symbolically marked with the *Mayun* ceremony. For this ceremony, which takes place a few days before the wedding day, traditionally the bride-to-be is segregated from the main household and confined to a separate apartment or a separate room, where she was surrounded by her age mates and was not required to participate in any household activity. She was in effect treated like an outsider or a guest and was made to feel a stranger in her natal home. She was expected to be bashful in the presence of elders, including her own parents. *Mayun* was an elaborate ceremony and may be regarded as rite of 'separation', as the bride-to-be was separated from her initial state and left in transition. It was a kind of threshold for a girl's social status, during which time rituals reinforced the significance of marriage for women. The bride-to-be was, to begin with, dressed in very simple clothes, either pink or amber, depending on the regional preference. She did not wear any jewellery, except a bangle in her right wrist, all to create a contrast with the wedding day when she would be fully decked with jewellery. The bangle she wore had attached to it an iron ring, some grains of rice and fresh green grass wrapped in a piece of cloth. Rice signifies prosperity and fresh green grass fertility, the two essential requirements of marriage for a woman, viz., that she should be provided for and have children.

The girl was groomed to be presented to her rightful 'owner' as a relaxed (she was withdrawn from all housework) and seductive person. Towards this end, her body was massaged with a special scented herbal paste twice a day – a practice that was designed to make her body supple and provide an alluring aroma. The first massage was also marked by a ritual in which seven *suhagans* (married women) put a little of the paste called *butna* on her palm, after which the Nai's wife rubs it on her body. The ritual was accompanied by singing of folk songs by professional singers attached to the family *by jajmani* relationship.

The songs referred to wishful thinking about the happiness of the girl to be married, and jokingly to the impending relationship between the families of the spouses. Among Indian Muslims a permanent joking relationship is established between the two families. Anthropologists regard this as a technique that societies have evolved to reduce the tension caused by the loss of a daughter to another family, and also to camouflage the implied hierarchical relationship between the families of the couple where the girl's family is given a lower status.

Unmarried girls and widows did not participate in the *butna* ceremony and while unmarried girls may be around and sing songs, widows were required to absent themselves from such joyful occasions, as widowhood signified misfortune and a bad omen. It may be noted that the boy to be married was not secluded in *Mayun*, nor *butna* is massaged on his body nor any restrictions are placed on the widower. Most such rituals are still performed at Muslim weddings with some minor modifications, such as the duration of *Mayun* has been reduced and the bride-to-be is not expected to be bashful. Although the rituals among the urban educated are performed with more frolic than seriousness, this does not mean that gender relationships have been radically altered.

Indian Muslim weddings usually spread over days, depending on the family's economic status, but the minimum was two days. A day before the wedding day *Mehndi* (henna) was celebrated when henna is put on the bride's hands and feet. A ceremony similar to the *butna* ceremony, where seven *suhagans* put a little henna on the bride's palm, takes place now except, in this case, a pan leaf was first placed on the palm and then the henna was placed on the pan leaf in order to prevent any irregular colouring of the palm. The ceremony was accompanied with singing. In the past, women from the singer caste used to sing at this ceremony, but now, with the breakdown of the *jajmani* system, women from the singer caste are no longer available and so friends and relatives sing the same folk songs. The *Mehndi* ceremony was accompanied with much fun and frolic. Sisters and younger relatives of the groom bring henna for the bride and sing traditional songs. Quite often a singing competition between the groom's and the bride's sides takes place and is the cause of much hilarity. *Mehndi* ceremony is normally a time for joy, when jokes between the relatives of the groom and the bride flow freely, followed by refreshments or a meal. A day before the girl's *Mehndi* ceremony, or the same afternoon, her sisters and relatives take henna to the groom also, but he only puts a tiny bit on his little finger just as an auspicious symbol.

On the night before the wedding day, women went to nearby mosques singing and carrying sweetened rice balls and earthenware lamps for placing in the mosques and for seeking God's blessing for the future happiness of the couple. It may be noted that women among the Muslims in India are not allowed to go into the mosque to pray; instead they say their *namaz* at home. Even on this occasion they do not offer a proper *namaz* in the mosque but just put their palms together and pray for the couple.

On the day of the wedding, the *baraat* (groom and his relatives and friends) comes ceremoniously in a joyous procession for the *Nikah,* which is followed later by *Rukhsati* or *Bidai* (bride's departure to her husband's house). Traditionally *baraat* consisted only of men with no woman accompanying the groom, but now-a-days, with the relaxation of *purdah* among urban educated classes, women also participate in the *baraat* and take gifts of clothes and jewellery for the bride. A Muslim bride is dressed in the clothes brought by the groom's family but she may wear the jewellery given by her own parents. The groom, in his turn, wears the clothes sent to him by the bride's parents along with henna the previous day.

The dowry system as prevailing among Indian Hindus was not practised in the past by North Indian Muslims. Hardly ever any financial transactions in money or kind were entered into before marriage. However, the girl's parents gave gifts on their own volition and suiting their pocket to the married couple. These gifts might include kitchen utensils and other household items, like bedding, linen, etc., in addition to jewellery and clothes. While it was not a matter of agreement, the brides' parents were expected to send their daughter to her husband with gifts according to their resources. In fact, it became an established custom that a bride may never enter her husband's house without some gifts from her parents. Equally it was customary that the groom bring a *bari,* i.e., jewellery and clothes for the bride, consistence with his financial status. In recent times, expectations from the groom are receding in importance, while from the bride's parents increasing. What is expected from the bride's parents now may include things like a TV set, other modern electronic gadgets, a car or a scooter, depending on the family's resources. Giving and receiving is becoming a status symbol among the Ashrafs as well as non-Ashrafs.

Among the Kameens not only is the incidence of giving and taking increasing, a tendency to settle in advance the items, to be given by the bride's parents, is also growing. Young men or their parents are getting more ambitious and often demand articles of comfort and status, such as electric fan, TV set, a scooter and even a car. If such demands are not met before marriage and the girl's parents are unable to meet them subsequently, ill-treatment of the girl and marital discord follows. These trends signify a progressive adoption of the regular dowry system among the Muslim non-Ashraf communities. Despite this, marriage continues to be absolutely essential for the girl and usually instead of spending on their daughter's education parents will save the money for her dowry. Furthermore, with modern symbols of status to be displayed at marriages, the occasion is becoming a much more expensive affair in all classes of Muslims, and the onus to meet the expenses is placed more on girl's parents than on boy's to parents. In effect, while the value of boys is increasing with changing aspirations of young men as reflected in their demand for bigger dowries, the value of women, their lives and their status is declining.

On the day of the wedding, as soon as the *barat* arrives the ceremony *of Nikah* takes place. Among the Muslims, *Nikah is* simply a civil contract and no religious authority is required to perform it. Normally, two adult men, accompanied by a *Maulvi* (religious cleric, who is optional and not legally required) come to the bride and take her consent to the marriage. The *maulvi* repeats the *Nikah* formula, which simply says, "You (names the bride), daughter of (names the father and not the mother) are to be married to (names the groom), son of (names the father of the groom and again not the mother) for *Mehr* (mentions the amount of the *Mehr)*, do you agree?" The bride is required to say 'yes' three times, but her distinctly audible consent was regarded to be against the requirement of modesty, so her consent was usually conveyed to the *Maulvi* and to the two witnesses by an elderly aunt. The bride normally cried along with other near relatives, at the time of the *Nikah,* which finalized her separation from her natal family. Women by themselves cannot be witnesses to a *Nikah.* In case two men are not available, one man along with two – not one – women can be accepted as witnesses. It may be observed that gender inequality is expressed throughout the marriage proceedings.

The same *Maulvi* and witnesses, after procuring the bride's consent, go to the groom, repeat the same formula and ask for his consent, which he gives audibly and emphatically as, unlike the bride, the groom is not required to be modest in this regard. Certain verses from the Quran are also recited in the male quarters. Sugar and dates are distributed after the completion of the *Nikah* among the male gathering (a custom believed to have been practised at Prophet Mohammad's weddings). An elaborate meal is served. Nowadays those women who do not observe *purdah* may come in the male quarters and more modern urban families may bring the bride too, after the *Nikah,* in the male quarters. After that the *Rukhsati* takes place, when the bride is taken to the husband's house. *Rukhsati* is accompanied by males singing a traditional song about the bride's severing herself from the natal family. This song is called 'Babul' and it pleads with the bride's father, *'Babul ham tore khoonte ki gayyan, jidhar banoho bandhjayen; Bhayya ko deene mahle do mahle, ham ko dine susral'* (Oh father, we are cows tied to your stake, you can tie us whereever you wish; To our brothers you have given palaces, to us *susral).*

Bride's arrival at the groom's house was also marked with rites of 'integration' and first a symbolic act of hostility took place. The groom's sisters block her entry into the house and would not let her enter until after strenuous bargaining resulted in a settlement and the requisite payment was made by the groom to sisters. All this was done in good humour. It signified the fact that an outsider (the bride) enters and occupied the place that initially belonged to the daughters of the house, and so the daughters of the house must resist and demand to be compensated. After the payment was made, the bride entered the house and she was seated in the hall with her face covered with the *ghunghat* (the edge of the *sari* used as a veil). The groom was then invited and was made to sit facing the bride. A platter of sweetened rice, decorated with slices of coconut, was then placed between them; it may be noted that the ritual value of coconut was borrowed from the Hindus. The groom took a pinch of rice and placed it in the bride's palm. He did this seven times and this ritually confirmed his role as a provider.

Relatives and friends of the groom, who gathered around the bride, then offered her gifts, and each time a gift was offered the bride removed her *ghunghat* to display her face, since most of them were seeing her for the first time. Remarks were whispered on the bride's physical appearance, her age and the jewellery she wore given by her parents. This used to be an ordeal for the bride, especially if she was not beautiful or was not wearing expensive jewellery. The groom did not have to go through any such ordeal. When the groom visited his bride at night, the bride was given some wax to hold in her hands, so that 'the groom's heart will melt like wax' goes the superstition. He was made to wash the bride's feet with milk, signifying both prosperity and respect that he may bring to her. Many of these rituals continue to be performed even now amidst jokes and laughter without the seriousness that was attached to it earlier.

It may be pointed out that the entire paraphernalia of ceremonies and rituals was and continues to be the domain of women. All of these are contrary to Islamic instructions and are completely the reflection of local traditions. Within India many regional and caste variations in ceremonies and rituals are encountered. Although birth and marriage celebrations affirm the lower status of women, they also provide them some space of their own as well as the experiencing of a sense of power. They get an opportunity to use their managerial skills beyond the purely domestic domain in organizing events and determining the sequence, manner and timings of rituals and ceremonies. All rituals had to be performed perfectly with regard to all details. This was taken very seriously, as it was believed that any deviation would bring bad luck. On such occasions women also had an opportunity to order their men around, demanding money for the events and for making available the requisite materials and goods. Above all these occasions were a great source of entertainment for women who had few avenues to entertain themselves. These occasions may be viewed as concessions granted to women to relieve their otherwise limited and oppressive lives within the confines of the *Zananah*. None of these ceremonies or rituals has the approval of the orthodox Muslims who pronounce them as *bidat* (contrary to Islam) and condemn them as superstitions. In this way they have tried to snatch away what little space women had carved for themselves. However, the force of tradition and culture has been strong enough to ignore the fundamentalists' reproaches. The Little and Great Traditions have co-existed and continue to co-exist.

References

Ahmed, I. (1973) 'Endogamy and Status Mobility among the Siddique Sheikhs of Allahabad, Uttar Pradesh', in I. Ahmed (ed.), *Caste and Social Stratification among Muslims*, Delhi: Manohar Book Service.

—— (2002) 'Theology, Law, and Sociology of Muslim Divorce Practices', in I. Ahmed (ed.), *Divorce and Remarriage among Muslims in India*, Delhi: Manohar Book Service.

Ahmed, L. (1992) *Women and Gender in Islam: Historical Root of a Modern Debate*, New Haven and London: Yale University Press.

Ahmed, N. (1909) *Banat-un-Nash* (in Urdu), Kanpur: Newal Kishore Press, first published in 1872.

—— (1967) *Miratui-ul-Uroos* (in Urdu), Lucknow: Newal Kishore Press, first published in 1869.

Ali, M.H. (1917) *Observations on the Mussalmans of India*, William Crooke (ed.), London: OUP, p. 186.

Balchin, C. (1994) *A Handbook on Family in Pakistan*, Lahore: Shirkat Gah.

Bhatty, Z. (1993) 'Status and Power in a Muslim Dominated Village of Uttar Pradesh', in Imtiaz Ahmed (ed.), *Caste among the Muslims*, New Delhi: Manohar Book Service.

Chhachhi, A. (1994) 'Identity Politics, Secularism and Women: A South Asian Perspective', in Zoya Hasan (ed.), *Forging Identities: Gender, Communities and the State*, New Delhi: Kali for Women.

Dube, L. (2002) 'The Meaning and Content of Marriage in a Matrilineal Muslim Society', in Lotika Sarkar, Kumud Sharma and Leela Kasturi (eds), *Between Tradition, Counter Tradition and Heresy*, Delhi: Rainbow Publishers.

Engineer, A.A. (2001) *Islam, Women and Gender Justice*, New Delhi: Gyan Prakashan.

Gennep, Van (1960) *Rites of Passage*, London: Routledge and Kegan Paul.

Hali, A.H. (1960) *Chup Ki Dad* (in Urdu), Delhi: Chanakya Publications, first published in 1897.

Hussain, R. (2000) 'The Effect of Marriage Preferences on Women's Autonomy: A Case Study', Pakistan's Population Issues in the 21st Century, Conference proceedings, Karachi.

Hyder, Q. (1975) 'Muslim Women in India', in Devaki Jain (ed.), *Indian Women*, New Delhi: Publications Divisions, Ministry of Information and Broadcasting, Government of India.

Ibbetson, D.C.J. (1916) *Punjab Castes*, Lahore: Government Printing Press.

Jeffery, P., R. Jeffery and A. Lyon (1988) *Labour Pains and Labour Power*, London and New Jersey: Zed Books and New Delhi: Manohar Book Service.

La Fontaine, J.S. (1985) *Initiation: Ritual Drama and Secret Knowledge across the World*, London: Penguin.

Lateef, S. (1990) *Muslim Women in India: Political and Private Realities, 1890s to 1980s*, New Delhi: Kali for Women.

Memissi, E. (1987) *Women in Islam: A Historical and Theological Enquiry*, New Delhi: Kali for Women.

Metcalf, B. (1992) *Perfecting Women*, Delhi: OUP.

Minault, G. (1999) *Secluded Scholars: Muslim Education and Muslim Social Reform in Colonial India*, Delhi: OUP.

Mukherjee, P. (1988) 'Sex and Social Structure', in Karuna Ahmed (ed.), *Socialisation, Education and Women: Explorations in Gender Identity*, New Delhi: Orient Longman.

Raman, V. (2002) 'Understanding Hindu Muslim Relations: The Banaras Story', in Lotika Sarkar, Kumud Sharma and Leela Kasturi (eds), *Tradition, Counter Tradition and Heresy*, Delhi: Rainbow Publishers.

Singer, M. (1959) *Traditional India: Structure and Change*, Philadelphia: American Folklore Society.

Thanvi, A.L. (1992) *Heavenly Ornament*, Berkeley: University of California Press.

Yaseen, M. (1958) *Social History of Islamic India*, Lucknow: Upper India Publishing House Ltd., p. 126.

7

Anti-Imperialist Humanism

The Feminine in Rabindranath Tagore's Theatre

Esha Niyogi De

In this paper I study the role played by femininity in Rabindranath Tagore's (1861–1941) play *Red Oleanders/Raktakarabi* (1924), and also set the gender imagery of this play in the context of the anti-imperialist politics of Tagore's creative imagination. My position is that images of women and femininity in this play and other writings by Tagore were part and parcel of his lifelong conceptual pursuit to rethink human collectivity against the grain of a world riddled by empire, capital and orthodoxy. What Tagore struggled for through his imaginations of the feminine was a polyphonic and internally dialectical authorial voice that both critiqued western masculine imperialism and was self-critical about the reactionary male nationalist perspectives that were proliferating in his colonized context. Through his depictions of the rational and corporeal attributes of female characters, in other words, he was at the same time attempting to be self-reflexive with regard to all the ways sovereign and separatist identities took shape in the imperialist and native patriarchal contexts of his time, and also to imagine how collectivity could re-emerge against and beyond such orthodox subject positions.

In this 'self-searching' position on men and masculinities, Tagore, of course, did not stand alone in his context. He was in tune with what Tanika Sarkar describes as the 'intense self-critical re-appraisal of Hindu malehood ... with no parallel in Victorian England'[1] which was occurring in course of the growth of a critical awareness about forms of human subjection amidst modern-educated anti-imperialist Indian thinkers. Still, Tagore's self-critical evaluations of masculine power do stand out amidst his peers' in that they were not an end in themselves. Rather, they were an integral part of his larger struggle to conceptualize a radically non-coercive human collectivity based on his experience of a world riddled by the manoeuvres of empire and the lures of capital. In looking at this struggle through the lens of what was central to Tagore's intellectual being – his literary activity – we note that it not only was complexly gendered but that its gendered vision was also transcultural and trans-regional. His practice and poetics rejected or selected from and mobilized various traditions of performance and representation including Indian learned and folk genealogies (the Sanskrit *rasa* theory, regional folk appropriations of Vaishnava *bhava* theory) and post-Enlightenment European theories (romanticism, symbolism, verisimilitude, allegory). On the one hand, they invoked non-illusionist and depersonalized concepts from Indian aesthetical and performance traditions to critique the masculinism in the sovereign individualist perspective privileged by contemporary European theories and to call for the surrender of subjective authorship; on the other hand, they invoked (and often gendered as female) such ideas as individual agency, independent reason, human equality and revolutionary historical change that were prevalent to European representational practice.

Tagore's migratory, and what at first glance appears as contradictory transcultural practice had a specific direction. His productions partook of the growth, on the grounds of empire, of a liminal language of what I have termed *anti-imperialist humanism*.[2] Like some other activist intellectuals in modernizing colonial India, Tagore was selectively translating European humanist discourse, and he was mobilizing non-humanist Indian aesthetics and philosophy to resist and self-critique the sovereign identities (foreign and native) born of imperialist modernity and capital. In this critical and transcultural approach to European modernity, he was not alone but one among a line of anti-imperialist and internationalist thinkers in India and elsewhere in the non-West. This diverse company includes the African-American W.E.B. DuBois, the Algerian Frantz Fanon, the Chilean feminist Gabriela Mistral, and from Tagore's own context of colonial Bengal the Anarchist Kazi Nazrul Islam and the early feminist Rokeya Sakhawat Hossain, to name a few. Reflecting upon worldwide experiences of subjection, these radical modern non-European intellectuals tried above all not to reinvent separatism by declaring non-western cultures to be unilaterally superior to western imperialist culture. Instead, they attempted to correct the roots of separatism in a post-imperial world through looking across cultures and societies and evaluating right and wrong, relatively successful or failed notions of human community and empowerment.

This paper is part of a larger study of the ways that European humanist discourse – of individualism, equality, universal humanity, and revolutionary historical change – were appropriated and critically mediated by such Indian anti-imperialist thinkers in the years of colony and the early independent Indian nation–state formation. My study debates the wholesale anti-humanism prevailing throughout the otherwise disparate positions of such influential postcolonial and subaltern theorists as Ashis Nandy, Dipesh Chakrabarty, Partha Chatterjee, Homi Bhabha and Gayatri Spivak. In a recent publication I have detailed my specific disagreements and agreements with these respective theorists, and have also presented an alternative model of culture-specific anti-imperialist agency.[3] I will not revisit these issues in this paper. However, I wish to emphasize here that my study has been motivated by the concern that the anti-humanism in the prevalent models – stemming from these theorists' over-reliance on western academic critiques of European humanist modernity (especially Michel Foucault's undoubtedly important critique of the modern historical subject) – has led to the neglect of radical non-western translations of European humanist discourse such as Tagore's. In viewing the sweeping anti-humanism and anti-historicism from a feminist perspective, I have been even more concerned about their political implications. For while the anti-humanist position has conduced theoretical models that are cultural-binaristic (Chakrabarty, Chatterjee) or ethnic-absolutist (Nandy), and remain inattentive to women's issues in pre-modern and non-western patriarchies, it has led to the sidelining of the more critical, anti-separatist and transnationalist strands of thought that emerged from the grounds of empire. In my view, the latter certainly merit revivification in our globalized world of late imperial capitalism.

Focusing on Tagore's aesthetical politics of translating European humanist concepts, I show through my discussion of *Raktakarabi* that he struggled to challenge exactly what Michel Foucault identifies as the coercive aspects of post-Enlightenment personhood (sovereign individualism, disembodied and instrumental reason, the collusion of knowledge with institutional power),[4] while he also was appropriating what he saw as the emancipatory potential (for women and the marginalized) in such European notions as personal autonomy, equality and liberatory historical change. The gender imagery of such theoretical creative works as this play presents an especially provocative register of Tagore's transcultural imagination of an emancipatory humanist collectivity for two reasons. Firstly, it shows how he strove to critique and to dialectically mobilize indigenous and Indian aesthetical and pre-capitalist social models against the grain of contemporary European masculinist models of representation and authorship, and it implies his alertness about his own complicity with the sovereign authorial voice and the objectified gaze. Secondly, it illustrates that while Tagore endorsed through a gendered lens such humanism-based (Kantian) ideals[5] as individual agency, the independence of reason from coercive social structures, and the autonomous human agent as the harbinger of revolutionary change in masculinist and patriarchal social structures (imperial capitalist and nativist), he also saw these ideals as provisional and process-oriented rather than as finalizable in and by any one person. From a non-essentialist perspective, *Raktakarabi* suggests that the ideals of individual agency and the autonomy of thought and emotion (Tagore, unlike Kant, refuses to bifurcate emotion and reason) are to be collectively striven for, and also to be critiqued and revised from multiple cultural perspectives and social standpoints. They are not fully achievable by any one person since all people are situated within power structures and potentially complicit (at least partially so) with hegemonic perspectives.

The story of *Raktakarabi* unfolds in the land of *Yaksha* (the spirit who guards gold deep under the earth in Hindu mythology). A young woman named Nandini (literally, 'the giver of happiness') has been brought into the land. She is the most vibrant and colourful presence in the narrative, decked in red oleanders, occasionally bursting into song, and lending the role to dance choreography. In this dystopia, Nandini finds a king conducting his operations concealed behind an iron mesh; she hears from behind the mesh occasional howls and groans of people in pain; around her, she sees numerous men known by numbers not names incessantly toiling to dig deep under the earth for gold, or drowning exhaustion in alcohol while being told by the priest that the way to divine grace is by maintaining an unshakable composure through trials; and she witnesses garishly extravagant celebrations in the worship of the flag *(dhwaja)*. She also encounters a professor supported by the king who endlessly cultivates knowledge in 'physical science' (*bastutatwa;* literally translatable as the 'study of matter'). Through most of the play, Nandini awaits the arrival of Ranjan (literally, 'the act of giving happiness'), the male companion from whom she was torn and brought over. The semantic implication of the names of these two outsiders is clear. Even though happiness in the transitive or the happening (Ranjan) is missing, its fount (Nandini) still exists. While we do hear that people have caught glimpses of Ranjan passing down the road playing upon the strings of his *sarengi,* we never see him alive. When the iron mesh finally uplifts, we see revealed Ranjan's dead body lying where the king unknowingly killed him. This revelation marks the watershed in the narrative. Asserting that Ranjan surely will return, Nandini leads a revolution joined by the king himself, the professor, and many others. She collectively moves forward on the prophetic resolve that they will break down the mega-structures of this land of accumulation. In closing the play implies, however, that this struggle will be to Nandini's death. While she herself, not any other historically-situated individual, will incarnate the prophecy the collective struggle will continue for revolutionary social and conceptual change.

From the point of view of genre this play elaborating verbal and visual images, such as that of the red oleanders, on an otherwise minimalist stage, certainly reminds of European

Symbolist theatre. It resonates with such guiding notions of symbolism as 'synaesthetic' imagery, impressionist simplicity, and the evocative use of words, shapes, and theatrical gestures to suggest meanings beyond 'immediate and concrete reality'.[6] Indeed, the play's combination of poetic language, music and choreography (as called for by the script) resonates specifically with Richard Wagner's concept of the *Gesamtkunstwerk* or 'total art work' that pre-figured Symbolist theatre.[7] Wagner drew on Schopenhauer's idea that the contemplative art of music could transfigure the degraded materialism of ordinary life through allowing 'an escape from the self and will'.[8] According to Walter Benjamin, the European tradition of literary Symbolism further developed the logic of Romanticism in that it placed the 'perfect individual within a progression of events which (was) infinite but ... nevertheless redemptive, even sacred'.[9] Precisely this genre's enshrinement of a singular, sacred and perfect-able individualism, however, makes it incommensurable with the literary framework of *Raktakarabi*. Tagore's play poses a contrast in two ways. To begin with, it presents a landscape of pain, death and revolution with uncertain and rather than a redemptive teleology promising to reinstate principles and practices that are better than what exist, while it also denies centrality and potential perfectibility to any one historically-located individual. Moreover, it emphasizes a collective rather than a self-contained individual-centred vision. While at the play's close, the individual protagonist Nandini departs on her struggle unto death, other voices collectively take up her visionary refrain. With regard to the politics of collectivity in this play and others by Tagore, it is noteworthy that both his practice and theory of stagecraft were radically at odds with the disembodied character of the Symbolist and Wagnerian operatic stages.[10] Theorizing and working against the grain of the remoteness of performer from audience in modern European stagecraft (Realist proscenium and Symbolist),[11] Tagore drew on rural theatre (*jatra*) and rural and urban street performance traditions of Bengal to theatrically imagine an eclectic and embodied confluence of performers and spectatorship. His plays and dance dramas traditionally placed all the singers together with performers on the stage, or they happened in open spaces where performers and audiences intermingled (a tradition still surviving at Shantiniketan, the university campus he established).

All in all, I see in *Raktakarabi* not a conventional Symbolist play with a homogenous-individualist telos, but rather a two-pronged allegorical theatre that appropriates and mediates the humanist ideal of the individual from a transcultural perspective. On one trajectory, it is what Benjamin characterizes as a baroque allegory, a reflexive aesthetical structure assembled of 'ruins' and 'fragments' that bear the 'imprint of the progression of history'.[12] The play's landscape of accumulation and its principal subjects reveal the fragmentation born of individuals reduced to masculinist possessors. Implicating the male author's own subject position, the baroque allegory relentlessly uncovers the various ways in which to know and represent under capitalist governmentality means also to become inclined to possess and to use. On the other trajectory, the play is what I would call a normative allegory in the prophetic mode. It allegorically envisions the contours of an Indian culture-specific modern individual from an anti-imperialist, pro-woman and pro-ecological perspective. I should add that the vision of social and cultural change this play presents resonates with some key aspects of such visions of universal rights as articulated by contemporary empire- and capital-centred feminists like Chandra Talpade Mohanty.[13]

On the baroque trajectory of the play, Nandini, the feminine fount of happiness, becomes the contrapuntal signifier allegorizing what is erased or foreclosed in the process of possessive knowing and instrumental reasoning. In this respect, the professor's and the king's relationships respectively to Nandini are relevant. The professor presents the predicament of a self-critical intellectual inert within the power and control his knowledge brings. In contrast to the bureaucrats and the mine workers of *Yaksha* land, the professor is quite self-aware about what is going wrong with his world. But he fails to command the critical energy to think how to set things right. Thus, he speaks of the way capital accumulation and governance are dehumanizing people such that they keep violating the earth driven by their 'baggage of need' (*darkarer bojha*), and he admits that like everyone else around him he too succumbs to the baggage of instrumental rationality by devoting mind and body to respite-less and unhappy work.[14] At fleeting moments he also knows the world through the blissful eyes of

Nandini and in terms of her 'free and unburdened time' (13). As he says with an erotic pang, the 'net' of his scholarly pursuit is ripped by emptiness when she suddenly departs. Yet the professor reverts to his intellectual and practical inertia by staking the pessimistic conviction that the one who understands that 'to survive is to be able to kill is the one who does survive' (71) in this world. He also asserts that this killer-subject is the centre of 'humanism' *(manusatya)* in his context (77). Why despite his momentary reciprocity with Nandini's presence the professor fails to command the drive to resist the institutions of accumulation, predatory knowledge, and power becomes clear once we see him in relation to the king.

The voice of the king behind the iron mesh is radically conflicted. He oscillates between the inclinations to possess and to control, on the one hand, and on the other to effectively bond with Nandini and all she stands for. No doubt, it is he who has brought Nandini to *Yaksha* land. Throughout he interacts with her from behind the mesh, responds to her calls, and calls and reaches out his hand to her. We also hear him tell her how exhausted and overburdened he is. Beyond this, Nandini narrates a resonantly erotic scene of her encounter with the king behind the mesh. She narrates that he took her hand and caressed it, and that silently and with eyes closed he kept running his fingers through her long flowing hair (51).

We should note that the woman's flowing hair (*elochul*) implies a deviation from the discipline of keeping hair braided that formed a part of women's regimen in caste Hindu households of village Bengal. It is arguable that the opening of hair was seen as a way of further opening to pollution the body of a woman which already was seen as more open and pollution-prone than a man's (certainly a belief existed amidst some Bengali Hindus that a woman's open hair caught the evil eye of spirits especially at some moments of the day).[15] In this regard, it also is significant that open hair was a familiar sexual trope used by Tagore in his poetry. Through this trope, he frequently evoked in his creative writing the Vaishnava erotics of the Radha-Krishna *lila*.[16] Drawing on the aesthetical ethics pervading popular performances traditions of eastern India, Tagore sought to mobilize the Vaishnava ethical ideal that a state of worldly-self-surrender is achievable through the inversion of the social hierarchy of *prem* (love). While mainstream Hindu social custom places procreative love for the preservation of the *bamsa* (patriline) and *kula* (clan) above sexual-and-spiritual love-as-play, namely, *lila*,[17] Vaishnava philosophy inversely posits that *lila* or illicit love (*parakiya prem*) is what enables human confluence with divinity. For only in this site can one be truly unencumbered by the self-serving rationality of dynasty, property and related carnal desire. Although Tagore's erotic imagery of the king with Nandini once more evokes the Vaishnava poetic trope of self-surrendering love-play, its moment in this work is short-lived. We hear from Nandini that immediately thereafter the king drastically changed his tune and asserted that what he desires most of all is to 'know' her (51). The knowledge of her that he seeks is not at all affective and reciprocal but fiercely mechanistic. In his own words, he want know Nandini 'back and forth' and to break her down 'part by part' (22).

In his own fiery elucidation of the play's meaning, written in the *Manchester Guardian* in response to the charge of western audiences that the work was too abscure (1924), Tagore himself sheds light on the king's interaction with Nandini. He describes Nandini as a 'real woman' who is pursued by 'an abstraction ... an acquisitive intellect (which) plies its psychological curiosity into the elusive mystery of love through vivisection'.[18] In view of this comment, the king's abrupt shift from his erotic immersion in Nandini's corporeal presence to his predatory analysis of Nandini's psychology of happiness carries a deeply disturbing meaning. The implication of this shift is that for the masculine subject of a capitalist society such as the king – who is, in Tagore's words, an 'abstraction' of a man guided by 'the spirit of organisation' (120) – both erotic relationships and rational interactions with others amount to the same attitude. For such institutional subjects all relationships, whether mediated by self-conscious reason or by emotion and desire, are a matter of claiming an object to possess and to use. And it also is precisely on this attitude that the professor converges with the king. While he occasionally does manifest a self-forgetful erotic rationality in respect of Nandini, the professor in his turn also wants mechanistically to know her and vivisect her meaning and that of her name.[19] On this baroque trajectory of the play, Nandini the feminine presents of allegory of all the human elements and possible ways of life that are infracted and ruined as capitalist governance rears its masculinist subjects and constructs eyes of possession and objectification.

However, this baroque allegory exposing the ruinous subjects of imperialist capital and knowledge still is only one of the strands of the play. It is complemented by a normative allegory in the prophetic mode. This is an allegory of how collectivity could re-emerge against institutionalized masculine positions, and what the characteristics would be of the autonomous person (one who potentially is independent of organized power) who leads the revolutionary change. This normative strand unfolds through the delineation of Nandini's modernity. We learn that the king has glimpsed in Nandini's 'thick youth' (*nibid yauban*) a form of the 'new' (*nabeen;* the word also means 'fresh,' 'recent,' 'young') which is at odds with his own conception of progress. The king's conception is that time moves forward (and yields products) at an exponential rate (in the king's language, two words are used interchangeably to designate the modern, the connotative *nabeen* and the more denotative *bartaman* or 'present/contemporary' (72). Although he has caught fleeting glimpses Nandini's alternative form new time, the king is driven to admit that he is unable to grasp it. In frustration, he alleges that the professor's 'physical science' (72) is to blame, presumably for not providing the tools for elucidating this alternative newness. At first glance, this imagery of a (feminized) modernity which fleetingly intoxicates and yet eludes the scientific approaches both of modern governance and its knowledge base bears striking resemblance to the 'whirlwind of modernity' as a 'dialectical motion' against existing structure and received concept that Marshall Berman has identified in nineteenth century Europe.[20] However, we understand that Nandini's modernity is not simply a movement working on the basis of a binary opposition to unsettle the dominant present and its knowledge forms once we consider Tagore's own Bengali commentary on this play.

In his 'Prolegomenon' to the first edition of the play (1924), Tagore states that the work is a re-telling of the politico-economic narrative which he sees in the Hindu epic, *Ramayana* (*Raktakarabi*, 117). In his own play he has re-presented what he sees in the epic as a conflict between the agrarian hero Ram and the demon Ratnakar (literally, the holder of gold) over the abduction from Ram's breast of the feminine Sita. Tagore maintains that he has revivified what the epic prophetically staged through this conflict, namely, the clash between a 'civilization of living through the tilling of land' *(karshanjibi sabhyata)* and another 'civilization of living by the means of attractions' (*akarshanjibi sabhyata;* although the more obvious meaning of the prefixed word *akarshanjibi* in this context is 'non-agrarian,' I keep the pun intact in the translation because it makes the word a potent metaphor for industrial capitalism). This genealogy of *Raktakarabi's* Nandini, as uncovered by the author, certainly illuminates her role from several directions.

To begin with, it explains that Nandini's palpable and erotically charged presence in the narrative performatively re-creates the attractiveness of the fertile body (of human and non-human nature) which is being devastated by capital accumulation in this land. Enhancing the palpability of this attraction, Nandini indeed is markedly sensualized in the midst of the other characters. She is very vocal throughout-uttering what we may call gut reactions to the 'peculiar' (*adbhut*) existence of people around her, often breaking into song and lending the role to dance choreography – and she also is obviously sexualized in contrast to other characters. Appearing in colourful attire, she wears at the parting of her hair red oleanders that are the colour of the marital sign of the *sindur* signifying menstrual blood and fertility. Furthermore, she sings as a refrain the play's thematic harvest song:

> [The month of] *Paush* beckons to you:
> Come, O Come, O Come.
>
> See you not, her basket is laden with crop:
> Loss, O loss, O loss!

It is this refrain that will be taken up, upon her exit at the play's close, by the collectivity of women and men involved in the anti-capitalist revolution for social and mental change.

Where Nandini defies a utopian and androcentric reading as a fertility goddess who calls for the community's return to the fertile land and procreative nature, on the other hand, is that her time has been named as new and future-oriented in a way not understood by the modern governors of capital. This implies that Nandini is a revolutionary Sita – appropriated from the androcentric Hindu epic and given a new lease of life as the prophet of a more sustainable form of progress. She stakes the principle that progress should resist the clash and the discontinuity of civilizations. The implication is that while the progressive-minded people take in their stride the reality of modernization, they should mobilize to decentre human work and life from the organizing structure of (i.e., institutions upholding) accumulation and its 'attractions'. Nandini's agency in decentring organized space is further reaffirmed by the Vaishnava resonance evoked by her extra-marital relations with Ranjan, as indexed by the red oleanders he had motivated her to wear. Deriving from the Vaishnava tradition, both Nandini and the wanderer Ranjan with the musical *sarengi* are shown to be people of the road, who also evoke on the margins of *Yaksha* land (in the madman, Bishu, for example) the urge to wander (164). This is not to be mistaken for the ego-centred wanderlust common in European Romantic Symbolism since in Tagore's imagination no individual after all is able to take to that perfect road of freedom, and the Ranjan who might have is dead when he arrives in the narrative. It seems to me that Nandini and Ranjan's reported and imagined meanderings take on another meaning. They open precisely the space in which to explore possible alternatives to the organized (colourless and de-sexualized/unfertilizable) confinement occupied by the meshed-in king, the encrypted gold-diggers, and the book-suffocated professor.

All in all, then, *Raktakarabi* is an unconcluded dialectic of allegories. A normative allegory – presenting in a prophetic mode alternate principles of time, space, nature and the individual knower – is set against a baroque landscape of progressivist knowledge and its human ruins. The point of the tussle between these respective strands of imagination is to stake a complex set of principles through which a more holistic and sustainable human existence can be envisioned for the future by means of meticulous critiques of the imperialist present and its masculine identities. By allegorizing the principles of correction as feminine, moreover, Tagore is striving for self-critique. He is reflexively attempting to take responsibility for his own proclivity, as a man and male author of privilege, to assume the possessive eye, to make the error of becoming the 'killer humanist' who precipitates the ruin of humanity through both representation and interrelated social practice. In this light, it is also noteworthy that Tagore displaces the androcentric myths alike of the *Ramayana* and the Vaishnava Radha-Krishna *lila* by making Nandini (Sita/Radha) the prophetic agent of the revolution-without-end while showing Ram/Krishna/ Ranjan to be absent. Moreover, he presents the re-formation of the ruinous organized landscape as a revolutionary process led by the woman.

What the prophetic mode of the normative allegory implies in this play, as I see it, is that any fully coherent and comprehensible formulation of principles for social and aesthetical change is bound to be susceptible to the possessive institutional perspective of its individual author, or for that matter of a collective speaking as an individual. Therefore, while people should stake principles, at the same time they should keep in view an open-ended and a trans-local frame of reference.

It is especially significant in regard to referentiality that in his English commentary on *Red Oleanders*, written in the *Manchester Guardian*, Tagore states that Nandini is the play's sole completely 'individual person' (123). Provocatively, he adds that Nandini indeed is the true individual, who poses the starkest contrast to the man produced of 'organization,' because she presents the 'divine essence of the infinite in the vessel of the finite' (123). My foregoing discussion of the dialectic at the heart of Tagore's anti-imperialist imagination should have clarified that the latter statement ought not to be taken as Orientalist nostalgia. Instead, it should be read as suggesting that Nandini allegorizes a provisionally formulated principle of the holistic individual. She presents a transculturally mediated appropriation of the European humanist ideal of the individual who is free of stultifying structures. For, on the one hand, her portrayal endorses the modern humanist notion of individual freedom and, on the other, suggests that to achieve this form of agency and freedom a person has to surrender the possessive and objectifying masculine eye born of capitalist modernity and empire. Therefore, the ideals of the individual are understood in this play by Tagore as a trans-historical goal of a collective and cumulative struggle which ought to be simultaneously ongoing in the realms of ideas and of social practice.

Notes

1. Tanika Sarkar, 'Hindu Conjugality and Nationalism in Late Nineteenth Century Bengal', *Indian Women: Myth and Reality*, ed. Jasodhara Bagchi (Hyderabad: Sangam Books, 1997), p. 101.
2. See my delineation of this term in 'Decolonizing Universality: Postcolonial Theory and the Quandary of Ethical Agency', *Diacritics* (32: 2) (Winter, 2004), pp. 1–17.
3. Ibid.
4. See Michel Foucault, *Order of Things: An Archeology of Human Sciences* (New York: Vintage Books, 1970), especially chapters 2 and 3; 'Technologies of the Self', *Ethics, Subjectivity, Truth*, trans. R. Hurley, ed. P. Rabinow (New York: New York University Press, 1994), especially pages 224–25; and 'A Preface to Transgression', *Language, Counter Memory, Practice*, ed. Donald Bouchard (Ithaca: Cornell University Press, 1977), pp. 29–52.
5. See the delineation of these ideals in Charles Taylor, *Sources of the Self: The Making of the Modern Identity* (Cambridge, Mass.: Harvard University Press, 1989), pp. 355–90.
6. J.L. Styan, *Modern Drama in Theory and Practice, Vol.* 2: *Symbolism, Surrealism, and the Absurd* (New York: Cambridge University Press, 1981), p. 2. The theory of 'synaesthesia' is to be found in the work of Rimbaud and Baudelaire, both of whom were writing in the decades prior to this play.
7. Ibid., p. 6.
8. Taylor, op. cit., pp. 443–44.
9. Walter Benjamin, *The Origin of German Tragic Drama*, trans. John Osborne (London: Verso, 1977), p. 160, 178, 180.
10. See Styan, op. cit., p. 8. See also the Symbolist versions of stage design especially pages 10–24.
11. For Tagore's critique of the way contemporary proscenium stagecraft created between performer and audience, see his commentary on Bengali theatre *Satabdir Natyachity*, eds. Debashish Majumdar and Shekhar Samaddar (Calcutta: A. Mukherjee and Co., 2000), p. 25.
12. Benjamin, op. cit., p. 180.
13. C.T. Mohanty, *Feminism without Borders* (Durham: Duke University Press, 2002), pp. 2–3.
14. Rabindranath Tagore, *Raktakarabi* (Calcutta: Visva-Bharati, 1924).
15. Sarah Lamb. Uma De tells one such occasion of the early twentieth century in her ancestral home in a village of Jessore, East Bengal (now

Bangladesh). A pregnant woman had bathed unusually late one day and kept her hair unbraided till the night. Soon afterwards, she miscarried and gave birth to a dead son. Ever since then, she was bitterly accused and subjected to physical abuse by her in-laws of bringing down the evil eye on the family offspring by exposing her hair to the spirits at dusk. *Interview*, Los Angeles, 30 August 2000.

16. See, for example, his well-known poem 'Sagarika' which depicts how a freshly-bathed beauty sitting by the riverside with her damp flowing hair lures to shore the wandering boatman, a familiar figure of Bengali Vaishnava poetry, *Sancahita*.
17. Ronald B. Inden and Ralph W. Nicholas, *Kinship in Bengali Culture* (Chicago: University of Chicago Press, 1977), p. 24.
18. Reprint, *Visva-Bharati Quarterly*, October 1925, p. 123.
19. The framework of Tagore's critique of knowledge resonates with Sandra Harding's point that one of the characteristic features of modern western science is the 'shift from an organicist to a mechanistic model of nature' and that important aspects of western scientific knowledge 'can be attributed to the successes of predatory expansionist policies'. See her work, *Is Science Multicultural?: Postcolonialisms, Feminisms, and Epistemologies* (Bloomington: Indiana University Press, 1988), pp. 55–56.
20. Marshall Berman, *All That is Solid Melts into Air: The Experience of Modernity* (1982, New York: Penguin, 1988), p. 21.

8

On the Question of Women in Films

Gulzar in Conversation

Sukrita Paul Kumar and Malashri Lal

SPK–ML: As a film-maker, have you consciously worked out your position vis-à-vis women and, if so, has there been any planned effort in pursuing it?

Gulzar: No, mine is not a conscious effort in picking up the subject of woman for my films. And yet when I look back at my work I find that it turns out to be a common subject for me. The process may begin with one's fascination for a story or a relationship and you start working on the script, realizing only later that the subject of your choice is a common link across your work. I am one of those very few directors who generally picked up woman-oriented subjects. Perhaps this came to me from my guru, Bimal Roy. There used to be very few directors who worked on that subject. In my case, however, in my very first film *Mere Apne,* the protagonist was an old woman, played by Meena Kumari. I approached different producers to make this film. I had to struggle to make it, since there was no dramatic story or romance, no heroine except the old woman, but perhaps that is precisely what made me take up the subject.

When I look back, I realize that my training began during school time. Even then, I was sensitive to the position of women, their tragedy and suppression. I could relate my mother's situation to one of the short stories that I read in those days, Munshi Premchand's *Idgah.* In *Idgah* there is a small boy called Mahmood who watches his mother making *chapattis* everyday and sees how her fingers are burnt. When he goes to the *mela* along with his friends, all the children are busy buying toys and playing around, but this boy spends the money he has saved on buying a *chimta* for his mother. When his mother asks him what he had brought from the *mela,* he answers, 'I have bought a *chimta* for you, so that you may not burn your hands while making *chapattis.'* Even when I was in school, I could relate this to my own mother who also used to make *rotis* on *tandoor.* In Punjabi houses, this was an everyday activity, and I had seen bum marks on my mother's arms and wrists. Premchand's story sensitized me to my mother's predicament. I realize that earlier this was only a part of my subconsciousness. Since then I have cherished a special feeling towards 'woman,' by this I don't refer only to the heroine of the romance, but I see her in a variety of roles – as friend, sister and beloved. Having made my beginning as a film-maker with a film such as *Mere Apne,* with the old woman in the centre, there was no looking back. Subsequently, there were many films of mine around a 'woman' character.

SPK–ML: It looks as though for you literature and films have happened alongside each other. Are there any other stories and novels that inspired you to make films which are woman-centred?

Gulzar: I think another important film that came my way was *Khushboo.* It was based on Sharatchandra's novel, *Pandit Moshai.* Sharatchandra had some influence on me right from my school time; I had read a number of his works: *Manjali Didi, Badi Didi* and *Pandit Moshai.* What touched me in *Pandit Moshai* was the helplessness of this girl whose husband left her and married someone else. But the author does not project her as an object of pity and that is the most beautiful thing about Sharatchandra, that he maintains the dignity of the woman. I really appreciate the way the self-esteem of the girl is kept up. Sharatchandra establishes value for this self-respect for which the girl becomes so likeable! I believe, I imbibed a lot from this writer who helped me become alert to the need to recognize the dignity of woman, first, by her own self and then, also by others. I think this settled somewhere in my subconscious and surfaced actively when I selected the subjects for my films, though I did not consciously graft this out.

SPK–ML: What about your critics or viewers, did they pick up on them and do you think your films adequately spread the awareness with which you made these films?

Gulzar: I think they did because that is how I treated women characters in my films. It is true of almost every film of mine because of this basic attitude remains a part of you no matter what theme you choose. If I search around this subject in my work, I think of my film *Aandhi*, the story of a career woman. To create the drama effectively I planted the husband opposite her – typically he doesn't like his wife going out. This attitude is similar to another film of mine, *Kitab*, based on the novel, *Pothik* by Samaresh Basu. In *Aandhi*, the husband has to realize the importance of his wife as a public figure and her role in society. The point that I put across is not just about her working and earning, but her role in the society. The husband understands it finally, and when she wins the election and she doesn't want to go, he says, 'Look, you have a responsibility and I don't want to see you defeated. I am with you wherever you go, whether it be at home or outside. I'll come along with the child, when she comes from the hostel; we'll come and meet you, but go ahead and do your work.' Moving further down into my career as a film-maker, showing the terrorist movement in Punjab, in one of the scenes the boys are waiting at their hideout for the missileshooter for their final attack. Nobody expected that the missileshooter would be a girl. This was in my film *Maachis*.

SPK–ML: This kind of role switching makes a great impact on the viewers especially through the powerful medium of the film.

Tell us, did you have a message to deliver about gender roles when you planned this scene?

Gulzar: No, it was not consciously done, but again, subconsciously, I just didn't differentiate between man and woman while framing this character and her job. While plotting the role, it just didn't occur to me that conventionally this is not a girl's job. It came to me quite automatically and there she is, at par, hand in hand with the other comrades! But, I actually think that a woman is always there, right at the frontline. Don't we have the example of Barkha Dutt who did such a courageous job of reporting directly from the front in Kargil!

SPK–ML: Do you see a progression in the depiction of women in your movies – from *Mere Apne* to *Meera* and then *Maachis* and beyond?

Gulzar: I think there has been a steady advancing of the position of woman seen in my films. Starting from *Mere Apne* upto *Meera* and *Maachis*, there has been a gradual shift and growth of space for women. Looking back at the last forty years, I see that the position of women has indeed improved. An increasing number of groups are working for the freedom and equal rights of women. But this is not something that can merely be discussed theoretically; equality cannot be divided with a knife! If there are ten areas where the woman may be leading the man, there are ten others where the man may be leading. It is not something that can be measured, weighed and divided. Equality for woman has to come with an inherent conviction and it is linked closely with respect for her as a person; the respect has to come from within. I feel that education in the urban society has made a lot of difference, but if we go into the interiors of the country, the conditions have not changed much. Probably progress in our country is slow in every department, and equality for woman may really take a long, time because it seeks a change of mindset and because it is the man who has to change. The man has to understand, especially the middleclass man, who is literate but not educated. Men are so bound with their traditions and refuse to change because it does not suit them.

SPK–ML: You seem to see a very clear rural-urban divide. Do you think that urban society is more liberated and a greater freedom is granted to the woman in the city as compared to the rural woman?

Gulzar: One thing which I see obviously is that the upper class apparently enjoys equality, because there are no inhibitions there. The same is true of the low class; men and women work together without any inhibitions. For example, women in the hilly areas work outside and men do household chores. The switching of roles comes so naturally.

SPK–ML: Men and women may be working together in many instances, but what about the oppression and wife-bashing that goes on among all classes?

Gulzar: This again is true more of the lower middle class, not so true of the absolutely working class. In fact, in the working class, the woman may be seen beating the man. She'll make him sit outside the home if he is drunk. Among the absolutely low working class, dwelling in slums, there are problems of survival – they are constantly confronting the question of life and death; where is the scope of working out equality of sexes? Both man and woman struggle to survive and fight the day-to-day battle of living.

SPK–ML: Do you think films, and especially popular Hindi films, represent the realities of society? In that, can one say that films record a sociological history?

Gulzar: Of course, our films do reflect the society of the times they are situated in. Don't you see so many changes in the present-day cinema as compared to the earlier? The image of the mother, for instance, has changed in today's films. Earlier, the heroines used to merely sing songs and may be dance, now along with the dance, some profession is attached to them. A girl may be shown working as a telephone operator, another may be an officer in some big corporate house, the image in both cases is that of a woman working outside the house. Our films are freely using this image of the woman, different from the earlier one.

SPK–ML: But you think that conceptually there is a tremendous departure in the projection of a woman in popular cinema – doesn't the popular cinema still view woman as an object, still not depicting her as a subject with her own existential angst and identity?

Gulzar: But I do see a change, and when I am talking of this in the context of the Hindi film, I do think that now since a profession is attached with the heroine, the scope of expression of her identity expands. Then there is that image of the mother – you now see her signing cheques and speaking English. However, in popular cinema, there are no woman-oriented films. I sometimes feel annoyed with the heroines, with what they accept as roles for themselves. They surely don't need to do that for money. They can easily afford to refuse such roles. Our heroines have to be educated. They can help significantly to change the scenario by doing more meaningful roles and preserving their own dignity. In this profession they may win more recognition than even the director. They have to understand their own strength.

SPK–ML: So, what you are suggesting is that women who accept these roles, have themselves to be educated first for the right choices to be made and not compromise their social responsibility for money or glamour?

Gulzar: Yes, there are a few women like Jaya, Shabana or Tabu who understand what they have to do. Others who are well-placed and educated but not 'educated' in the real sense, have to realize the meaninglessness of their roles. They have to learn to go beyond their individual selves to understand the damage they might bring to the cause of 'women' by generating images of woman as object, even though glamorized. They think of it as a career: I am at the top, at no. 1 or no.2. They have to realize that acting is much more than that. Even for their own gratification!

SPK–ML: Despite the gains from commercialism and glamorization, have the abounding numbers of the male-centred or hero-oriented films provoked a dissent ever in the movie world? If not from the heroines, from the directors or even from the heroes? Has this ever become a matter of concern in Bollywood?

Gulzar: If one is in commercial cinema, there is no running away from the straight equation of demand and supply. They say that heroine-oriented films don't work well while hero-oriented films go well in the market. Heroine-oriented films are referred to as family films. But indeed, there is some change from the earlier films, say in the films of Sooraj Barjatiya. In films like *Hum Aapke Hai Kaun,* women characters have come across as live, though this film too, was after all done totally for commercial purposes and not for the sake of propagating a certain image of women. The moment films are termed as family films, they need to go deeper into the characterization of women of India, to be more respectful to the role they play at home and develop an understanding of their compulsions sensitively.

SPK–ML: Your participation in these deliberations on Women's Studies raises the idea of incorporating and in fact sensitizing first the academics and then the viewers of films to women in media. Films are a powerful medium, and popular too. In what way do you think it would help the Women's Studies programmes to include film appreciation and workshops from the point of view of arousing feminist consciousness?

Gulzar: It could certainly help in raising awareness. One point that I have missed out earlier, and wish to record now is, how in the last two decades, there has been an ever-increasing number of women writers, directors and even technicians, sound recordists, camera-women and editors (Renu Saluja is one of the top editors in the film industry). They are very competent. Interestingly, more and more girls are joining the technical departments!

SPK–ML: Do the women directors show greater sensitivity to the roles of women in their films? And, is there a strong community consciousness amongst women who are making films?

Gulzar: Women do get their due respect in the film industry. Perhaps they do not need to come together to seek or demand their space in any special way. I think many women directors have come out with depiction of women with a serious concern for their individual identity. Women like Kalpana Lajmi, Deepa Mehta, Meera Nair and Meghna Gulzar, all of them have picked up various relevant issues. But why should only a woman pick up women's issues? Men should choose these subjects, like we did in our times.

SPK–ML: Aren't the male directors bothered by the cruel modes of oppression women of various classes go through?

Gulzar: Some of them are Shyam Benegal for instance. But as it is, there's a need for better understanding and evolving of good, sensible Hindi cinema.

SPK–ML: What is happening at the grassroots doesn't seem to affect the film-makers who are into depiction of so much glamour. Why is this so?

Gulzar: At the grassroots, women certainly should be made more aware.

SPK–ML: Coming back to a point we discussed earlier regarding the impact of films, films reach the deep interiors of the country, they reach the masses. The cues and messages, the signals they project about gender roles are very important. And yet a large percentage of films are insensitive to the depiction of the women in particular. What are the measures to be taken to make some headway in improving the situation, because if the film improves, the society may well change. There'll be fresh orientations.

Gulzar: The priorities in the system have to be worked out. One cannot isolate films from the system. The priority of education for children for instance. Child labour is a problem. Lots of things have to be put in order and the issue about equality of woman too is of primary concern. Perhaps Women's Studies could evolve more and more programmes in a bigger way and create film appreciation courses for social understanding.

SPK–ML: Do you think that the film world too needs to have Women's Studies courses for greater awareness?

Gulzar: Yes, there are many who can be and should be educated. There was a time when the educated families wouldn't send their children to films, though it is no longer true. I think in these times of electronic media, good cinema can go a long way in educating people through entertainment. But there is nothing to feel disheartened about. I do see a lot of hope around with a lot of gender issues being brought out into open discussions. Though I do wish that this awareness could reach the grassroots as well. It concerns us all as a grave issue – for the nation – the question of equality for women.

9

Interventions to Tackle Domestic Violence in India and the United Kingdom

Ann Stewart and Manjeet Bhatia

'The transnational circulation of people and ideas is transforming the world we live in, but grasping its full complexity is extraordinarily difficult ... . The international human rights movement against violence to women provides a valuable understanding how new categories of meaning emerge and are applied to social practices around the world'.[1]

The Protection of Women from Domestic Violence Act (PWDVA) was enacted in India in 2005. This Act was the result of many years of social activism on the issue of violence against women in India. The original Bill was drafted by a group of feminist lawyers (Lawyer's Collective) after extensive consultation with concerned voluntaries organizations (VOs) throughout the country. The Act takes a civil law approach and focuses on the protection of the woman, in particular empowering her with the right to stay in the matrimonial home.[2]

When the Domestic Violence Bill was introduced in the Indian Parliament, it generated a passionate debate. Within the Women's Studies Network (WSN), a British Council-sponsored initiative in India, the issue brought together a large number of women's studies departments in universities throughout India to discuss and develop models and strategies for effective interventions in the formulation of the Bill.

A need was felt to understand the different approaches that other nations had adopted to deal with the issue of domestic violence. Since the United Kingdom had a thirty years experience in addressing the issue, a collaborative effort, supported and sponsored by the British Council in India, was initiated to make links with academics working in the areas of gender and law in the UK through video conferencing. The exchange of ideas regarding the UK and Indian approaches to violence against women resulted in the formulation of a proposal that was selected by the British Council for grant from amongst other proposals.

A specific link between Delhi University's Women's Studies and Development Centre and Warwick University's School of Law was established.

Aim

Given the emerging approaches to domestic violence, the aim of the project was to consider the different types of co-ordinated responses to domestic violence which exist in England and in India. We sought to consider the role of women organizations in bringing domestic violence to the public attention in both England and India, and their contribution to the development and management of these initiatives. We had very limited resources and could only undertake a very small amount of primary research with key informants. Coventry in the UK, and Jaipur and Bangalore in India were the three cities selected for survey. In addition, some Delhi-based VOs interventions were also studied.

The approach in the United Kingdom[3] to violence against women was determined by the activism of the women's movement during the 1970s and 1980s which brought the issue out of the private sphere of the family into public policy agenda. The dynamics of the sustained pressure that women's organizations put on policy makers became an integral part of the process of formulating legislation.

Domestic Violence and the Law

The Protection of Women from Domestic Violence (PWDV) Act, 2005 seeks to create an institutional framework for the protection of women. It provides a comprehensive definition of domestic violence (section 3)[4] based on the UN Framework for Model Legislation on Domestic Violence and the UN Declaration on the Elimination of Violence against Women. It recognizes the woman's right to live free from violence and also the right to reside in a shared household. Protection is not limited to spouses but extends to relationships in the nature of marriage and also a range of family members such as mothers, daughters, sisters and widows. A magistrate is empowered by this Act to issue a protection order and/or custody order and/or residence order as well as grant compensation and monetary relief. Breach of this civil order becomes a punishable (criminal) offence (section 31). The Act adds to existing laws so that other criminal offences and civil proceedings are not affected.

The novel elements in this framework are the establishment of Protection Officers (POs) and the recognition of service providers. The central role played by women's organizations and other social activist organizations is institutionalized through registration with state level government as service providers who can record Domestic Incident Report (DIR) and forward it to magistrates, arrange for medical examinations and ensure the provision of shelter, if necessary. The police, in addition to their existing criminal law enforcement powers, are required to record a DIR and assist in the enforcement of court orders. State governments are responsible for the appointment of POs and the registration of service providers and generally expected to publicize the Act. States are also required to provide the appropriate budgetary support.

Thus, this framework seeks to harness state resources to assist women who experience violence. It encourages the incorporation of VOs into state procedures and recognizes the limitations of reliance solely upon reporting to police under existing criminal provisions.

In England, there have been in recent years increased efforts to provide co-ordinated responses to domestic violence. While there are as yet no specific criminal offences relating to domestic violence, there has been civil legislation on domestic violence since 1976.[5] A woman can report violence to the police who can use their powers if they consider that a criminal offence has occurred or she can initiate a civil action to obtain a non-molestation and/or occupation order. These processes are channelled through different procedures and courts. Very recently, in line with the greater emphasis on the criminalization of domestic violence, a breach of a non-molestation order constitutes an arrestable offence.

There are a wide range of agencies involved in the handling of different aspects of domestic violence. Organizations within the non-governmental sector provide advice and assistance, run shelters, offer counselling and advocacy services, nationally or locally, generally or to specific communities or groups. Local government service providers such as social workers and housing officers have statutory responsibilities in this area. Health service professionals are increasingly involved in policies to detect and support those experiencing violence. Central government is involved in the provision of financial support not only through the welfare system but also through a myriad of policy initiatives aimed at tackling domestic violence. Much effort is concentrated on improving the response of the justice system (police, prosecutors, courts, probation and prison services). There are now inter-ministerial and inter-departmental groups to consider the policy implications of domestic violence. Statutory organizations such as the police liaise with activists at both national and local levels and activists and academics are closely involved in discussions relating to policy.[6]

Each of these bodies has their own objectives and culture. There is now a recognition that a co-ordinated response to domestic violence is essential to tackle the range of issues which women face in these circumstances and to provide effective protection and support.

Contexts

In Britain, it is estimated that one in five (21%) women and one in ten (10%) men have experienced at least one incident of non-sexual domestic threat or force since the age of sixteen. If financial abuse is included, then 26 per cent of women and 17 per cent of men had experienced domestic violence since the age of 16.[7] The presence of children in the household is associated with nearly double the risk of domestic violence for women.[8] It was estimated that there were

12.9 million (from a population of approximately 60 million) incidents of domestic violence against women in 2001. The estimated cost of domestic violence in England and Wales in 2001 was £ 23 billion.[9] Only 50 per cent of domestic violence incidents are reported that constitute 17 per cent of all reported crimes. It must be noted that women who are in existing relationships are particularly unwilling to report.

Vigorous lobbying by activists over many years ensured that domestic violence in UK is now much less likely to be treated as 'merely domestic' by the police. However, a recent research study on one police force showed that only one in 27 reported cases of domestic violence results in a criminal conviction. Of the 869 incidents recorded at least 70 per cent of those charged were repeat offenders but only four resulted in a custodial sentence, whereas the majority of convicted offenders were fined. Chronic offenders were not stopped from violence and harassment by this process and victims felt let down and shocked by the sentences.[10] Equally women face considerable difficulties if they feel strong enough to take a civil action against the perpetrator. They must identify a sympathetic family lawyer who will assist them with the procedures for taking out an injunction (for a non-molestation or occupation order). Legal aid is limited to those on state welfare benefits or the women will be required to contribute to or pay all the costs. Court injunctions are ignored by some men which means that the women must return to court for enforcement. Obtaining an injunction can cost in the region of £ 2,500, which is beyond the means of many UK women.

The considerable academic research on many aspects of violence against women shows that there continues to be a failure to achieve positive outcomes for women, in other words, stopping the violence and securing her safety and well-being.[11]

The statistics on the prevalence of violence against women in India show a similarly depressing picture. According to National Crime Record Bureau's (NCBR) 2003 report, out of the total incidents of crime against women reported, 23.4 per cent women were molested and even higher, 36.1 per cent were tortured. According to NCBR's 2002 figures, 121 women were sexually harassed, 31 women and girls trafficked, 45 women raped, 40 women and minor girls abducted, 21 women murdered, and 135 women faced torture by husbands and in-laws everyday. One woman faced torture in her marital relationship every 11 minutes. Every 3.2 minutes a crime was committed against women in the year 2002. These figures have to be understood in the context that majority of the cases of violence against women go unreported. According to a voluntary organization 80 per cent of the cases of domestic violence are not reported to the police.

Coordinated Response of Different Agencies Needed to Deal with All Aspects of Domestic Violence

In UK, over the years, coordinated responses of government agencies as well as voluntary sector have evolved. There are active reviews and experiments for effective interventions.

In India, committed voluntary organizations (VOs) succeeded in bringing different agencies together to deal with specific issues. However, there are some successful experiments, specially in states of Rajasthan and Maharashtra, of collaboration between VO and government agencies leading to some formal structures in place. PWDV Act seeks coordination among several agencies.

It is predicted by NCRB that by 2010 growth rate of crime against women would be higher than population growth by then.

Activists have again moved these issues out of the private sphere and insisted on action by the state. As Anjali Dave points out: 'The state responded sporadically and experimentally with a wide range of institutional developments. These included the setting up of family courts, special women's courts, legal aid cells and lok adalats as well as amendments to the Indian Penal Code (Sections 498A, 304B and 376) within the judicial system and within law enforcement, the establishment of vigilance committees, all-women police stations, crimes against women cells, family counselling centres in police stations and special cells. The voluntary sector also responded through the Central Social Welfare Board, family counselling centres, short stay homes and awareness generation schemes.'[12]

Although there are now specific criminal offences associated with violence against women in particular under Section 498A of the Indian Penal Code, there has been widespread concern that this has not been an effective provision in relation to domestic violence partly because it tackles 'cruelty' and is still associated (incorrectly) with issues of dowry abuse. The conviction rate is very low and there is a continuing discourse of 'victim blaming' associated with this provision.[13]

There is dire need for coordinated action between all the agencies particularly between the police and women's organizations.[14]

Thus, in India, we were interested to see how the proposed institutional structure associated with the PWDV Act, particularly the PO and registration of women's organizations as service providers, would 'fit' with existing initiatives involving VOs with co-ordinated responses of one sort or another. In England, we were interested in seeing the way in which VOs contributed to co-ordinated responses in one area which was the subject of a new initiative to provide a specialist domestic violence court.

Coordinated Responses

Coventry, England

Coventry is city in the centre of England with a population of about 2,30,000 people. In 2003, 88.5 per cent of households were white, 7.9 per cent Asian, 2.1 per cent black and 1.5 per cent mixed or other. In 2003–04 there were 5,053 recorded incidences of domestic violence. The Coventry Domestic Violence and Abuse Partnership (CDVAP) is a multi-agency partnership which co-ordinates Coventry's response to domestic violence. It has representatives from the police, the health service in particular midwives and health visitors (because they enter homes), education services (children at school), social services (social workers), probation and housing services and the voluntary sector (women's organizations and others). It draws up its own Strategy and Action Plan to cover all aspects of domestic violence, including the need for accommodation for women at risk of domestic violence. These multi-agency forums exist in one form or another in many local districts in England. Their overall aim is to identify people at risk of harm, then develop effective ways to manage and reduce it. (However research shows that the results are patchy). The Coventry forum seems to work well: the police are proactives and the voluntary sector is very involved.

In addition, Coventry established one of the first specialist domestic violence courts in England which provides a focus for criminal justice strategies.[15] This magistrate's court sits one day a week and deals exclusively with domestic violence issues. Magistrates (lay persons) and prosecutors have all received specialist training in the area of domestic violence to enable them to understand the complex issues involved and to treat domestic violence seriously. The Crown Prosecution Service has a protocol on domestic violence which it uses as a guide for all its actions in relation to domestic violence. According to Janice Nichols, chair of the Coventry Domestic Violence and Abuse Partnership (March 2007),

> We're building on our work over the last few years with initiatives including proactive police visits to the homes of perpetrators to warn them that officers are on their case and the use of CCTV at incidents to gather powerful visual evidence.
>
> To help improve the conviction rate of offenders, we have established a local specialist domestic violence court where prosecutors and magistrates are aware of the sensitive nature of abuse within relationships and in the last 10 months our Independent Domestic Violence Advisor has supported 73 victims who have either gone through or are going through the criminal justice system.

In Coventry there are three domestic abuse officers, one in each police state, entrusted with responsibility for overseeing domestic violence work. The performance of the police in handling domestic violence has improved substantially in recent years partly as a result of strong central guidance from the Home Office and also from the Association of Chief Police Officers. There have been a plethora of new initiatives, some based on lessons learnt from the voluntary sector on how to understand domestic violence. These initiatives are directed at a number of elements: ensuring the women's safety, improved evidence gathering and prosecution (and reducing attrition rates in the justice system). Speedy prosecution and conviction can contribute to increased safety and possibly reduce repeat events.

The police nationally are adopting a risk assessment and management approach to domestic violence. This requires officers who attend incidents to assess the level of risk (on a scale of indicators). Policing and prosecution strategies are then based on the level of risk. In Coventry 50 per cent of reported incidents are repeat offences. These assessments are shared with other agencies at the CDVAP meetings. The police are also now required to meet centrally agreed performance indicators on arrests in the area of domestic violence.

> Successful prosecutions in domestic violence cases in UK have increased from 46 per cent in December 2003 to 65 per cent in December 2006, with specialist court prosecutions rising to 71 per cent.

Generally, there has been pressure on the police from women's organizations to improve their performance. In Coventry there are a range of women's organizations including those drawn from the minority ethnic communities. These groups seek to hold the police and other state agencies accountable for their actions and to increase awareness of the particular issues which face specific women, such as those who have recently arrived in the UK, and whose immigration status may still be insecure. Women's groups have had a marked effect on overall police culture although there are still major problems.[16] The government is also keen to see improved performance under the pressure coming from both civil society and the state. Det Chief Insp Ron Winch, from Stoney Stanton Road police station (March 2007) said,

> The effects of domestic violence are extremely serious and can last for many, many years. We investigate each case thoroughly and do our very best to bring perpetrators to justice while also supporting victims.
>
> By working with partner agencies in both the public and voluntary sectors we are making real inroads to improve the way we investigate and prosecute perpetrators and change their behaviour while also putting in measures to protect victims and help them regain control of their lives.

In India, we interacted with several VOs, lawyers, judges, academics, etc. Coordinated responses of most of the VOs alone are included here for want of space. Individual professionals, however, gave important insights into the issue and the processes of addressing it.

Jaipur, India

With Police and Community

We looked at the well established Jaipur initiative by women's organizations working in and with the police to provide a co-ordinated response.

In association with the police the MSSK, or *Mahila Surakhsa Avam Salaha Kendra* (Women's Security and Advice Centre) provides the much-needed conduit between community and the system of justice, in particular, with police. In the process, police, judiciary and local community get connected. This interaction opens the possibilities of changes in value system. MSSK had been a very successful experiment that has been extended to nine other districts of Rajasthan.

MSSK functions as a bridge between formal structures (especially police), judiciary and other services. The centres, through its networks, provide counselling, free legal service, medical and trauma assistance, and rehabilitation. These have appointed counsellors at the MSSK which have police assistance whenever needed, i.e., sending notice, making a visit, lodging an FIR, etc. Counsellors maintain record of each case. The centres keep evolving strategies to meet newer challenges.

The VOs running the MSSK at Jaipur had been running the short stay home even before the first counselling centre was started. There is full-time caretaker at the short stay home. The inmates share day-to-day work of the home of cleaning and cooking. They do small errands for the home and some remunerative work that the rehabilitation unit of the VOs arranges for them. They are also given some training to undertake such work. Short stay home is like another home for all age group women and their young children. These 11 organizations meet regularly and even for any special deliberations, such as implement the new domestic violence law. This home has voluntary help from lawyers, doctors, psychiatrists, etc. The inmates are referred or accompanied to these professionals as and when needed. The broad social base of these interventions helps sustaining these efforts over the years.

Vishakha, a Jaipur-based NGO and also closely associated with other VOs at Jaipur, has extended the MSSK model to other nine districts and one rural area of Jaipur. In addition, they conduct regular training and contact programmes with the counsellors, hold meetings with the local with community (wherever necessary), and organize medical help and meditation classes for women. They are able to incorporate domestic violence as a major concern in their broad-based approach to social issues. Unlike other VOs running MSSK at Jaipur, Vishakha receives funding from donors.

Bangalore

With Community

We also consider the position in Bangalore to provide a contrast in social and economic contexts and also in the approach of local activists who have adopted a less collaborative approach to date with state personnel. According to Women's Voice, Bangalore,

> Mahila (all-women) police stations were not effective for want of government support and sensitive trained personnel.

Coordinators interacted with VIMOCHNA and Women's Voice at Bangalore. Both the organizations have their local set ups and area-wise coordinators. These local units are now proactive in taking up women's issues and building community pressure on the erring husbands and other relatives. Women's Voice regularly conducts workshops on legal literacy and works out the methodology of participatory approach with the women of the area.

Both the organizations believe in helping woman as a friend, guiding her and helping her in all aspects. If she decides to launch complain, she is accompanied to police station, FIR is registered and case is followed up, sometimes even after settlement for a few years. Community partnership also helps women and the VOs to remain in touch. Some women who want a break from the past are left alone.

Women's Voice has introduced women into neighbourhood watch scheme. Women keep watch on any kind of violence against women in their area and intervene at the local level. If the case requires advice they bring it to the central unit of Women's Voice.

Women's Voice also organizes cultural programmes including street theatre once a year for general awareness of its members.

Leadership and the teams of both Women's Voice and VIMOCHANA are highly motivated and socially aware which sustains their efforts in the face of indifferent approach of government on protecting women against domestic violence.

VIMOCHNA was not very supportive of law-based approach. Its members felt that justice is deeply embedded in the local context and cannot be generalized by the law. According to the activists of Women's Voice and VIMOCHNA,

> Middle and upper class women are in particular vulnerable as they are not aware of their rights and are reluctant to accept that they are facing violence.

Delhi

Innovative Involvement

Prayatan, a Delhi-based voluntary organization, has made a youth brigade of unemployed boys between the ages 14–25 years to act as alert community to check domestic violence and work in partnership with the VO staff to curb and support the violence survivor. These boys have been given special training by the social work department of Jamia Milia Islamia University at Delhi. The boys take help of elderly women of the neighbourhood to intervene when so required. Coordinators of the VO regularly interact with these boys. Strategies and approaches to handle the cases are discussed in these interactions. Involving men in addressing the issue of violence against women gives social recognition to the existence of such violence in the community.

This has proved to be a double-edged strategy. This constructive work has given the boys visibility and acceptance in their community which otherwise was treating them vagabonds. On the other hand, possibility of their perpetuating such violence is also checked. Involvement of youth thus tackles domestic violence cases and prevents them by educating the possible perpetrator. More importantly, involvement of men gets social recognition and community awareness of the violence perpetuated against women.

To sum up, the socio-economic context for the implementation of legislation differs significantly in the UK and India. In particular women are enabled to leave violent situations in the UK because they have access to greater economic and in many cases social resources. They are also supported by a developed welfare state. However women still face major levels of violence. Many find it difficult to leave and many choose not to. The institutional setting for the implementation of specific legal strategies has been in existence for longer than in India. In the last ten years there has been a greater commitment on the part of central government to tackle the issue and this has resulted in a plethora of initiatives aimed at the domestic violence sector as it can now been seen. VOs involved with domestic violence are increasingly integrated into the governance of domestic violence policies with state institutions. They receive state funds to support their advice and advocacy roles, to undertake training roles for the domestic violence sector and to provide shelter. They play a central role in the development of coordinated responses to domestic violence as partners in a joint enterprise although they still maintain a critical distance and act as vocal critics of policies where necessary.

In India VOs work in a different environment and view state institutions differently. The legislation in relation to domestic violence is based on the assumption that most women will not leave their homes. It is also based at least implicitly on an assumption that law enforcement in this area is going to meet with resistance from within the state. It is however clearly influenced by transnational thinking on the need for the development of state-based institutional support and collaboration between the VOs and the state through the provision of POs and service providers. VOs' views on this approach are varied reflecting their wider views on the role of state law in India and the contribution of a human rights approach. Clearly there is a much stronger sense of pluralism – of a wish to work with local communities which have differing value systems. There are tensions between a lawyer's view of the domestic violence law and voluntary's organization's view. Generally, however, the new law is seen as providing an opportunity for positive developments.

Implications for the Development of the PWDV Act India

Our very limited research took place just before the coming into force of the PWDV Act in India. There was at the time limited knowledge of the rules which would provide the basis for the establishment of Protection Officers (POs) and service providers. It was also unclear how women's organizations would respond to the idea of being registered service providers. We looked at an electronic-based discussion among voluntary organizations on the role of the new Act facilitated by Action India.[17] Some of the crucial issues raised are summarized below:

Understanding of the Law

- The law is not well understood, there is need to simplify the law to make people understand it. Many VOs are working in this direction, by bringing out posters and translating the law.
- Lack of sufficient budget allocation for strong institutional set-up, capacity building, sensitizing of personnel and awareness building.
- Need for more meaningful allocation of powers to the courts and let the POs be answerable to the presiding officer in the court
- Service providers, POs and special magistrates are not able to reach out to the victims, in dire consequences and in situations beyond control.

Creating Conducive Environment for Effective Implementation of PWDV Act

- Overall supportive environment at all levels is required for the victims to be able to reach out to the POs.
- Even today, the police, the judiciary and counsellors work on the basis of traditional system. Gender sensitization of these functionaries is crucial.
- Gram panchayats (local self-government), Aanganwadi workers (local functionaries) and SHGs may be recognized as associates of the POs and are legitimized to give support to the victim.
- District Protection Officers should have a committee that can visit different blocks weekly and can tie up with Anganwadi workers to get information and to enable them to be aware of the new legal provisions.

Understanding Social Hurdles

- Alarming social misconceptions, law is being considered as a threat to Indian family structure and strong social and cultural values.
- Training and orientation programmes for different stakeholders must include common people.
- Women who are victims of violence do not report the matter either out of ignorance, lack of confidence or for fear of being discarded by the in-laws and the family.
- Equally pertinent is women's own perceptions. She needs to understand whether 'social security' acceptable at the cost of worst possible forms of violence, atrocities, insult and humiliation.
- There is social apathy about the issue.

Role of Media

- Media has crucial role to play to raise awareness and counter negative publicity.
- Media advocacy need to organize press meets, conferences, press releases frequently once in every month in a creative way.
- Leading newspapers should be invited to participate in workshops on domestic violence. Media needs to link cases to the Human Rights Issues and the Domestic Violence Act.

Training of the Functionaries

- All POs and other appointees responsible for the implementation of the Act must be professionally trained.
- The training module should be developed on (a) woman-friendly implementation of the Act, and (b) gender sensitivity.
- Basic Information Kit should consists of the (i) overview of the Act, (ii) rules of the Act, and (iii) the budget.

Budgetary Aspect

- The Finance Ministry, in consultation with women's groups, should immediately undertake an exercise to calculate the minimum budgetary requirements for all key ministries and departments (WCD, Law, Health, Home) and create a specific budget line called 'implementation of PWDV Act'.

- Delhi State has appointed two POs in each of its nine districts.
- POs are fresh appointed, as demanded by VOs.
- POs are young post-graduate pass-outs. They do not have independent office and support structure and would need experience and training before they see themselves as eyes of the magistrate and act independently enough.
- Family Counselling Centres (FCCs) of State Social Welfare Board are listed as service providers. VOs have objection to the conciliatory approach to the family issues of FCCs.
- There is dire need of training of POs, police, service providers and magistrates.
- Courts are receiving many domestic violence cases of which only 10 per cent are through POs. Rest is handled by lawyers.

It is not clear as yet how the role of PO will develop. Much will depend on the level of state commitment to the selection and training of such officers. Will they be enabled to gain expertise in the area of domestic violence and become a focal point for processing actions? Will they foster multi-agency coordinated responses to domestic violence within their districts? How will they develop their work with the VOs given that women's groups have developed their own understandings of local domestic violence issues and networks with local communities? Will these VOs want to become service providers within a state institutional context? VOs have years of experience and networks that can facilitate the implementation of the new law if the government provides sufficient support generally for the implementation of the law.

There have been a number of developments since we completed our link which point to the need for further in-depth research. How are VOs using the new facilitative framework to support and protect women? How are the judiciary and the law enforcement bodies responding to the new context? The first Supreme Court judgment might suggest that there is going to be resistance to key elements within the law.[18]

The PWDV Act process also raises interesting analytical questions relating to the global production of human rights ideas and approaches to violence against women with which we started this report. As Merry[19] points out, transplantation is both global and local at the same time. It involves appropriation and translation. Appropriation means taking the programmes, interventions, and ideas developed by activists in one setting and replicating them in another setting. Translation is the process of adjusting the rhetoric and structure of these programmes or interventions to local circumstances. Appropriated programmes are not necessarily translated, but they are more likely to be popular if they are. However, if they blend into existing power relationships completely, they lose their potential for social change. Therefore, resistance is to be expected and in some ways welcomed because the rights based on the protection of their bodily integrity along with ideas of autonomy, choice and equality which women seek whether in England or India can never been fully indigenized into a patriarchal system. So 'inside the specific culturally resonant packaging is a core that radically challenges patriarchy'. Further research is necessary on the way in which this construction of the culturally resonant packaging of the PWDV Act is used or resisted by those involved in the delivery of justice for women.

Notes

1. Sally Engle Merry (2006) *Human Rights and Gender Violence: Translating Inlet-national Law into Local Justice*, Chicago: University of Chicago Press, p. 1.
2. For further discussion, see Rajeswari Sunder Rajan (2004) 'Rethinking Law and Violence: The Domestic Violence (Prevention) Bill in India 2003', *Gender and History*, 16 (3): 769–93.
3. For discussion involving law-based strategies, it is most appropriate to limit the discussion to England, Scotland, Wales and Northern Ireland as they all have their own devolved assemblies which to a greater or lesser extent develop their own policies and procedures.
4. It covers physical and sexual abuse, verbal and emotional abuse and economic abuse (e.g., deprivation of the necessities of life such as food, disposal of one's own assets, etc.).
5. There are a wide range of possible criminal provisions relating to assault, actual bodily harm, grievous bodily harm, sexual assault, rape and harassment. The Domestic Violence, Crimes and Victims Act

2004 gives police the power to intervene in domestic incidents by making common assault an arrestable offence. The present civil law is contained in the Family Law Act 1996 amended by the Domestic Violence, Crimes and Victims Act 2004 which comes into force fully in July 2007.

6. A. Mullender (2004) 'Trackling Domestic Violence: Providing Support for Childern Who Have Witnessed Domestic Violence', *Home Office Development and Practice Report*, 33: 1. London: Home Office.
7. Alpha Parmar and Alice Sampson (2001) 'Tackling Domestic Violence: Providing Advocacy and Support to Survivors of Domestic Violence', *Home Office Development and Practice Report*, 34: 1. Figures from the British Crime Survey (2001).
8. Ibid.
9. See Kelly Liz and Linda Regan (2008) 'Violence/Against Women: A Briefing Document on International Issues and Responses', *1006 British Council*. This is a very good source of information on the area and is available on www.britishcouncil.org
10. Marianne Hester et al. (2003) *Domestic Violence: Making it through the Criminal Justice System*, Sunderland: University of Sunderland and Northern Rock Foundation.
11. See, for instance, the National Domestic Violence Delivery Plan, March 2007 which is produced by central government. It sets out a range of national objectives to achieve a co-ordinated community response (covering a wide range of activities from building capacity within the 'domestic violence sector' to provide support, training health professionals, increasing reporting rates and arrest rates, supporting victims in the criminal justice system to developing evidence-based knowledge tie research). The report then assesses progress on these. See also Marianne Hester and Nicole Westmoreland (2005) 'Tackling Domestic Violence: Effective Interventions and Approaches', Home Office Research, Development and Statistics Directorate.
12. See Anjali Dave (2005) 'Feminist Social Work Interventions: Special Cells for Women and Children', in Kalpana Kannabiran (ed.), *The Violence of Normal Times*, New Delhi: Women Unlimited.
13. See, for instance, Shalu Nigam (2005) *Understanding Justice Delivery System from the Perspective of Women Litigants as Victims of Domestic Violence in India*, New Delhi: Centre for Women's Development Studies which considers the justice delivery system from the

perspective of women litigants and finds it underutilized, highly ineffective and also manages to re-victimize the complainant.

14. One such is the Special Cell for Women and Children in Maharashtra, for more details on this initiative, see Dave, op. cit.
15. These courts enable DV to be tackled within a multiagency framework which is designed with the specific needs of DV victims in mind. There are now 60 such courts in England and Wales. See Dee Cook et al. (2004) *Evaluation of Specialist Domestic Violence Courts/Fast Track Systems*, UK: Cardiff University.
16. Consultation with survivors of DV reveals the continuing problems with police performance. See Women's National Commission (2003) *Unlocking the Secret: Women Open the Door on Domestic Violence*, London: WNC.
17. This summary is based on the e-Discussion in which more than 75 responses were posted. Members enthusiastically responded to the three questions emanating from the topic 'implementing the PWDVN, by providing numerous suggestions on the specific mechanism of the Act, discussing its strengths and constraints and sharing experiences. The discussion was moderated by Gouri Chowdhury of Action India and was part of Solution Exchange consultation site maintained by UNDP.
18. See *S.R. Batra vs Smt Taruna Batra* 136 (2007) DLT I (SC) and the critique prepared by the Lawyers Collective WRI, www.lawyers collective.org
19. Merry, op. cit.

10

Anti-Sikh Riots of 1984 Revisited

Gender, Violence and Politics of Representation

Amrit Kaur Basra

The brutal killing of Mrs Indira Gandhi, Prime Minister of India on 31 October 1984 by her two security guards, who were Sikhs, was followed by an organized violence in many parts of India. The situation was more explosive in Delhi where, between 1 November and 3 November, hundreds of Sikhs were burnt alive, women were molested, gurdwaras were desecrated, and properties were looted and burnt. As the nation mourned the death of Prime Minister, it appeared as if Sikhs were no longer regarded as the part of Indian nation. The dazed Sikh community in Delhi, with the help of sympathetic fellow citizens, tried to cope up with the violence that had visited their bodies and souls. The aftermath of the violence saw concerted efforts by organizations like Nagrik Ekta Manch to help displaced victims of violence. Alongside processes to codify voices of victims and demand to punish the guilty also started.

This is the revised and enlarged version of the paper presented at National Seminar on 'Agency, Autonomy and Power: A Dialogue on Women and Body' organized from 23 February 2010 to 25 February 2010 by WSDC, Delhi University.

Twenty-nine years have passed by. The struggle to seek justice by the Sikh community is still continuing. It is the time to revisit these riots again. The main purpose of the paper is to explore the relationship between gender, violence and politics of representation. The initial silence on these riots gradually gave way to codification of victims' voices. During the last 29 years information has been available in many forms like written records, oral testimonies and visual representations. The paper, while taking into account all these resources, focuses on the 'living histories' of Sikhs who lived through violence in 1984 and, since then, have reorganized their lives.

The paper is divided into four segments. The first segment explores the nature of available resources and by focusing on oral narration coming from within the community provides a theoretical framework to analyse them. It remains a fact that the anti-Sikh riots of 1984 were not communal riots, yet the inside story provided by social scientists in studying communalism, communal riots and communal politics is useful in exploring many strands of violence and politics associated with their interpretation. The next section focuses on the structure of violence that was perpetrated on the Sikhs with focus on women in different parts of Delhi between 31 October and 3 November 1984. The third segment traces the processes of rehabilitation of riot victims in particular and Sikh community in general. The demand to punish the guilty was entwined with the demand to probe into the causes of riots. It brought into focus the role of state's machinery in protecting its citizens. The responsibility of the state to redress the grievances of victims also came to the forefront. This segment by studying these aspects throw light on the relationship between state and society. The last segment in relationship with foregoing objectives looks at the Sikh community from within. By focusing on the lives of few individuals, it show how Sikhs and women in particular have coped with the violence that threatened their existence in 1984 and moved ahead in their lives to claim their rightful place in Indian democracy. However, all have not been successful in this endeavour. On the basis of the above-mentioned analysis, the paper concludes that the role of state machinery in igniting and spreading violence against Sikhs in 1984 was evident. During these riots and thereafter, Sikhs have encountered violence in multiple ways. The politics of representation only created discursive space for political parties and to some extent for intelligentsia to indulge in accusation and counter-accusation to establish secular credentials. In fact, the male-centric representation has been more dominant and as it is evident in case of widows, they have been left to cope with the memories of violence and stagnant present and uncertain future of their siblings. The voices of victims were pushed to the background. Presently, while for many, it remains only a point of reference, but for Sikhs in Delhi, it is connected with the demand to get justice and upholding of their identity.

Sources and Interpretation

As stated before, written records, oral testimonies and visual representations constitute main sources. The codification of oral testimonies can be traced from 31 October 1984 with the unfolding of events in Delhi. The process is still continuing. However, there is need to make a distinction between structures and processes that have led to the recording of oral testimonies. From personal subjectivity and those of others, known to me, it can be underlined that those who lived through those times have experiential narratives at their disposal. There were eyewitness accounts by journalists. One can mention the names of Arun Shourie, Prannoy Roy, Rahul Bedi and Shekhar Gupta in this regard. They reported the large-scale massacre of Sikhs in Jehangirpuri.[1] Within days that followed these riots, human rights activists had recorded testimonies of victims. Among them were Poonam Muttreja who cofounded the Nagrik Ekta Manch,[2] Rajni Kothari of People's Union for Civil Liberties and Govinda Mukhoty of People's Union for Democratic Rights.[3] They were also involved with the processes of rehabilitation. The academic community and students belonging to the University of Delhi also made identical efforts. The voices of victims were recorded unmediated by the ideologies of recorders. Uma Chakravarti and Nandita Haksar's efforts in this regard were exemplary. These recorded narrations have been published and provide valuable information.[4]

Oral testimonies are also available in the recordings of various commissions and committees that were set up by the state. The witnesses' accounts can also be culled from court proceedings. There is need to make a distinction between official discourses available in the form of findings of various committees and commissions, narrations of political leaders[5] and accounts of eyewitnesses.

In this regard, efforts made by H.S. Phoolka, who has been fighting on behalf of Sikhs to obtain justice for them from judiciary, are significant. He has been instrumental in making the findings from official records public and has written his experiences as well.[6]

There are also accounts provided by media. There is need to contextualize these records. The changing nature of reporting can be seen over the period of time.[7]

It remains a fact that recording of anti-Sikh riots and their analysis has been a continuous process. By studying news magazines like *Manushi* and *The Sikh Review* since 1984, an attempt can be made to understand the contours of narration at the level of representation.[8]

For interpreting the above-mentioned sources, there is a need to contextualize them at the level of time and space. The oral testimonies are 'life histories' of Sikhs. They constitute narration entwined with 'self' and 'society'.[9] The feminist scholarship on anti-partition riots is also useful in interpreting oral testimonies. The works of Urvashi Butalia, Kamla Bhasin and Ritu Menon have shown that women who had experienced violence in 1984 found it difficult to recollect them.[10] The role of a researcher both as an insider to create a congenital space for recording oral testimonies and also as an outsider so as to not determine their narration becomes crucial in this regard.

The available records reflect on the centrality of violence. The nature and structure of violence has been explored in several scholarly writings. In the process, the role of state and its agencies has been pointed out.[11]

The anti-Sikh riots of 1984 were not communal in nature. It was an organized pogrom by the state overtly and covertly. Yet during the riots and afterwards, Sikhs were perceived as a monolith. Uma Chakravarti has observed that these riots resulted in the making of Sikhs as a minority.[12] There are several writings on communalism, communal riots and communal politics that provide valuable information in understanding the structure of the anti-Sikh riots of 1984. Asghar Ali Engineer, for example, who has worked extensively on communal riots, has pointed out the role of space in shaping violence.[13] Gyanendra Pandey has shown the mechanism that goes into the construction of communal discourse across time. The official discourse as evident in the utterances of leaders belonging to the Congress and other political parties can be decoded in the light of inferences provided by Gyanendra Pandey.[14]

On the basis of above-mentioned details, the paper interprets oral testimonies as available in multiple sources in relationship with context shaped by time and space. In the process experiences of Sikhs during anti-Sikh riots of 1984 and their relationship with those events over the period of time can be pointed out. The focus on inside voices in relation with other narration also helps in understanding the politics of representation and life histories of Sikhs since 1984.

Structure of Riots: Spaces and Violence

The available evidence helps in constructing the structure of anti-Sikh riots that erupted on 31 October 1984 with assaults on Sikhs and their properties. The spatial spread out, the behaviour of rioters and the vulnerability of targeted Sikhs point out the nature of organized crime. The role of rumours in abetting violence was also evident. It was asserted that Sikhs were celebrating the assassination of Mrs Gandhi by distributing sweets. They had poisoned water in many parts of Delhi.[15] It was also alleged that a train with dead Hindus had arrived from Punjab. In this way violence perpetrated against Sikhs was sought to be linked with the situation in Punjab.[16]

The spatial spread of riots engulfed all parts of Delhi where either Sikhs were residents or were caught in public spaces. The religious identity of Sikhs was targeted. Even during violence, many who were forced to cut their hair were also killed. They were identified on the basis of marks of turban on the forehead. The assault began with targeting of the cavalcade of Giani Zail Singh, the then President of India.

Sikhs were rendered destitute in both public and private spaces. The rioters had complete information about the inmates of Sikh households including women. In a systematic way, residences, schools, gurdwaras and other institutions owned by Sikhs were attacked, looted and damaged.

Rioters were fully equipped with weapons to inflict maximum damage. Local Pradhan, councillors and leaders belonging to the Congress party led them.

The behavioural aspects of rioters indicated that they did not fear police. In fact, except for a few places, police sided with the rioters and abetted crime. It was evident in East Delhi. The arrival of the army also did not improve the situation as no coordination was established between police, administration and the army.[17] The crowd consisted of individuals ranging from 50 to 400. They would appear suddenly, encircle targeted spaces and then indulge in acts of arson, looting and killing. At several place, crowd encircled the areas and searched for male and even female inmates of the houses.

The savagery was evident in torturing and burning alive of young Sikhs and even children. In most cases, kerosene was poured and males were burnt alive. In areas like Palam, old Sikhs were caught and burnt alive by placing tyres around their necks.[18]

The trauma felt by the Sikhs caught in violence was tremendous. They tried to negotiate with rioters. In areas like West Patel Nagar, Paharganj and Trilokpuri, Sikhs pleaded for their safety. They tried to get help from police but in vain. In several places, help was extended by neighbours who provided shelter. However, when rioters threatened them, they also found it difficult to support them. In areas like Rajouri Garden, where everyone remained alert, rioters could not enter.

Worse fate awaited women of all ages. They were left to see killing of their male counterparts. Many were kidnapped. Many were raped in front of their children.

Gurdwaras were also not spared. They were seen as exclusive religious spaces of Sikhs. In many areas like Shalimar Bagh, Guru Granth Sahib was also desecrated. In this way, in the absence of any supportive machinery and indifferent administrative set-up, Sikhs were subjected to organized pogrom.

On the morning of 31 October 1984, I was in Nehru Memorial Library searching books for my research. I was enrolled in M.Phil course in the Department of History, University of Delhi. It was around 10.30 a.m. that I heard somebody saying that the Director of the library had left for the residence of Mrs Indira Gandhi.[19] After some time, I noticed that the number of readers in the library was thinning. I then decided to go back home and left library around 11.30 a.m. I boarded a bus from nearby bus stop for reaching Central Secretariat. From there, I took another bus to reach my residence at Rajouri Garden. I did not know that events that were unfolding would force me and residents of my locality to remain indoors for next week.[20]

Sardar Patwant Singh[21] at his residence located in Amrita Shergill Marg was informed by his secretary Indira Mehra about the shooting of the Prime Minister by her two Sikh bodyguards. He immediately decided to call Lt. General (Retd.) Jagjit Singh Aurora, Air Marshal (Retd.) Arjan Singh, foreign diplomat Gurbachan Singh and Brig (Retd.) Sukhjeet Singh.[22] After holding a meeting, they decided to issue a press statement condemning the assassination of Mrs Indira Gandhi by prominent Sikhs. For this purpose, George Varghese, editor of *Indian Express*, was contacted. There was a lurking fear that Sikhs might be targeted in the wake of assassination. To thwart any such happening, they decided to meet the Union Home Minister, Narasimha Rao.[23]

Even the President of India, Giani Zail Singh was approached. While the administration had become alert about the deteriorating situation and the army was also contacted but the entire focus was on the wounded Prime Minister and after her demise on making arrangement for her funeral and on ensuring safety of foreign dignitaries who had gathered in New Delhi to participate in the last rites of the slain leader.[24]

The wounded Prime Minister was shifted to All India Institute of Medical Sciences. Her death was announced at 1.30 p.m. on All India Radio. The media also announced the identity of killers who were Sikhs. Rajiv Gandhi reached hospital at 4 p.m. and Giani Zail Singh returned from abroad at 5 p.m. On the same day, Rajiv Gandhi took oath as the Prime Minister of India. The body of the slain leader was kept in state at Teen Murti Bhawan where slogan-shouting crowd converged to pay homage.

Sikhs were also deeply saddened by the tragic death of Mrs Indira Gandhi[25] and were part of the crowd that had gathered in front of All India Institute of Medical Sciences to know about the condition of wounded leader. However, as the behaviour of crowd became hostile, they became aware of their vulnerability.

By 4 p.m., nearly 4,000 people had gathered outside the All India Institute of Medical Sciences. Suddenly, a group of 30–40 men formed a column. They moved in the direction of INA market. They caught a Sikh scooterist and burnt his scooter. The same group moved in the direction of Sarojini Nagar. Plying buses were stopped and Sikhs were assaulted. Their turbans were burnt.[26] The cavalcade of Giani Zail Singh was attacked near All India Institute of Medical Sciences around 4.45 p.m.[27]

It thus became clear that Sikhs were vulnerable in public places. They had to fear for security. This was the reality for those who were coming from outside in their private vehicles and even in public transport.[28] Many Sikhs were killed at the railway station and their bodies were left there.[29]

By 2.30 p.m. an electronic goods shop in Rajouri Garden market was attacked. It only alerted the locals about the impending danger.[30] The slain body of Mrs Gandhi laying in state in Teen Murti Bhawan was telecast by Doordarshan. The crowd shouting slogan 'Khoon ka Badla Khoon se Lagein' could also be heard. At personal level, it was difficult for my family to cope up with the situation. The death of slain leader was mourned but what awaited Sikhs like us was also not clear.

My brother did not return home from duty from Palam where he was working with Bharat Petroleum. He was called back from Palam, when he had just come out of his office to return home on 31 October 1984. The situation had deteriorated and he was to remain at his workplace for next week.[31]

H.S. Phoolka, a young lawyer at the High Court, had come to know about the death of the Prime Minister by afternoon. He went to Naraina where his wife worked. Her duty ended by 5.30 p.m. When both were returning back on motorcycle, a car occupant warned them that Sikhs were being assaulted at the interjection of Aurangzeb Road and Tughlaq Road. With great difficulty, passing through by-lanes, they reached their rented accommodation at Kotla Mubarakpur. Their landlord cautioned them to remain inside. However, within the next two days, it became explicit that like other Sikh residents in the vicinity, they were also not safe and had to negotiate for their safety with the help of friends.[32]

In this way, the nightmare for Sikhs had begun and on 1 November, it took the shape of organized violence directed at them.

In South, North and West Delhi, properties were looted and Sikhs were attacked. However, alert residents were also able to resist. Gurdwaras were also burnt. In few places when Sikhs tried to defend themselves, they in turn were targeted by the police. It happened with Manmohan Bir Singh Talwar, Mahavir Chakra awardee for his contribution in the war of 1971. His residence in West Patel Nagar was attacked by a mob on the morning of 1

November. The crowd kept on swelling in number and remained determined to kill all the occupants. When he opened fire in self-defence, police came and asked him to surrender. He was put in jail.[33]

In Shahdara, a Sikh truck driver was dragged out of his vehicle and was killed.[34]

According to an official estimate 2,733, Sikhs were killed in Delhi. Out of these 1,234 were butchered in East Delhi and half of those dead fell under the jurisdiction of Kalyanpuri police station.[35]

In Kalyanpuri, a mob, armed with weapons and kerosene, entered Block 11 on 1 November. Local Sikh residents, mostly from Sikligarh and by occupation iron smiths, tried to defend themselves. Many of them possessed weapons. The police intervention resulted in forcible taking away of their weapons. It was done by Soor Veer Singh Tyagi, chief of the Kalyanpuri police station. The crowd led by Dr Ashok Gupta, a local municipal councillor, indulged in killing of Sikhs and looting of their properties.[36]

The most terrible carnage took place in Trilokpuri, a resettlement colony, which housed mixed population. In Blocks 30 and 32 Labana Sikhs belonging to Sikligarh from Sindh lived. Their traditional occupation was cot weaving but over a period of time many had shifted to other occupations. The locality also possessed two gurdwaras. The organized crime was preceded by holding of a meeting by local Congress leaders on 31 October. It was also attended by H.K.L. Bhagat. On 1 November rioters armed with iron rods, wooden sticks and kerosene reached Trilokpuri's Blocks 30 and 32. Before that, they had attacked and burnt gurdwaras. The local residents approached the police and were assured by police officer Soor Veer Singh Tyagi that normalcy would soon return. Rioters retreated for the time being but returned in the night. Many like Gulzar Singh tried to save themselves by hiding. A few also shaved off their beards and cut their hair. Yet, they were caught, doused in kerosene and burnt alive. The mayhem that continued on 2 November also caused the death of 400 Sikhs.[37]

The plight of women in these riots was worse. In Trilokpuri itself, they were asked to assemble at one place and then were taken to Chilla village. Many were raped during the riots and afterwards. There were gang rapes. One Gurdeep Kaur was raped in front of her son. Rajjo Bai and Indra Bai witnessed such instances. Similar treatment was meted out to many women even in Nandnagari. Everywhere, women as mothers and wives pleaded for the safety of their male members. In some cases, young boys were dressed as girls and were saved. It became difficult for pregnant women to look for safety and they had to be provided help by others.[38]

In Palam Colony, as per police estimate, 341 Sikhs were killed. The mob consisting of 400 to 500 people crowded the roads and searched identified houses. Sikhs were caught and burnt alive. Local goons were leading the mob.[39]

There were also attacks on gurdwaras in several localities. On 1 November a large Sikh gathering had collected outside Gurdwara Sis Ganj: Maxwell Preira deftly handled the situation. While Sikhs were asked to go inside the gurdwara, the mobility of crowd was also checked. At his order, the police opened fire which resulted in killing of one person and compelled the crowd to retreat.

The seize of Gurdwara Rakab Ganj continued for five long hours. Two Sikhs, father and son, were caught by the crowd and burnt alive. Kamal Nath, prominent Congress leader was present on the spot. Even when Police Commissioner Gautam Kaul was present, very little was done to disperse the crowd.[40]

In Shalimar Bagh too, a gurdwara was burnt and Guru Granth Sahib was desecrated.[41]

Violence subsided by 4 November. There were few instances of loot and stabbing in West Patel Nagar, Shahdara, Badarpur and Anand Parbat.[42]

The violence that visited bodies and souls of Sikhs in Delhi has continued to stir them, even though 29 years have passed by.

Politics of Representation: Issues of Identity of Guilty and Punishment

The violence that was inflicted on the Sikhs led to the realization that they were not safe within their personal and public spaces. Despite efforts by concerned citizens, many were rendered homeless. The Sikh residents of resettlement areas like Nandnagari, Trilokpuri, Sultanpuri and Delhi Cantonment virtually lost everything. They were crowded in relief camps set up by activists. Gurdwaras provided shelter. There were half-hearted measures by the administrative machinery. The issue of relief and rehabilitation came to the forefront.[43] The Government of Delhi appointed a relief commission on 4 November. On 6 November, a scheme for rehabilitation was announced. An amount of ₹ 10,000 to the kin of the dead and ₹ 5,000 for the wounded was announced. On 7 November ₹ 40 lakhs were released for distribution from the Prime Minister Relief Fund.[44]

At civic level, students, academic activists and local neighbourhood communities tried to comfort dazed Sikh community. The relief camps were flooded with widows and children. Steps were also taken to record their voices. The most persistent demand that emerged from civil society was to probe into the causes of riots so that the guilty could be punished. Data was collected and offenders were identified.

It was evident in the report published by Gobinda Mukhoty and Rajni Kothari in November 1984. Aptly titled 'Who are the Guilty?', it identified Congress leaders, local goons and police officers who instigated the mob. It was concluded in the report that the riots were not spontaneous but organized.

Among the Congress leaders, H.K.L. Bhagat, Minister of state for I&B; Sajjan Kumar and Dharam Das Shastri, both MP; Babu Ram Sharma, Mangat Ram Singhal, Ashok Kumar and Jagdish Chander Tokas, members of Municipal Corporation; Lalit Makan, Mahender Yadav and Sukhan Lal Sood, Metropolitan Councillors; Faiz Mohammad Ratan, a Youth Congress leader; and Ishwar Singh were identified.

Similarly, among the police officials who instigated the mob, included, ACP, Shakarpur and SHOs of various police stations, viz., Shakarpur, Sultanpuri, Sadar Thana, Kalyanpuri, Durgapuri and Trilokpuri.

A few local goons were also identified.[45] In this report, it was asserted that violence was organized by the Congress party with the help of administrative machinery and it was not spontaneous. The political parties opposed to Congress also took a similar stand. Over a period of time, the politics of representation revolving around the genesis of anti-Sikh riots has revolved around the issue of identifying the guilty and punishment to be given to them. However, while the victims of violence have been struggling to get justice, the emergent political discourse has concentrated on vote bank politics. The issue of violence has been provoked by political parties mainly to target the Congress party. The entire party has been held responsible for causing violence. It remains a fact that issue is still alive and the stand taken up by civil society in 1984 has proved correct, yet the political discourse that emerged from the outset has remained immune to the main issues connected with the rights of Sikhs under the Indian State. It is also clear that the Congress party, whenever it has remained in power, has shown no intention to own up the guilt.

The assassination of Mrs Gandhi was seen as a threat to the nation. It was alleged that Sikhs had invited violence on themselves as two Sikh bodyguards of the Prime Minister had attacked her. Thus, for the crime of two, the punishment met out to entire community was justified. It was made explicit by Rajiv Gandhi who had become Prime Minister of India in 1984. In his public address at the Boat Club near India Gate, on 19 November 1984, he announced 'when a mighty tree falls, it is only natural that the earth around it does shake a little'.

For him, riots exhibited anger of people and he complimented the crowd indulging in violence for containing it soon.[46]

There was projection of ongoing tension in Punjab. Under Rajiv Gandhi-Longowal agreement, even when decision was taken in 1985 to set up a Commission to probe into the causes of violence, it was becoming clear that there was no intention to punish the perpetrators of violence.[47]

The functioning of commission set up under the chairmanship of Ranganath Misra made it explicit. While the activists saw it an opportunity to set the records right and to protect human and civil rights of the victims of carnage, it became clear very soon that the commission was determined to work at its own pace and also to reach its own conclusions.

H.S. Phoolka got involved with the issue of obtaining justice to the victims when he visited a relief camp at Farash Bazar. He met victims who were mostly from Trilokpuri. The aim was to help the victims file their affidavit before Misra Commission so that they could get compensation. A Citizens Justice Committee, consisting of Soli Sorabjee, Rajni Kothari, Govinda Mukhoty, N.D. Pancholi, Dinesh Singh, Justice V.M. Tarkunde, Justice R.S. Narela, Khushwant Singh, Lt. General, J.S. Aurora and Gyan Singh Vohra, was formed in 1985. H.S. Phoolka as Secretary of the Committee helped in preparation and filing of 500 affidavits. The proceedings were held in front of camera and while victims were scrutinized, individuals who were identified as perpetrators of violence were treated respectfully. The members of the Citizens Justice Committee were also not allowed to question these people. It made the members withdraw from the proceedings of the Committee.[48]

The findings of the Committee came up with sharp criticism by political leaders and concerned citizens. While Janardan Thakur called it an 'eyewash',[49] Khushwant Singh refused to attach any credibility to it. For him, 'Although born a Sikh, I express my anguish as an Indian. It is more as an Indian than a Sikh that I feel let down because in the long run, it is my country that will pay the price of failure to bring the guilty to book by condoning massive miscarriage of justice'.[50]

A.G. Noorani blamed Justice Ranghanth Misra for grave judicial offence. In his view, the report was a 'wilful, systematic flouting of the law and precedence established since the Commission of Inquiry Act was enacted in 1952'.[51]

Under pressure, the government set up another committee. Between 1985 and 2005, three commissions and seven committees were formed. The situation changed with the appointment of Nanavati Commission in 2005. Each commission/committee had brought to the surface negligence of duty by police, non-action by administration and abetment of violence against Sikhs by Congress leaders and even police. Yet no concrete action was taken to punish the guilty. The reality was outlined by Sardar Manmohan Singh, Prime Minister in 2005 in the upper house, 'We all know that we still do not know the truth and the search must go on. Justice has been denied to Sikhs'.[52]

At the level of government and political parties, the riots of 1984 have been used as a reference point to indulge in allegations and counter-allegations to attack each other and to proclaim secular credentials. While opposition parties mention the violence of 1984 to assert that justice has been denied to Sikhs, Congress leaders, whether Sajjan Kumar or Jagdish Tytler, have asserted that they did not participate in the violence of 1984 and that Sikhs were and have been their traditional supporters. The situation becomes more murky, when Sikh leaders of Congress and BJP are found to be indulging in a similar game. The victims are only used as a context to draw political mileage.[53]

It was in 2005 that Sardar Manmohan Singh speaking on the violence of 1984 apologized to the Sikhs: 'I have no hesitation in apologizing not only to the Sikh community but the whole Indian nation because what took place in 1984 is the negation of the concept of nationhood as enshrined in the Constitution'.[54]

The struggle to get justice by Sikh victims and mainly widows has turned out to non-ending. H.S. Phuka formed Carnage Justice Committee after 2005 to continue his struggle on behalf of victims.[55] The financial help to fight cases of victims was provided by Delhi Sikh Gurdwara Parbandhak Committee. Yet there have been few convictions.

The intensity of coverage in media was seen whenever cases relating to prominent Congress leaders like H.K.L. Bhagat, Jagdish Tytler and Sajjan Kumar have come up for hearing.

Jagdish Kaur, whose husband Kehar Singh and son Gurpreet were killed by a mob in Delhi Cantonment Raj Nagar area, filed a case against many persons including Sajjan Kumar. Balwan Khokhar, area Councillor and kerosene dealer, was accused of leading the mob that indulged in killing of five Sikhs – Kehar Singh, Gurpreet Singh, Raghuvender Singh, Narender Pal Singh and Kuldeep. The case was fought by CBI. Its prosecutor R.S. Cheema called it a planned communal riot in which the victims were isolated. He called it a religious cleansing, as survivors did not return back to their area of residence.

In his judgement, delivered on 30 April 2013, District Sessions Judge J.R. Aryan acquitted Sajjan Kumar on the basis of non-conclusive evidences. Balwan Khokhar, Girdhari Lal and Captain Bhagwal were given life term whereas Mahender Yadav and Kishan Khokkar were sentenced to three years' imprisonment.

Once the crowd that had gathered outside the court came to know about the verdict, there was a huge protest. Phoolka called the judgment 'unsatisfactory'.[56]

It has been found that there is more media coverage for accused leaders. Both Tytler and Sajjan Kumar have been given wide coverage and both have maintained that they had nothing to do with violence of 1984. Judiciary has not found them guilty.

Life Histories

Time is a continuum and so have been the lives of Sikhs who lived through those times and are still associated with violence in multiple ways. They remember those events but their memories have been entwined with events that have taken place since 1984 in their lives, that of community, society and nation. The variegated life experiences of Sikhs across locales in Delhi have been moulded by class, status, educational and cultural norms.[57]

Those who suffered partially at the level of material resources have rebuilt their lives. However, initially physical and mental trauma was identical for everyone. Silence engulfed them. I still recollect that in my classes in M.A., we were four Sikh girls but none of us talked about violence. Grief was personal yet collective. One of our friends who got married in 1984 had suffered heavily during the riots. Their house and press were burnt down. The family migrated to Chandigarh but returned after few years, as she got a job in the University of Delhi. Another went to join the Indian Railways and the remaining two of us are part of the academic community in the University of Delhi.[58]

At my personal level, I still recollect that commuting in buses for Sikh males was traumatic, whereas Sikh women could not be identified easily. There was an overwhelming concern for gurdwaras. Crowds consisting of women, would collect on the outskirts of wired spaces encircling Gurdwara Bangla Sahib in 1984. The police would allow small groups to go inside. I, also, was part of many such groups. The affinity of Sikhs with their religion was strengthened and there was greater consciousness about their religious identity. At the same time, distance from Hindus was also becoming explicit.

The educated Sikhs, who have been part of academic, administrative and other spaces, have continued their deliberations on the issues. Through media, conferences and writings, they have continued with their demand to identify the guilty. There has been a major concern as to why Sikhs were targeted in 1984.[59] H.S. Phoolka has given his entire life to seek justice for the carnage victims. At individual levels, Sikhs belonging to the upper and middle classes are not living under the shadow of violence of 1984.

Life had come to a standstill for widows and children belonging to resettlement colonies. Rendered without shelter, bread earners, widows were deprived of security. Their children were orphaned. They were also relocated in Garhi[60] and Tilak Vihar. While in Garhi, many households have improved their lives with the passage of time, Tilak Vihar is a grim reminder of anti-Sikh violence of 1984. In this locality boys can be seen loitering around. Very few girls who were married have been successful in leading their lives. There is lurking fear for young girls. Even when helping hand has come from the community yet financial uncertainty continues. Most of the inmates still live in the shadow of violence.[61]

Between individual and collective memories the relationship with events of 1984 have been variegated. For individuals like me, dissemination of information on anti-Sikh riots of 1984 is indispensable. There is need to point out the responsibility of state towards its citizens. For others like Jarnail Singh,[62] who threw shoe at P. Chidambaram, it is essential for the government to accept its failure in protecting its citizens and accept its role in abetting crime against them. For women belonging to lower income groups, it has been a journey of struggle to live their lives and to fulfil responsibilities towards children and elders in the family. For Nirmal Singh, who resides in USA, there is need to build a memorial in the memory of those who lost everything in 1984.[63]

By and large, the Sikh community does not hold grudge against anyone. They are also beholden to those who stood by them. They only want justice. While they are not living in the past yet they cannot forget it.

Conclusion

The foregoing narration provides the conclusion that the role of state machinery and Congress leadership in structuring organized violence against Sikhs in 1984 was explicit. The role of concerned citizens who stood by them and later on started struggle to ensure justice for victims is also explicit. However, the aftermath of the event resulted in politicization of demands put forth by the civic community. The riots were dubbed as spontaneous and role of Congress leadership was denied. The emergent political discourse remained at the level of waging allegations and counter-allegations. The violence affected the entire community but its impact on the bodies and sensibilities of women was distinct. In the aftermath of violence, widows were left with responsibilities of bringing up children. Amidst these experiences, the Sikh community has also continued its struggle at variegated levels and has overcome the processes of isolation and discrimination.

Notes

1. These journalists published the account in form of a book. For details, see, Arun Shorie et al., *The Assassination and After*, New Delhi: Roli Books, 1985.
2. For her narration, see, Poonam Mutreja, when Delhi burnt, as told to Sheela Bhutt, last updated 25 February 2005, rediff.com, India News.
3. It constitutes one of the earliest accounts based on the happening of events between 31 October to 10 November 1984. Many of the activists had tried to contain violence and had become involved with acts of relief and rehabilitation of victims. They had interviewed the survivors. See, the report of a joint enquiry into the causes and impact of the riots in Delhi, published jointly by Govinda Mukhoty and Rajni Kothari, *Who are the Guilty?*, Delhi: Sunny Graphics, 1984.
4. Uma Chakravarti, an eminent historian and activist, was then teaching at Miranda House. Nandita Haksar presently is an eminent lawyer. Both, along with students had interviewed a wide array of individuals including victims and young activists. The records were published as a book. For details, see, Uma Chakravarti and Nandita Haksar (eds), *The Delhi Riots: Three Days in the Life of a Nation*, New Delhi: Lancer International, 1987.
5. The Government from 1985 to 2005 had set up three commissions and committees to probe into the causes and nature of violence as to identify the guilty and punish them.
6. He has been involved in fighting cases on behalf of victims of carnage since 1984. His efforts can be studied from the book he wrote along with senior journalist Manoj Mitta, *When a Tree Shook Delhi: The 1984 Carnage and its Aftermath*, Delhi: Roli Books, 2007.
7. The media initially remained biased. There were very few newspapers that exposed the involvement of politicians and workers in the riots. For this paper, newspapers like *The Hindustan Times* and *The Times of India* have been studied.
8. Madhu Keshwar, Editor of *Manushi* witnessed these riots and in her magazine, highlighted brutalities committed against women. *The Sikh Review* set up in 1953 is a theological, educational and socio-cultural monthly magazine.

9. For more details, see, David Arnold and Stuart Blackburn, *Telling Lives in India: Biography, Autobiography and Life History*, New Delhi: Permanent Black, pp. 1–21.
10. Urvashi Butalia has extensively worked on partition riots.
11. Ritu Menon and Kamla Bhasin, *Borders and Boundaries: Women in India's Partition*, New Delhi: Kali for Women, 2007 reprint. Jean-Marie Domenach et al., *Violence and its Causes*, UNESCO, Paris: Imprimerie des Presses Universitaires.
12. Chakravarti and Haksar, op. cit., pp. 2–24.
13. See, for instance, Asghar Ali Engineer, 'Communal Riots: Review of 2001', *Economic and Political Weekly (EPW)*, Vol. 32, No. 2, 12 January 2002, pp. 100–4.
14. Gyanendra Pandey, *Construction of Communalism in Colonial North India*, Delhi: OUP, 1995.
15. This aspect was explored and negated in the report *Who are the Guilty?*, op. cit.
16. For this aspect, see Lt Col. Partap Singh, 'The Gathering Storm over Punjab', *The Sikh Review*, Vol. 38, No. 433, 2 February 1990, pp. 51–53.
17. It was noticed by Lt General (Retd) Jagjit Singh Aurora and Brig. (Retd) Sukhjeet Singh. On 2 November when they found that no joint operation control room had been setup between the army and police.
18. One such instance was noticed by my brother, Gurcharan Singh.
19. Professor Ravinder Kumar, eminent historian was the Director.
20. Based on personal diary.
21. A prominent Sikh and historian Sardar Patwant Singh remained closely involved with issue of violence that was inflicted on Sikhs in 1984.
22. Ajay Ashraf, '1984 Revisited: The Guilty Men of Delhi', *The Sikh Review*, Vol. 41, No. 479, 11 November 1993, p. 43.
23. Ibid.
24. These aspects have come to surface in the reports of many commissions and committees that looked in the role of administration and police in particular to know as to why riots could not be pre-empted and once started could not be controlled.
25. This aspect was stressed by many women of riots. For details, see, Chakravarti and Haksar, op. cit. See Rajni Kothari, 'Culture of Communalism in Gujarat', *EPW*, Vol. 37, No. 48, 30 November 2002, pp. 4823–25. Ashutosh Varshney, *Ethnic Conflict and Civic Life:*

Hindus and Muslims in India, New Haven: Yale University Press, 2002.

26. An eyewitness account of Dev Dutt, journalist, see Mukhoty and Kothari, op. cit., pp. 32–34.
27. Ibid., pp. 13–14. The photographs can be seen in the book written by Mitta and Phoolka, op. cit.
28. Dr Mohinder Singh presently honorary Director, Bhai Vir Singh Sahitya Sadan and Judge, Minority Education Commission was returning with his family in a car from Chandigarh. He had to lie down below the seat. At that time, he was heading towards Guru Nanak Research Centre. On reaching Delhi, he was taken by Professor Bipan Chandra to his residence.
29. For visual details, see Mitta and Phoolka, op. cit.
30. Based on my personal diary.
31. Ibid.
32. See Mitta and Phoolka, op. cit., pp. 91–96.
33. Ibid., pp. 40–46.
34. Ibid., pp. 19–22.
35. Ibid., p. 26.
36. Ibid., pp. 25–27.
37. Ibid., pp. 72–78. For more details, see, Chakravarti and Haksar, op. cit.
38. For details, see, Madhu Keswar, *Religion at the Service of Nationalism and Other Essays*, Delhi: OUP, pp. 1–15.
39. Chakravarti and Haksar, pp. 53–56.
40. Mitta and Phoolka, op. cit., pp. 49–54.
41. Ibid., pp. 82–102.
42. Mukhoty and Kothari, op. cit., pp. 28–32.
43. P.C. Alexander, 'Assassination and the Massacre', *The Sikh Review*, Vol. 41, No. 466, 10 October 1992, p. 39.
44. Mukhoty and Kothari, op. cit., pp. 26–27.
45. Ibid.
46. Mitta and Phoolka, op. cit.
47. Shri Janardan Thakur, 'Mishra Commission: A Deliberate Eyewash', *The Sikh Review*, Vol. 35, No. 399, March 1987, pp. 49–51.
48. Mitta and Phoolka, op. cit., pp. 122–46.
49. Thakur, op. cit.
50. Khushwant Singh, 'Mishra Commission', *The Sikh Review*, Vol. 35, No. 399, March 1987, p. 52.

51. A.G. Noorani, 'Mishra Commission under Fire', *The Sikh Review*, Vol. 35, No. 401, May 1987, pp. 48–53.
52. Mitta and Phoolka, op. cit., p. 6.
53. This has been seen in context of Gujarat Riots of 2002. On several occasions, leaders from Congress and BJP used riots as reference points to attack each other leading to vitiating of atmosphere. On this aspect, see, Upendra Baxi, 'The Second Gujarat Catastrophe', *EPW*, Vol. 37, No. 34, August 2002, pp. 3519–30.
54. Mitta and Phoolka, op. cit., p. 7.
55. Kuldeep Nayyar and Rajendra Sacchar had also joined it.
56. For details, see, CNN-IBN Live, 1984, Anti Sikh Riots: 3 Convicts Get Life Term, 2 Jailed for 3 Years, last updated 9 May 2013.
57. *The Times of India*, 11 April 2013 and 30 April 2013.
58. Based on personal diary. Other available evidences also provide identical information.
59. Inferences are based on formal and informal interaction with prominent Sikhs including Jaswant Singh Neki in the Bhai Vir Singh Sahitya Sadan.
60. Sukhmani Singh, 'Children of the Holocaust', *The Sikh Review*, Vol. 38, No. 443, 11 November 1990, pp. 37–45.
61. Ibid.
62. For details, see, Jarnail Singh, *I Accuse ... The Anti Sikh Violence of 1984*, Delhi: Penguin Books, 2011.
63. Nirmal Singh, 'Sifting the Dust of 84 Pogrom for Some Positives', *The Sikh Review*, Parts I, II and III, Vol. 61, No. 709, 1 January 2013, pp. 51–65; Vol. 61, No. 710, 2 February 2013, pp. 33–46 and Vol. 61, No. 711, 3 March 2013, pp. 46–52.

Part III

Taking it Forward: Retrospection and New Areas

11

Gender Inequality

Manjeet Bhatia

If we break the phrase 'gender inequality' into two words, gender and inequality, it would be clear that the two draw on different concepts. One is a social phenomenon and the other is based on liberal principles.

Gender is a grammatical term, metamorphosed by feminists to describe that aspect of social phenomenon that goes without notice and that subtly carves out our identity based on sex. We would generally understand that men are independent, courageous, powerful, logical and aggressive. In contrast women are seen as dependent, fearful, emotional and meek and passive. If we reflect a little, it would be clear that not all men and women would fit in such descriptions and if we need to understand how these identities are formed we need to have a new tool of analysis. That is gender.

The one who first described this difference between sex and gender was Ann Oakley.[1] Oakley borrowed this terminology from a US-based psychiatrist and psychoanalyst, Robert Stroller, who worked with individuals whose sexual identity was either biologically or psychologically ambiguous. Following Stroller, Oakley defined sex 'as the anatomical and physiological characteristics which signify biological maleness and femaleness' and gender as socially constructed and not a 'direct product of bociological sex'.[2] Gender is 'a culturally shaped group of attributes and behaviours given to the female or to the male'.[3] This process of social construction is named gendering.

Gendering involves subtle prescription of customs, rituals, ideologies, social behaviour, and social institutions such as of marriage, religion etc. As a result, we are silently gendered. 'As we grow up, ideas of masculinity and femininity become central to the way we think about ourselves. Many of us actively reject interests which we recognize as untypical of our sex: girls do not really fight to play games, or engage in physically strenuous activity. Neither do boys appear eager to learn cooking or interest themselves in the details of housework and care of children. From their adolescent and post-adolescent years upwards, girls seek to look beautiful, appealing, and sometimes cultivate a deliberate passivity. Boys, in turn, court a macho ideal, swagger into an aggressive masculine identity with which they may or may not feel comfortable.'[4]

Notion of equality, on the other hand, was given to us by the classical liberal philosophers.

With Enlightenment and break up of the old order in the west, classical liberalism emerged as the dominant ideology that brought individual to the centre stage. Equality among individuals became one of the basic principles of governance and justice.

We should be able to understand the concept of inequality against this principle of equality. Can we? Let us see.

For building a new social order philosophers speculated the situation of man in the natural state and took all men equal in the state of nature.

John Locke describes the state of nature as one 'of equality, wherein all the power and jurisdiction is reciprocal, no one having more than another; there being nothing more evident, than that creature of the same species and rank, promiscuously born to all the same advantages of nature, and the use of the same faculties, should also be equal one amongst another without subordination or subjection' (Locke, *Treatise*, 8).

Such equals to protect their interest arrive at a general will to get in the social contract in which all are equal before the law. Equality thus achieved is the 'conventional' one as against the 'natural' in the state of nature. Rina Singh tells us thus: 'Universal moral worth translates into equality before law (the public sphere), which in turn is to guarantee equality of individual freedom (the private sphere).'[5] Equality thus got translated in the democratic nations as equality for all.

If we read more carefully, these philosophers of the Enlightened era also protected the patriarchal families in which man was the master of all those who comprised family.

Commentators of such social contract theorists do not mention that *women are excluded from this contract*. Liberal philosophers see relationship between men and women as natural and not conventional. Carole Pateman understands that Locke (*Second Treatise*) clearly differentiates 'political power' (in the public) from 'paternal power' that is over the private family sphere that is based on '... natural relationship that ends with maturity, and hence freedom and equality, of (male) children.' Pateman further laments that commentators are not able to see this division of 'family' and 'political' as also a 'sexual division'.

Thomas Hobbes makes it even more explicit as he states that family is '... created not through procreation but by conquest, and a family consists of a master and his servants: that is, all those, whatever their age and sex, who fall under his absolute jurisdiction.'[6]

These philosophers, who were representative of a new order, where through social contract equality of the state of nature was recognized, could not disengage themselves from the ideas of Aristotle, who according to Gerda Lerner completed the historical subordination of women by calling them 'mutilated men' and 'lacking soul'.

Lerner tells us that 'without offering much evidence' Aristotle finds male as active and female as passive sex,[7] and women devoid of principle of soul, which is the creator and shapes the inert matter (female's contribution).

'It is clear [to Aristotle] that the rule of soul over the body, and of the mind and the rational element over passionate, is natural and expedient ... again male is by nature superior, and the female inferior; and the one rules and the other is ruled.'[8]

They continued to see state as 'man writ large' implying all that is associated with man is alone what state is in a larger form.

Liberals who were champions of individual freedom and equality could not see this 'sexual division' of 'public' from 'private' that had played major part in subordinating women and denying them opportunities to grow.

Liberal theorists justified this dichotomy of public and private sphere. Thus, denying women universal equality, Hobbes understood that women are conquered by men in the state of nature and who have thus lost status of free and equal individual. Only free and equal individuals can participate in the original contract of forming a civil state.[9]

Similarly, other liberal philosophers have also justified natural exclusion of women from public sphere and thus denying them universal equality. Locke further provides the basis of this denial to women by arguing that age or talent difference among men are not relevant to their political equality, whereas the natural differences between men and women subjugates women to men.

Rousseau who thinks that we all are free in the state of nature is not in favour of social equality of sexes; as such equality would distract men from their duty.[10]

It is very clear that creation of civil society in which such values found place could not free itself from baggage of patriarchy. The freedom in the state of nature was sexist and not representing moral worth of individuals.

Yet, the concept of equality, defined by liberal philosophers, became the benchmark for human democratic societies. Thus women's concerns, rights and representation in social-cultural institutions remained a non-concern for centuries till some of earlier feminist writers like Mary Wollstonecraft and J.S. Mill drew attention of the intellectuals and feminists took the issue onboard. Feminist scholars brought to light the sexist bias of democracies in particular, the primary agenda of which was aimed at setting individual free from subordination.

We are now more clear that the notion of equality given to us by liberals cannot give us the concept of inequality as this notion does not even recognize gender-based discrimination. To them, in considering and defining equality, a relationship between men and women or women as an individual was never part of their agenda. So we cannot bifurcate *gender* and *inequality*. It needs to be understood as a separate concept, i.e., *gender inequality*.

Gender Inequality

Gender in reality is a dual existence of men and women. In actual practice, gender behaviour is in relation to the behaviour of the other gender. In other words, it is a relational category and thus a social category. We can pictorially depict it as under:

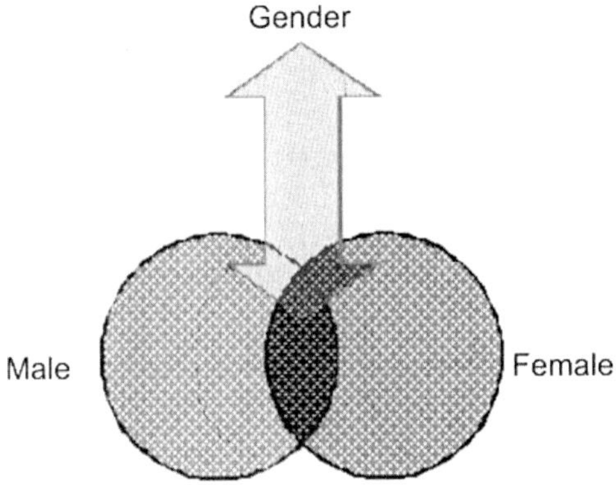

The above diagram shows that gender relations are based on interaction between men and women, but it does not tell us that these interactions have power inbuilt into them. There is no equal participation in these interactions, and globally gender relations are heavily tilted in favour of men. Feminists had to coin this concept to focus on the reality of domination of women in these relations.

'[Gender] Inequality [thus] notes that women are denied what is granted to men. It focuses our attention on the injustices of letting men vote when women could not, of giving men access to higher-paid jobs while restricting women to low-status work, of encouraging boys to train as engineers while girls learn to type.'[11]

As is obvious from a very brief description of inequality between men and women, such historic inequality has far-fetched outcome, especially for the subordinated gender. I would now take up an example from Indian sub-continent to describe gender inequality.

Declining Sex Ratio

World over sex ratio is counted as number of males per 1,000 females as females are naturally stronger sex and have greater chances of survival as compared to male sex. But in India it is reversed. We count number of females per 1,000 males and census after census this ratio is declining. The latest census 2011 puts child sex ratio (0–6 years, child sex ratio gives the clearer picture as it takes care of adult movement) at 914 girls/1,000 boys. In economically progressive states of Haryana and Punjab it reaches below 850.

Indian sub-continent has history of son preference. Religion, culture and institution of marriage had been historically creating and maintaining this preference. Hindus believe that in order to attain heavenly abode one must get cremated by his son. Culture of patrilocal* institution of marriage treats girl child as guest in her natal home and outsider in her matrimonial home. She is thus discriminated in her natal home in terms of education, health and in other aspects as compared to male child.

The skewed sex ratio is the glaring symptom of this gender discrimination where females are not allowed to born. Male child is preferred over the female child. They are easily eliminated by sex-selective abortions without anyone knowing publically. Here, doctor-client nexus works inspite of law against such selective abortions.

Such discrimination in the natal family results in gender inequality where women start their life at back foot as compared to men. As a result, women lack in the field of education, employment, health, political participation and worst kind of violence is perpetrated against them due to their lesser social worth. And in the name of protection they are discriminated against in the familial set-up.

Feminist scholars have very rightly challenged the public-private divide that has kept women in the state of dependence. In spite of individual freedom and equality as the guiding slogans of the Enlightenment, women were kept in the darkness and thus excluded from participation in public arena and associating domesticity with nature of women. Pateman has widely written on this divide which is at the root of gender inequality:

There is close association of liberalism and feminism. The roots of both doctrines lie in the emergence of individualism as a general theory of social life'[12] yet there are differences on where

* Patrilocal marriages are where women join the marital partner in his house leaving her natal family. She, thus, more than her husband, is faced with a new situation and relationships to negotiate in order to make space in this new familial set-up.

the line in public and private should be drawn or whether it should be drawn at all.

Nature/Culture

Most of those who justify the public-private divide rest their arguments on women's nature being more suitable for nurturing, domesticity and close to nature as against men's nature more suitable to culture. Feminists have argued against this distinction on the basis of which women have been kept out of public arena. Pateman classifies these arguments in two groups: one that are anthropological and the other given by radical feminists.

Human beings endeavour to conquer nature modify or cultivate nature. Thus, to remain close to nature had been placed lower to culture. To be cultured is placed higher than to be closed to nature.

S.B. Ortner tells us that women are associated with nature because of the work that they do is close to nature as compared to that done by men. Women's role of childbearing, child rearing and housekeeping, for example, brings them closer to nature. Whereas, culture involves creation, is associated with men and is placed higher to nature.

Ortner argues that opposition between nature and culture is itself a cultural construct and given in nature.

Radical feminist takes sexual difference as the only basis of women's subjection to men.

Shulamith Firestone, in her famous work, *The Dialectic of Sex* (1970) argues that the nature/women and culture/men distinction lies in 'biology itself-procreation'. The natural or given inequality is the basis of oppression of women. She thinks that by confining women to procreation men have freed themselves 'for the business of the world'[13] thus creating and controlling culture. So for Firestone solution lies in relieving women from the burden of reproduction by innovative technologies. Her main argument is that women suffer from 'a fundamentally oppressive biological condition'.[14]

Pateman rightly observes that biology in itself cannot be liberating or oppressive. There is meaning acquired by biology in specific social relationships.[15] Firstones' reduction of men and women to biological categories denies the 'complex history of the relationship between men and women'. In other words, biology is also historically constructed.

Morality/Power

Yet another divide which associates women with morality and power with men, makes women repository of morality. Uma Chakarvarti[16] very rightly points out that women live in 'mortal fear of being categorized as *bad woman*'. Similar pressures are not faced by men or young boys. For instance, to be a *bad boy, bad brother* or *bad father* does not have same connotations as a *bad girl* or a *bad mother* would have. I understand young girls are socialized more under the fears of societal sanctions than for their own sake, whereas boys have much more freedom to interact in a social space. In a society where a woman's identity is drawn from or is dependent upon male members of the family, to be categorized as a *bad woman* not only speaks of not playing her ascribed roles of a girl, wife, or a mother but also of having loose character. Her identity in patriarchal society primarily hinges upon her sexuality and to be categorized as a *bad woman* denudes her of her social existence.

On the other hand, liberal theorists have contrasted the public/political sphere with power, force and violence, with the society/private with freedom and voluntarism. The opposition between morality and power then contrasts physical force and aggression, the natural attributes of manliness, expressed in the military force of the state against love and altruism, the natural attributes of womanhood, which are expressed in family, private sphere where women are located and who ensure such morality.[17]

Such attributive distinction is maintained even by liberal feminists. For instance, while lobbying for reservation for women in Panchayati Raj Institutions (PRIs) in India, one of the arguments given in favour by activists was that, women, who have moral superiority, would cleanse politics. As women are not corrupt, any corruption by a woman leader becomes very important news. Whereas this is not only not represented by the conduct of women Chief Ministers in India, it also exposes the myth of natural attributes and denial of exigencies of politics. On the other hand, it also shows that such public/private divisions are social constructs.

Gender inequality leads to discrimination against women in most of public, private institutions.

Personal/Political

Feminists argue that this inequality is the result of the public values actually ruling the private. The famous slogan of feminists is *personal is political,* implying that relations of power, that rule the public, also rule the private. This understanding is crucial for understanding gender inequality.

Pateman tells that feminists showed us that how personal circumstances are structured by the public factors, for instance, laws on rape, domestic violence, child custody, maintenance, divorce etc. Personal problems thus need public interventions.

I would particularly site the example of domestic violence. Family is considered as an abode of love and understanding and thus has been kept out of the state purview by the liberals. Family, according to liberals, is a natural institution governed by nature. But increasingly feminists the world over have found family subjugating women and even perpetrating worst kind of violence against them.

A recent Indian law against domestic violence – Protection of Women from Domestic Violence Act, 2005 – based on the experience of voluntary women's organizations, recognized four kinds of violence against women in domestic sphere, namely, physical, economic, emotional and sexual. A recent study by the author shows that women are facing all of these at the hands of her own relatives. It also reveals that without the intervention by the state this violence would have never been addressed,[18] if personal is kept out of the public view.

Before this law was passed, there was no definition of the term 'domestic violence' that comprehensively reflected a woman's experience of violence in intimate relationships.

The above discussion clearly recognizes that personal relationships are also infested with power – power that liberals gave us to understand that it was associated with politics and public sphere alone.

Feminists rightly argue that the so-called *personal* is also governed by power relations. What more can establish this than that there is violence in domestic sphere and women need to be protected in this sphere by the state.

In fact, both the spheres of personal and political are interrelated. The public values are practised in the personal too. The domestic life, according to Pateman, is at the 'heart of the civil society rather than ... separate from it'.[19] ... 'family as a social category belongs to civil society, not outside it.' Civil society, according to Pateman, can be divided into 'social (private)' and 'political (public)'.

This separation of private/personal from public has ruled democracies for centuries and has blocked development of just gender relations. Most of civil societies treat family relations out of bound for the public and men continue to rule that private sphere with values of the so-called public sphere. Women are made completely dependent on men.

What does dependence upon male members entail?

A woman is maintained by her husband, and prior to that by her native family. It is recognized by law. So, she legally demands maintenance in the face of divorce from her husband. Is she an object that has to be maintained? In Hindu marriages woman is given away to the groom. This ritual is called *Kanyadaan* – gifting the girl. Both these practices indicate non-participation of woman to say the least.

Such prescribed gender behaviours illustrate gender inequality in which men dominate in constructing these relations. Since it is a relational category, it cannot be constructed without the 'other', historically, though the 'other' had always been female gender, and primarily dominated by male gender.

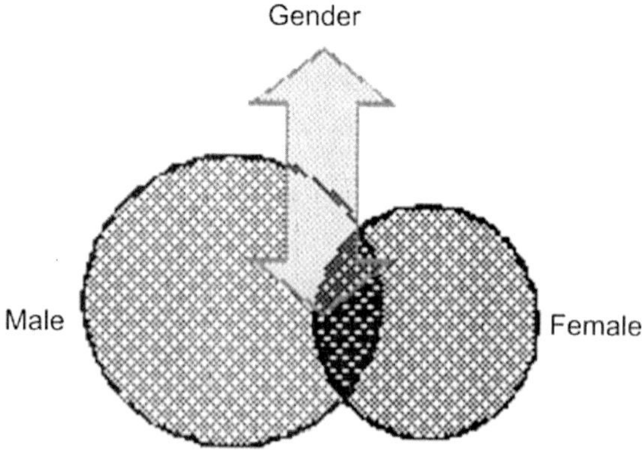

We can correctly depict these relations by the above diagram where male has more role in defining these relations.

In independent India there had been a major government sponsored fact-finding exercise to ascertain the status of Indian women. Well-known academicians and activists were entrusted with this job. They came out with their report in 1974, which is popularly known as *Towards Equality*.[20] This report was an eye-opener that showed women lacking in education, employment, health and political representation. It also highlighted the cultural discrimination against Indian girls and women. It was the first comprehensive document on the status of Indian women. This report had far-reaching effect on further research, policy interventions and special provisions for women. Several women-specific research and action-based institutions came into existence. The University Grants Commission intervened by introducing Women's Studies Centres in universities. The Government of India introduced several schemes for women's empowerment in each of its five-year plans. It also made a major policy intervention by reserving not less than 33 per cent seats at all levels of local governing units for women.

These interventions in India and many others in different nations and by UN have brought gender question to the centre stage though gender equality is still elusive.

Conclusion

Gender is not given by nature. It is rather acquired. This process world over has relegated women's role to domesticity. Women are expected to reproduce, nurture and keep the house clean and tidy. Such division has also been justified as natural – natural that is based on sex. Giving us to understand that women are justifiably ruled/ controlled by men and men having higher faculties of reason create culture.

It is obvious that such creation would represent woman as dependent and secondary to man.

It is for feminists and some sensitive philosophers who could break this dichotomy and use the same tools of scholarly exercises to question this deep-seated discrimination towards one gender – the female gender.

The classic works of liberal philosophers that brought individual to the centre stage in constructing civil societies not only continued but also justified patriarchal families.

As a result, gender inequality is seen in all public institutions and practices despite breakaway from monarchies. It would be out of scope of this essay to elaborate on these inequalities. However, an overview of these and their social constructions can be depicted. One may broadly see some fundamental inequalities (constructive) that lead to other (implicative) inequalities. We can show them by a flow chart as follows:

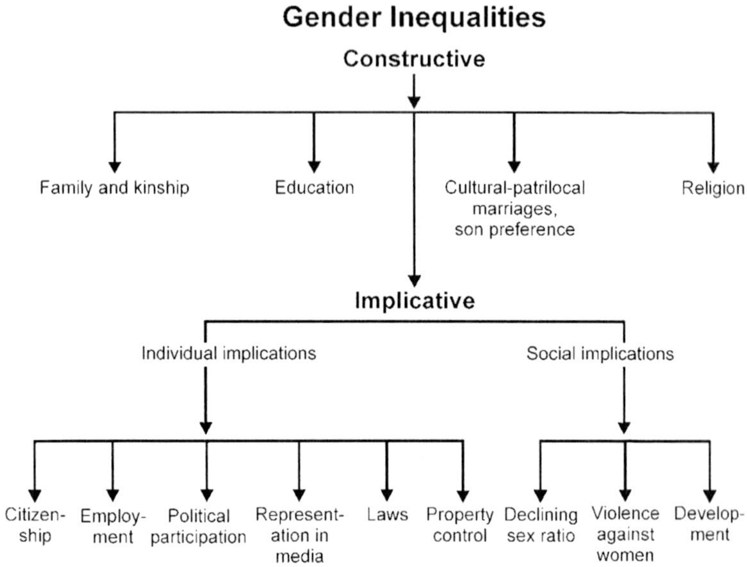

These inequalities reflect in political and judiciary institutions as well. In fact, we need to assess in some ways the price human civilizations has paid by perpetuating gender inequality. On the other hand, it is not easy either, to speculate a gender-equal society for notion of equality has to be reformulated that includes social in civil society.

Notes

1. Oakley, Ann, *Sex, Gender and Society*, London: Temple Smith, 1972.
2. Jackson, Stevi and Sue Scott (eds.), *Gender: A Sociological Reader*, Routledge, London, 2002, Introduction.
3. Humm, Maggie., *The Dictionary of Feminist Theory*, second edition, Edinburgh University Press, 2003, first published in 1989, p. 106.
4. Geetha, V., *Gender*, Stree, Calcutta, 2002, p. 3.
5. Singh, Rina, *Gender Autonomy in Western Europe: An Imprecise Revolution*, Macmillan Press Ltd., London, 1998, p. 2–3.
6. Pateman, Carole, "God Hath Ordained to Man a Helper': Hobbes, Patriarchy and Conjugal Right" in *Feminist Interpretations and*

Political Theory, (ed.) by Mary Lyndon Shanley and Carole Pateman, Polity Press, UK, 1991.

7. Lerner, Gerda, *The Creation of Patriarchy*, Oxford University Press, 1986, p. 206.
8. Aristotle, *Politics* (trans. by Benjamin Jowett) in W.D. Ross (ed.), *The Works of Aristotle* (Oxford, 1921) p. 125b, 4–6, 12–16 in Gerda Lerner, ibid., p. 208.
9. Pateman, op. cit.
10. Rousseau, J.J., Politics and Arts: Letter to M.d' Alembert on Theatre, trans. Allan Bloom 1977, as quoted by Rina Singh in notes of *Gender Autonomy in Western Europe: An Imprecise Revolution*, Macmillan Press Ltd., London, p. 189.
11. Phillips, Anne, *Feminism and Equality*, Basil Blackwell, first published, 1987, Introduction.
12. Pateman, Carole, Feminist Critiques of the Public/Private Dichotomy, in *Feminism and Equality*, ed. by Anne Philips, Basil Blackwell, first published in 1987, UK, pp. 103–126.
13. Firestone, S., *The Dialectic of Sex*, W. Morrow, New York, 1970, p. 232.
14. Ibid., p. 255.
15. Pateman, op. cit., p. 111.
16. In a recent lecture.
17. Pateman, op. cit., p. 113.
18. 'Domestic Violence in India: Cases under the Protection of Women from Domestic Violence Act, 2005', *South Asia Research*, 32(2), *SOAS*, London, 2012.
19. Pateman, op. cit., p. 119.
20. *Towards Equality*: Report of the Committee on the Status of Women in India, Ministry of Education and Social Welfare, Department of Social Welfare, GoI, New Delhi, 1974. CWDS has recently brought out updated edition that is published by Pearson, New Delhi, 2012. The project was sponsored by Ministry of Women and Child Development.

12

Happily Unmarried

Interrogations of the Single Women in South Asia

Tanya Caulfield

This paper examines, from a contemporary feminist perspective, the phenomenon of single women in South Asia. My research demonstrates that South Asian female sexualities are both multiple and complex yet this is rarely taken up within 'conventional' society. It is accepted that women will follow established customs and social practices in ways that do not depart from tradition. However, women who engage in one of, or a range of, sexual practices are considered different and/or deviant by society. I consider the possibilities of diverse female lived experiences and variations of actual situations that may be manifest in established structural and cultural arrangements and how women might construct their lives in the context of prevailing notions of femininity and pressures towards marriage. This paper is a partial

This article is based on field research undertaken in Delhi during 2002 and 2003 for my PhD dissertation at the University of Queensland, Brisbane, Australia. My research focuses on issues of gender in South Asia, particularly those generated by the emergence of single women in Delhi, as a complex social phenomenon linked to processes of modernization.

explanation of the slow but increasing emergence of single women as a perceptible socio-cultural group in Delhi based on the narratives provided by middle class women. I consider women in Delhi as an anthropological case study of recent changes that have occurred through modernization processes and which are located within a broader understanding of women in South Asia. Despite social perceptions of single women as abnormal and ill-fated, I explore the ways in which single women are shaping and negotiating their being along non-traditional lines of conduct as socio-economically independent women by rejecting patriarchal values and ideologies that regulate women's intellectual freedom and expression in Delhi society.

For a relevant and contemporary understanding of single women's lived experiences in Delhi, I relied on informal interviews, observation and questionnaires. Many of the single women with whom I spoke lived in women's hostels. These women's hostels enabled women to shape their private and social lives in individually desired ways. The living arrangements of single women living in Delhi was an important factor the way these women perceived their actual situations and how such conditions influenced their social beings. Therefore, in order to frame my examination of single women in Delhi, I consider my informants' living spaces in order to situate my analysis within a broader socio-economic framework that offers insights into their negotiations of the constraints of their home lives.

Single Women's Living Arrangements

The majority of my informants lived in working women's hostels run by government and independent organizations that were located in inner-city locations and provided housing to women of all backgrounds. Many women told me that single women found it difficult to rent or purchase properties in Delhi, because property owners did not want to rent their properties to single women as they were thought to be suspicious and participating in unacceptable practices. My informants told me that as people would also talk or gossip about single women's behaviour and the type of people they invited into their homes, their privacy in rented properties was limited. Sadly, buying a house or apartment was often not an option for many due to limited incomes and the increasing property prices in

Delhi, so hostels were designed particularly for working women who were unmarried, widowed, divorced and hailed from other regional locations. The hostels offered reasonably priced housing and provided a secure and comfortable environment in which women might maintain happy and friendly relationships with other women. While many hostels organized seminars that focused on the development of women's personality and confidence, some hostels conducted courses on health, beauty and banking too. My informants told me that not only hostels were safe places where like-minded women came together, but they also gave them the freedom to live as single women in a society that restricts women's socioeconomic potential. Whilst acknowledging the necessity of and the services provided by working women's hostels, I soon learnt how single women's lives were restricted and shaped by hostel arrangements and the social preconceptions that produced them.

In order to speak with women living in the hostels, I had to adhere to a number of regulations and procedures. After dropping in to a government working women's hostel, I was told by senior hostel staff that I had to first obtain permission from the Director of Social Welfare Department of the New Delhi Municipal Council. Having drafted a letter of my intentions with the hope that she might assist, the Director, after many cups of tea and biscuits and general talk about her recent visit to Australia, was only too glad to help. She immediately phoned a hostel and told the hostel warden about my study. I was quickly given the phone to speak with the warden in order to arrange a meeting time and the likelihood of speaking to single women residents.

Initially, I was struck by the terminology and conception of a 'warden'. Western concepts of 'warden' define the term as an official who is in charge of something or someone and is responsible for the enforcement of particular regulations (Collins English Dictionary, Fourth Edition). My perception of a 'warden' is defined within institutional contexts such as correctional facilities. I also associate the term with restrictions and indifference. However, in order to speak with the women living in the hostels, I had to first contact the female wardens at every hostel about my research intentions. Every warden expressed their beliefs regarding single women in South Asia before allowing me to meet with the women. One warden told me, 'all women want to marry but some women are unfortunate in that they cannot marry due to dowry or unattractive physical features'. She then said, 'divorced and or widowed women find it difficult to remarry as men do not want to marry women who were once associated with other men'. I met some single women whom the warden believed to be significant to my study. In the presence of the warden, I introduced myself to those who were willing to participate in the interview. However, I noted that while speaking with the women the warden would interrupt and advise the potential informant that perhaps speaking with me would be upsetting. For the warden, all single women had a deep desire to marry. The situation of 'being single' therefore was distressing to all women. On meeting Olivia, for instance, the warden told her that she should not speak with me due to her previous experiences of divorce. However, Olivia, like all the potential informants, explained to the warden that she wanted to participate as she was happy being single.

In a meeting with another hostel warden, again I was told that although women may choose to remain single, they subconsciously desire to marry. The warden alleged 'single women are deluded in thinking that remaining unmarried is a healthy and rewarding life option'. She then stated, 'class differences make it possible for some women to be single'. She further argued, 'all women marry for reasons of economic, emotional and physical support, sex, and male children. Upper class women, for example, can obtain all these elements without getting married'. When questioned about upper class women and their ability to have children, the warden explained that it is acceptable for upper class women to have relationships outside of marriage that produce children. It is also common for upper class single women to adopt children as did the Bollywood actress Sushmita Sen. The warden explained that this was due to women's careers and economic independence. However, from the warden's understanding, middle class women can only obtain support, sex and children within the institutions of marriage and family. It is therefore difficult for middle class women to remain single. When I suggested that there is the potential for middle class women to make subjective decisions that allow them to negotiate their lives as single women, I was simply told that all middle class women marry unless there are problems with their looks or the inability to provide dowry.

All wardens explained to me the hostel regulations which determined the times and meeting places of my interviews with the women. Many interviews took place in a common lounge, library or garden as I was not allowed to be alone with the women. On one occasion, an informant invited me to her room to conduct the interview as she said that she would feel more relaxed in her own environment. The informant offered me tea and began talking to me about her life whilst showing me photos and personal items that were important to her. However, the warden became aware of this and we were told to conduct the interview in the common lounge. Despite my informant's argument that there was nothing wrong with having a female company in her room, we were forced to move to the common area. Many women told me that the hostels did not allow visitors in their rooms and there were specific times in which they could entertain visitors in common areas. However, it seemed to me that for women who were able to shape their lives as single women by rejecting social ideals that pressure them towards marriage, the imposition of hostel regulations limited and directed women's social beings in ways that were deemed necessary to protect women's actual situations.

Furthermore, some of the hostels had established contracts that determined the length of stay for its residents. Depending on the hostel, women were expected to leave after a specific time to find new lodgings. As many of my informants told me that it was difficult to find places to rent as single women, I perceived hostel regulations to imply that being single was a premarital phase for women. That is, women experience a time in their lives when they might undertake paid employment and live away from the family. However, it is expected that women will marry and live with husbands and family. The women living in the hostels told me that the temporary accommodation did not provide them with future security in that single women were forced to constantly move and re-establish their personal spaces. Many of the women said that they did not feel settled in the hostels and therefore did not feel as if the hostels were 'home'. Personal belongings were minimal as the majority of women shared rooms with other women. The set rental contracts and the minimal living conditions reflect the assumed temporariness of being single. From my observation and understanding of my informants' narratives, the lives of single women were shaped by the daily procedures of hostel life and their relationships with women both working and living in the hostels. The limitations and supervision of women's living spaces ensued the hostels' conjecture of the ephemerality of being single.

'Being Single' in Delhi

As my research indicates, women's experiences are multiple and varied thereby shaping and framing their lives in diverse ways. In an examination of single women's narratives, I identified specific issues and themes emerging from their stories. Although expressed in different ways, the narratives reveal that women have similar desires and needs which contribute to their multiple and complex modes of being. Issues such as the importance of a career, female education and independence indicate that women in contemporary Delhi society have more life options as opposed to the predetermined familial role of wife and mother. Despite traditional patriarchal ideologies, which define women's beliefs and behaviour within prescribed gender roles, many women in Delhi negotiate independent socioeconomic situations in order to remain unmarried. For many women being single was a life choice. By choosing to pursue an education in order to achieve career ambitions or by repudiating the roles assigned to women, single women directed a significant part of their lives towards goals that rewarded them social, economic and emotional security outside the sphere of the family. Single women reworked South Asian definitions of femininity in order to establish lives free from many of the perceived constraints of traditional expectations.

Nonetheless, while many women told me that being single in Delhi was generally an easy way of being, their narratives suggest that being single is intensely complicated and complex. The lives of single women are delineated by broader socio-cultural and economic systems that work to limit women's potential expressions of individuality. The ways in which women negotiated being single were circumscribed by notions of honour, socio-economic structures, family arrangements, women's oppression, and their active human agency in relation to cultural ideologies. These underlying themes and concepts, which I now consider, shaped the ways in which women in Delhi lived as single women. Single women in Delhi forged their lives within a broader theme of life choice and thereby according to their personal values and desires, thus revealing the actuality of multiple independent female subjectivities in contemporary South Asian societies.

Notions of Honour and Shame

Women's narratives reveal the ways in which women actively shape their understandings of female sexualities and negotiate their social beings as single women within the constraints of South Asian societies. Whilst shaping their lives in ways that are perceived to be different, single women maintained ideas of 'honour' in their life trajectories. Married women retain respectability and status through marriage and childbearing and are defined in relation to their husbands and families. A central theme of the standards and criteria for appropriate female behaviour is that men should control women and their sexuality. Ideal women, argues Wadley, 'are those who do not strive to break these bonds of control. Moreover, the salvation and happiness of women revolve around their virtue and chastity as daughters, wives and widows' (1988: 31). The sexualities of women who follow established ideals protect and uphold the honour of both natal and marital families. Women who diverge from social expectations are perceived as outsiders and therefore dangerous.

Some women with whom I spoke told me that marriage provided women with security and support and validated their social beings as respectable and moral women. While many agreed that being single was an ideal situation, many women said that the familial and social pressures to marry were so forceful that it was difficult to make the decision to remain unmarried. For many women, the social expectations of being female in South Asian societies are maintained and promoted through the institutions of marriage and family. However, the family gives little space to women who do not conform. Since women hold the power to destroy family honour through sexual misconduct, women's behaviour and manner are indicative of family virtue and community power (Dasgupta and DasGupta, 1996). Although women's status of being single was important for my informants, the honour of their families was also a significant factor in their negotiation of their social realities and experiences. For example, Rekha told me that she could not have a relationship with a man due to social attitudes towards sexual relationships outside the institution of marriage. She said:

> I think marriage is a very important part of life but I don't think if you don't get married you can't have a quality life. Certainly you can have. It doesn't mean you can't have friends in your life and it doesn't mean you can't have a love life, you can but it is like you can't express your love life to society because if my husband loves me and sends me some flowers, I would be proud and be able to express this. But if my lover sends me some flowers, you cannot express this so you have to say that a friend sent them. So that is a problem I think so marriage is a very important part of life.

By restricting individual desires and actions, as a single woman, Rekha recognized the potential harm of friendships with men due to social attitudes towards uninstitutionalized relationships. As female behaviour and 'uncontrolled' female sexuality reflect upon the whole family's reputation, the ways in which single women pursued their private and social lives were shaped according to recognized codes of female respectability.

While Rekha considered the consequences of her social behaviour as potentially damaging, Radha shaped her lived experiences and social identity according to community ideals of family honour and morality. Originating from a strict Hindu community in Tamil Nadu, Radha remained unmarried due to community principles that did not permit the marriage of its individuals to members of other communities. Although Radha claimed that she would have liked the opportunity to marry, she retained her family's honour within the south Indian community by not marrying out of caste. She said:

> If we marry outside the caste then our parents will look bad, so why hurt them? That is the belief of the whole community that we don't many outside of it. This is more so the older generation's view, nowadays that may be changing a bit.

Marriage patterns in South Asia vary according to caste/class, region and religion. In South India, there is the preference for the marriage of women with relatives, such as cross-cousins or uncles (Caplan, 1985). In comparison to women from northern India who generally marry inter-caste, South Indian women are married to men who are known and/or related to their family. Nishimura (1994) argues that women who marry cousins are cared for by their in-laws and are able to maintain their close relationships with natal families. 'The closeness of the kin and the affines acts as a web to protect married women in the Tamil family' (ibid.: 247). As Nishimura claims such a web not only protects women within the family, it also protects the purity and ideals of the community. Radha told me that she knew women from her community wanting to marry:

> Women are looking for a suitable partner but in our community, women won't marry themselves. They have to have their parents or family arrange a marriage within the same community and a particular sect. So they match all those things such as stars, qualifications, and background. But if no one wants to marry the girl then no one wants to marry outside of the caste.

Marrying out of caste disrupts and pollutes communal succession and identity. Radha's father, as the head of the family, maintained his family's social reputation and economic status by adhering to established caste ideals and standards. For Radha, this meant an education that would provide her with 'all the things a housewife should know' whilst also ensuring her family's honour as a daughter who should be proficient and accustomed to her future role as wife and mother. For a woman to enter her marital home without the knowledge and capabilities of what is considered to be women's work in the community would reflect negatively upon her family. Radha said, 'In education, women were taught to cook and stitch as this was considered to be a woman's job in the community. So if we went to our husband's house there would be no problem'. Radha's domestic education was also used within her natal family as a means to further her skills, and to inculcate an accepting attitude towards the established roles and behaviour of south Indian women. She said, 'At the age of sixteen I used to cook for the whole family – morning breakfast and all. My sisters used to also'.

Despite her 'traditional' education, Radha nonetheless shaped her social being as a single South Indian woman living in Delhi in ways that might be considered deviant by her community but in accordance to women's responsibility of maintaining family honour. During her education, Radha's movements were defined and regulated by family notions of morality and respectability. Radha was not allowed to visit the cinema or clubs with friends and was told to return home directly after attending college. Her family's honour depended upon her behaviour as an unmarried woman. The ways Radha's community perceived women were determined by women's situation within a family, that is, as a married or unmarried woman. As a single woman, Radha was susceptible to social criticism and accusations that might lead to dishonouring her family. She said, 'They didn't let us have any diversions such as going to a movie or a club which would divert our mind. Even college was a problem as they said go to college and study and come back –don't look at others'. An unmarried woman and her 'uncontrolled' sexuality are perceived as an inherent threat to the family and established social structures.

While Radha's situation might have been questioned within a social context, being single complicated Radha's perception of her social identity in relation to family and caste ideals of women's roles within the community. Radha understood that her choice not to marry out of caste and, as a result, to live as a single woman might affect caste and familial identities in two ways. Not wanting to hurt her father and uncle or make her parents look bad, Radha did not marry due to her inability to marry outside her caste, her living in Delhi and the unlikelihood of finding a suitable match from her community. Radha therefore chose to live as a single woman. However, by not marrying, Radha's single or 'different' sexuality was a potential threat to her family's honour. Radha argued that as a single woman she enjoyed her social and economic independence without the constraints of a family and therefore believed her behaviour was without limitations. However, Radha's lived experiences and social identity were regulated by her religious beliefs and caste practices which, in turn, constituted her interpretation and representation of how she could live as a single woman in Delhi. Radha said:

> Since our community is in the south we do not find people from our community in Delhi. So now I am living in a hostel and have good friends. Staying in hostels is the only choice to live as people don't want to rent out their properties to unmarried women. Sometimes I think after retirement what will I do, but because I have brothers and sisters and we don't want to go to the south, we will stay in Delhi together.

By living in a working women's hostel and working with her brothers as an IT consultant, Radha restricted her own movements and space in deference to the ideals of 'appropriate' female behaviour defined by her South Indian community and broader South Asian society.

While Radha negotiated and challenged her actual situation as a South Asian woman within the context of communal honour, Nalini's status as a respected single woman was maintained through her understanding of South Asian gender relations and the subsequent implications for single women in Delhi. Prior to moving to the hostel, Nalini rented a home in which she lived alone. Not only was her action perceived to be unconventional in relation to perceived notions of women's behaviour in society, it was also understood by men to be an invitation to take advantage of women who were not defined by the institution of marriage. Nalini said:

> God has made man to take advantage of these things such as women who are not attached to anyone because they think that she can go out whenever she likes. This problem exists and people try to take advantage such as if I am staying alone in a flat someone will try to come in.

Acknowledging that single women were vulnerable subjects of gossip and talk, Nalini did not allow visitors to her home and, in return, was not invited to the houses of men. In the same way that Nalini maintained her honour by rejecting such initiations, she also protected her living spaces from intrusions and the threat of violence. By creating a space that was safe and comfortable, Nalini was able to embody and reinforce her individual identity as an unmarried woman. As a result, she preserved her own reputation including her family's honour and status. However, whilst shaping her identity as an independent woman according to individual desires, and with the consideration of her family's reputation, Nalini's freedom of movement and choice of how her social and sexual interactions may evolve were limited by both familial and social perceptions of appropriate female behaviour and acceptable female environments. Nevertheless, by not disrupting the social order in which the expectations and roles of women are established, Nalini was admired within her social sphere. She said, 'Men became afraid and they didn't come and they would not invite me to their home because they know I am a single woman. I am well respected because of this'.

While South Asian ideologies construct female sexualities as potentially damaging and dishonourable when not under the control of men, single women engage in behaviour that preserves family honour yet allows them to live their lives in ways that are perceived to be different and unconventional. However, the narratives demonstrate that the actual situations and social experiences of single women in Delhi are still extremely restricted by family expectations of daughters, social precepts of appropriate female behaviour, male prejudices towards single women, and the regulations of hostels which reflect social attitudes of 'exposed' female sexualities. Processes of modernization have increased women's opportunities to remain unmarried through the expansion of women's increased participation in formal sector employment, which has enabled women to obtain economic independence. Despite these opportunities social attitudes and established ideologies of appropriate womanhood limit single women's potentiality of exhibiting different ways of being and shaping social identities as independent, modern women. My informants' actual situations and social experiences were different to those of married women in that single women's desires and aspirations were pursued within individually defined spaces that were external to the family. However, being single was regulated by individual and family honour. Single women's behaviour and movements were conducted according to social expectations of appropriate womanhood. While the reputation of their family was important in the shaping of their actual situations, they also told me the ways they negotiated social standards of being female in South Asia.

Manipulating Social Standards to Single Women's Advantage

In my conversations with women living in Delhi, I was told that in contemporary metropolitan societies women were able to negotiate their own socio-economic and emotional independence due to the advancement of female education and women's entrance into public workplaces. These factors enabled women to shape their lives in specific and varied ways. Women's options for a life other than marriage had expanded. However, despite socio-economic systems and arrangements that have generated life alternatives for women, I recognized that social ideologies and perceptions towards single women have little changed. Strong familial and social pressures on women to marry continued unabated. In order to live as happy independent lives, single women were compelled to establish their social beings in acceptable, yet different, ways. While recognizing ideologies and attitudes that govern female sexualities, Single women mediated their social beings and lived experiences within and outside established gendered spaces in order to organize and redefine their actual situations of being single.

Acting as agents of cultural practices and ideologies, single women reinterpreted elements of the dominant culture in order to establish and protect their independent status and social status. Kalpana Ram eloquently alleges that women are able to negotiate cultural ideologies to their advantage:

> Women are able to a certain extent ... manipulate and even exploit to their advantage the qualities patriarchy ascribes to them. This manoeuvrability is made possible by the fact that the dominant culture is itself full of internal contradictions, ironies and ambiguities, which create a potential space for the contestation of cultural meaning. (1992: 93)

Living within the confines of respectable femininity but challenging the norm by remaining unmarried, Nalini constructed individual standards of female appropriateness in accordance with established ideologies. By suggesting to others that she was unable to have visitors due to her family's wish for her to be alone in the house, Nalini was able to found her story on cultural perceptions of female virtue and morality but, at the same time, create a space independent to broader social perceptions and practices. Nalini's perceptions of social and sexual restrictions that affect women's respectability were defined by women's sexual behaviours and self-presentation in society. In her narrative, Nalini discussed, internalized and negotiated her perception of sexual purity that encoded, in Puri's words, 'expectations of what is socially and sexually appropriate for middle-class women' (1999: 76–77). Through self-surveillance and monitoring, Nalini ensured her respectability, and therefore, her family's status. Although Nalini's remaining single might be regarded as outside the boundaries of acceptable middle-class women's sexuality, by accepting and adhering to social expectations, Nalini took advantage of her established respectability in order to convert her 'different' social situation into an acceptable female identity.

As single women, many of my informants identified with social representations of South Asian women but rejected notions of women's dependence and objectivity. By accepting certain female life trajectories, single women were able to redirect their lives according to individual goals and desires. For example, Jani told me, 'I always had my career in my mind; I never thought about getting married'. These forms of women's agency can be identified within the perceived limits of middle-class women's social responsibilities and respectability. For example, some of my informants negotiated their 'being single' within the contexts of caring for their ageing parents. Although the role of carer may be regarded as limiting and perhaps suffocating, single women utilized this space in order to create independent and diverse lifestyles for themselves.

Pritam, for example, saw it as her responsibility to look after her family. Living in a women's hostel whilst working as a teacher, Pritam's conception of female sexuality was not defined by traditional notions of South Asian womanhood. Having been educated by Irish nuns and read numerous western social and philosophical theories, Pritam had strong beliefs regarding women's situation in South Asia:

> My early education was in an Irish missionary school. The Catholic nuns and the curriculum that was taught influenced my thinking and behaviour. Because of the nuns, I was introduced to western texts on philosophy and social theories. I was also inspired by the strong and determined character of the nuns. I think that these are attractive qualities for women. My interaction with the nuns and my reading, I believe, have contributed to my beliefs, particularly about women in South Asian society.

Guided by her opinions, Pritam created a space for herself as a single woman in accordance to her own beliefs and choices. Pritam argued that there were significant differences between single women and married women that defined and determined women's social spaces and experiences. 'Being single' provided Pritam with a strength and independence which she perceived as unique and different to that of a married woman's social being. Pritam was aware of the inequalities in socio-economic structures that negate women's worth and potentialities and was intent on gaining what she believed to be the right of every woman. In this way, Pritam enjoyed aspects of life in Delhi which she believed would be unattainable for married women. An obvious difference when compared to other single women was her open-mindedness regarding relationships with men before marriage. She said:

> I have had numerous relationships with men, many of whom wanted to marry me. But I refused all of their marriage offers because I believe in getting to know the person properly without the false pretences of material objects which many men offered me.

For many single women, being seen with a man was problematic in that it was potentially damaging for their reputation and detrimental to their family's honour.

However, Pritam negotiated her relationships with men in ways that situated her as a dominant and independent figure within the relationships. While this may be regarded as an irregular and diverse portrayal of South Asian womanhood, Pritam challenged established ideals of sacrifice and reticence in order to defend her situation of 'being single' from possible individual distress and suffering. Manipulating her dominance within her relationships with men, Pritam enjoyed her ability to see men whilst maintaining control of the situation as well as her respectability in society.

Many single women told me the ways they shaped their lives as single women with regard to perceived roles of South Asian women. Their 'being single' was defined by individual desires and experiences and the ways they used dominant ideologies to their own advantage. Single women shaped their actual beings according to, but unrestricted by, ideals of South Asian womanhood.

The Socio-economic Complexities of 'Being Single' in Delhi Society

The women with whom I spoke created individual spaces to shape their lives as single women. In defining their own social spaces, these women were able to make specific choices and freely express their identities in ways that characterized what they wanted from their lives as South Asian women. Single women not only created effective modes of being within established social systems and economic arrangements but also took advantage of modern and changing social circumstances in favour of their development. Although modernity is intermingled with deep-rooted systems and ideologies of 'tradition' and, in particular, ideas regarding women's roles in South Asian society, single women negotiated their private and public lives in order to engage in practices that they perceived as necessary to sustain successful and enjoyable lives. One way of achieving an independent livelihood was through education and employment. Many women in South Asia have progressed and reached new personal, social and economic standards due to processes of globalization and modernization. Such processes have increased women's self-perceptions, motivations and potentialities and have redefined contemporary South Asian women's priorities. Many of my informants had received a tertiary education in order to further their lives in paid employment. Employment outside the domestic sphere guaranteed women's economic independence and the ability to live as single women.

Whilst transgressing traditional standards of female economic dependence, women have entered male-dominated spheres in order to achieve a life free from economic reliance. Economic independence allowed women to control their own earnings in ways that would not be acceptable for married professional women. As Rekha told me, 'An individual's earnings are generally given to the family. Yet without the responsibilities of a family, single women are able to enjoy their money'. Uyl (1995) suggests that processes of modernization engender forms of monetization and market orientation. Together, notions of individualism begin to emerge in the form of private property and the growth of personal profit. Although my informants did not perceive their careers as a means to make money, it did allow them to have a disposable income beyond that used for the necessities of daily living to be spent in ways that satisfied them. Olivia's situation demonstrates the priority of looking after yourself in order to be happy despite a limited income. The profit which accumulates from having a career, from Olivia's understanding, was personal satisfaction rather than monetary gain. Oliva's self-worth increased due to her work and her identity as an independent working woman. She said:

> It is like you have leprosy – if you are not married after twenty-five there is something wrong with the girl. For me

> happiness is very important. Even though I don't have that much money, I do have my happiness. One shouldn't get married just to please their parents or society. One should take responsibility for their own actions and be prepared for your moves. You mature a lot if you have a job and are looking after yourself.

Olivia's perception of paid employment for women was consistent with the majority of my informants' understanding regarding women in the public sector. Many single women conceptualized the success of their lives in terms of having a career that enabled them to live as independent women. For some, their careers were an extension of personal interests such as dancing and learning while other women regarded their employment as an enjoyable and viable component of being single. Many single women pursued careers as a means to further their artistic and intellectual involvement with activities that they regarded as enjoyable and fulfilling. In this context, women's careers occupied time and spaces that would customarily be consumed by marriage. Career-oriented women perceived their work as a lifetime involvement that required a considerable amount of devotion and responsibility. For example, Sita's ambition to be a dancer began in the early stages of her life. In pursuing her love for dancing, Sita ignored social pressures to marry in order to have a career. She said:

> I would never think about marriage ... as I was thinking about my profession – my career. When I was growing up my interest was in music and dance so I didn't think about marriage as I was so busy with learning and giving performances everywhere. I gave performances all over India and abroad. So going and coming I had no time. I had no time to think about marriage because I was so busy with my work. My work is everything ...

The benefits of economic independence enabled women to pursue goals and activities in ways that were defined by their own needs and desires. Many of my female informants perceived their economic independence as a means to further self-evaluated aspirations and life ambitions within marked spaces which are not bound by patriarchal definitions of appropriate womanhood. As Gupta (1999) suggests, women have generally been defined in relation to their relationships with men, such as their fathers, husbands and brothers. 'In the eyes of traditional 'South Asian society, like many other societies, a woman is not a person in her own right; she is primarily her father's daughter, a wife or a mother' (ibid.: 23). However, the single women with whom I spoke were not economically reliant on men or restricted by family relationships. Their careers enabled them to engage in activities and practices in ways that marriage does not. For some single women, careers offered them the opportunity and economic capacity to pursue overseas travel independently or in conjunction with their work. Not only do such activities contribute to the fulfilment and satisfaction within the lives of single women, they are also linked to women's understandings of female potentialities and subjectivity. Single women associated their capacity to shape their beings in specific ways with the socio-economic independence they attained through their work and perceived their economic independence as necessary and significant to complete independence as single women. In modern society, independence and success are intrinsically connected with economic freedom. Women's options are increased when they are financially secure and are socially established in their career or work. The option of being single is then a matter of choice for women. Women can be single but the issue is whether or not they want to be.

The Perceived Limits of the Family

The restrictive aspects of the family were defined by my informants as an influential factor for their being single and framed within broader understandings of female oppression. The informants subjectively interpreted the expectations and roles of being a wife and mother in the family as potential hindrances to their conceived lifestyles. Female desires for personal achievements and lifestyles were invalidated by familial and social ideals of acceptable behaviour and presupposed duties of women. Women understood that they would have to make compromises as women in the family. Such compromises were related to women's careers, independent activities, individually defined spaces, and loss of self. Rekha, for example, believed that she did not want to give up her career for marriage in which case she would be dependent upon her husband. Like many of my informants, Rekha recognized the patriarchal structuring of society and the ensuing inequalities that restricted her movements and social being as a single woman in Delhi.

Negotiating her life in ways perceived as different but in accordance with social ideals of respectable female sexuality, Rekha enjoyed her lifestyle free from the obligations and responsibilities of family life. The concept of individuality was a significant aspect to Rekha's happiness and successful life as a single woman. Rekha's individuality allowed her to establish a social image and status that she claimed would not be possible as a married woman.

Furthermore, some women did not want to jeopardize their established lives as independent women for the institution of marriage which they believed to be oppressive and limited. For many single women, women's detachment from family concerns enabled them to pursue lives in unconventional, yet modern, directions. Sita, for example, perceived the family to be a frightening aspect of women's lives and aspect that she did not regard as necessary for her fulfilment. The inequality of family structure was a significant factor for Sita's reasoning to remain unmarried.

Opposed to living within the confines of the family, many of my informants believed that the ability to have successful careers and enjoyable lifestyles were consequent to their decisions to remain unmarried. For example, Nalini and Indira perceived married women to be solely focused on their families and subsequently were unable to consider issues that are outside the family context. Women's lives within the family were restricted by their perceived responsibilities in the home and limited by the socioeconomic dependence to family life. Single women perceived the duties of a housewife to be disruptive and unfavourable to their desires for a career or an independent lifestyle. For some single women per cent men's attitudes towards career-oriented women highlighted men's desired inequalities between husbands and wives. Established ideals in arranging successful marriage alignments suggest that men have higher qualifications, higher incomes, and higher caste than their prospective wives. One informant named Jasmine identified these gendered differences within marriages claiming:

> Men look for women who are submissive, uneducated and brainless so they can control them. They do not want women who are educated, career orientated, mature or even perhaps equal to them.

The independence of single women emerged as a significant factor from women's narratives and the inability to maintain their individuality within the framework of the family. Many of my informants told me that they had undertaken activities in their lives that they would not have been able to achieve as married women. For some women, this meant the ability to travel overseas and throughout South Asia as independent women. This, as Pritam argued, strengthens women's perceptions about themselves and helps in shaping an understanding regarding the situation of women in South Asian societies. In order to live happily as single women, my informants told me that they needed to be strong and confident to be able to live in a male-dominated society and to confront dominant social attitudes towards single women.

Conclusion

In contemporary Delhi society, there is an emerging phenomenon of women bypassing the institution of marriage in order to pursue education and career opportunities that have increased with processes of modernization. While 'being single' is still perceived by many South Asians as an unfortunate or deviant situation for women, many women are beginning to negotiate their social beings and lived experiences according to individual desires and aspirations. From my examination of women's narratives, it is evident that female sexualities are both complex and multiple and that there is the potential for women in South Asian societies to depart from traditional practices in order to construct their lives as single women within the perceived limits of established structural and cultural arrangements.

References

Caplan, P. (1985) *Class and Gender in India: Women and their Organizations in a South Indian City*, London: Tavistock Publications.

Dasgupta, Shamita Das and Sayantani DasGupta (1996) 'Public Face, Private Space: Asian Indian Women and Sexuality', in Nan Bauer Maglin and D. Perry (eds), *'Bad Girls'/'Good Girls': Women, Sex, and Power in the Nineties*, New Brunswick: Rutgers University Press.

Gupta, Sangeeta R. (1999) 'Introduction', in Sangeeta R. Gupta (ed.), *Emerging Voices: South Asian American Women Redefine Self, Family, and Community*, New Delhi: Sage Publications.

Nishimura, Y. (1994) 'Marriage Payments among the Nagarattars in South India', *Contributions to Indian Sociology (NS)*, 28 (2), July–December.

Puri, Jyoti (1999) *Woman, Body, Desire in Post-Colonial India: Narratives of Gender and Sexuality*, New York: Routledge.

Ram, Kalpana (1992) *Mukkuvar Women: Gender, Hegemony and Capitalist Transformation in a South Indian Fishing Community*, New Delhi: Kali for Women.

Uyl, Marion den (1995) *Invisible Barriers: Gender, Caste and Kinship in a Southern Indian Village*, The Netherlands: International Books.

Wadley, Susan (1988) 'Women and the Hindu Tradition', in R. Ghadially (ed.), *Women in Indian Society: A Reader*, New Delhi: Sage Publications.

13

Gender Imagery in American and Indian Advertising

Some Comparative Notes

Lucinda Joy Peach

The view that gender is socially constructed, and that the differences between males and females are produced by the social experiences people have, rather than biology alone, is held by many of us who teach from a feminist perspective. As a result, we understand that the images displayed in various forms of media socialize us and shape our understandings of both femininity and masculinity (Wysocki, 2002). Among various forms of media, advertisements in particular both reflect social ideas about gender as well as shape them. Advertising constructs a quasi-fictional world of gender imagery which provides models by which we gauge our personal identities (Griffin et al., 1994: 492).

Given the prevalence of gender imagery in advertising (ibid.: 491), along with the significance of advertising in shaping the dominant gender images in modern society, this essay will consider some of the normative dimensions of gender advertising. Since media depictions of gender have been considered by most scholars to be more pervasive and influential in shaping women's identity than men's, I will focus on images of women in advertising. Nevertheless, since the social construction of gender is a process in which men and women are mutually constituted in binary opposition to one another, consideration of advertising's influence on women's identity will necessarily include some consideration of men's identity as well.

Much of the research on gender in advertising has been conducted in the United States and Europe, and may not fully describe the ways gender is portrayed in advertisements across cultures. Indeed, there has been little attention paid to how western women are portrayed in advertising in other cultures and its impact on non-western women in those cultures (Frith et al., 2004: 1). Yet, the impact of western advertising on the global media is significant. It plays an important role as an agent of socialization, perpetuating culturally-specific or localized beauty standards such as thinness as universals. With the rise of international media corporations and the spread of international editions of women's magazines, these conventions are being spread quite rapidly around the globe (Shaw, 1999).

In addition, the almost exclusive focus on western media is unfortunate because the depiction of gender, and women's bodies in particular, may have radically different consequences in western and non-western cultural contexts. For example, scholarship conducted on depictions of gender in western contexts are rooted in an ethos that women have acquired certain rights in relation to their bodies, including the right to display them in public without fear of retribution or punishment and the right to take pleasure in them. These are rights which are not universal for women in many countries, especially non-western ones.

In South Asia, for instance, cultural traditions historically have dictated women dress modestly, and such traditions remain widespread today (Frith et al., 2004: 1). As the authors of a study of Indian magazine advertisements point out, 'while the "new" Indian woman may be similar to the western woman in so far as education and workplace aspirations are concerned, her cultural experiences may be different' (Singh and Schoenbachler, 2002: 7).

Magazines remain a popular medium for dissemination of cultural norms and values in both American and Indian societies. Women's magazines are among the most desirable of vehicles for advertisers, since they are aimed at the sector of the population increasingly more responsible for purchases. As an editorial on the Strategic Management Website proclaims: 'The strength of these magazines rests principally on the crucial role of women in the consumption process. The front cover of a magazine is the vehicle by which the consumer distinguishes one magazine from another and serves to label not only the magazine but also the consumer who possesses it' (Strategic Management Website Editorial, 2004).

Since the representation of gender has become such a dominant feature of modern-day advertising in India, it is often called the social resource 'used most' by advertisers. Yet, there has been very little published research on Indian magazine advertising at all, never mind gender advertising, despite recent feminist scholarship on the role of gender on other forms of media, including film, television soap operas, romance novels and stories in women's magazines, and so on. For all of these reasons, this essay will focus on gender advertising in Indian magazines and how well the analysis of American and other western advertisements seems to apply in this different cultural context.

Issues with Gender in Advertising

Jean Kilbourne, an expert on the impact of advertising, especially on girls and women, begins her book *Can't Buy My Love* (1999) with the following observations:

> If you're like most people, you think that advertising has no influence on you. This is what advertisers want you to believe. But, if that were true, why would companies spend over $200 billion a year on advertising? Why would they be willing to spend over $250,000 to produce an average television commercial and another $250,000 to air it?

While we might think that advertising does not affect the way we see the world, Kilbourne argues that 'we internalize these advertisements, and they unconsciously alter the way we perceive normalcy' (Bryant, 2004). In particular, advertising has a significant influence on our understanding and social experience of gender altogether.

Scholars and other observers of gender images in the mass media have noted a number of problematic aspects of the gender imagery in American advertising. These include the objectification of women and valorization of 'the male gaze,' the promotion of negative gender stereotypes, especially of women, the creation of harmful ideals, such as the 'beauty myth' with its unattainable standards of physical perfection, again, especially of women, the 'eternal youth' myth that valorizes only youth; and the effect of encouraging unsafe and/or unhealthy activities, such as extreme dieting and eating disorders, cosmetic surgeries such as breast enhancement and weight reduction, smoking, drinking, alcoholism, and so on. After discussing each of these, I will make some preliminary assessment of the extent to which these problems are also apparent in Indian magazine advertisements.

Objectification

Objectification refers to the process whereby persons are effectively turned into objects by the way they are portrayed. Rather than being valued as subjects, they are depicted and/or treated as objects. Women's bodies are more likely to be shown to advertise products than men's. More often than not, 'advertising portrayals depict women in a narrow range of primarily traditional roles, encouraging the view of women as sexual or decorative objects and creating unrealistic and undesirable ideals for women to uphold' (Williams, 1995; Hornor, 1998). Advertising often objectifies women by reducing them to their bodies, and often to certain parts of the body, such as breasts, torsos, legs, or buttocks, rather than the whole body. Many advertisements reinforce women's insecurity about the adequacy of their bodies by asking women to view themselves as a collection of discrete parts, each one in need of major renovation (Jacobsen and Mazur, 1995). Such portrayals emphasize the view of woman as an object to be disciplined, manipulated, and viewed by others, especially men (Rohlinger, 2002).

In recent years, men are also being objectified in advertising, although the message is different. Media portrays the ideal man as physically big and strong, and the ideal woman as small and taking up little space. The tough and powerful man considers compassion and sensitivity signs of weakness and displays what Kilbourne calls 'contempt for the feminine qualities' (Bryant, 2004).

An important aspect of objectification in media generally is 'the male gaze'. This refers to the way the camera focuses on the body of a woman as reflecting a hypothetical or actual male viewer. Indeed, Indian feminist scholar Mary John contends that 'the difference between the sexes has been associated with visual processes – to be sexualized as a "woman" is to be objectified as an image to be looked at, while the power of "man" is in his gaze, the pleasure and anxiety generated by the desire of looking' (John, 2000: 372). Sociologist Erving Goffman's now famous analysis of advertisements supports this assertion. Goffman's research showed that males are much more often depicted as looking directly at women than vice versa, and that this contributes to the objectification of women in real life (Goffman, 1979).

Goffman also attributed different types of gaze with male and female models in advertisements. Male models typically gaze directly at the audience. Conversely, female models often engage in the mental drift, in which the female model does not make eye contact with the audience but instead allows her gaze to focus in the distance, on a small object, or on the protective male character. This withdrawal entrusts the woman's physical and mental safety to the dominant, superior man, who may or may not be physically present within the advertisement (Rohlinger, 2002). Goffman's work also suggests that women engage in passive touch behaviour that positions them as ornamental objects in advertisements. He argued that this type of visual cue strips women of their instrumentality and reinforces their subordinate position in the social hierarchy.

While Goffman and other researchers have focused on western advertising, communication researchers studying images of women in Indian advertising have noted that the gaze differs across culture and gender (Frith et al., 2004: 2; Griffin et al., 1994). Nonetheless, the way that the male gaze objectifies women seems to operate similarly in American and Indian magazine advertisements. A study of gender in magazine advertising in the US and India by Griffin, Viswanath and Schwartz found that perhaps the most common way that the subordination or portrayal of women as accouterment to men was ritualized was through presenting women as the accessories of men. The frequency with which such poses by women as subordinate or accessories of men were used was very similar in Indian and US advertisements, occurring in 30 per cent of their study sample (Griffin et al., 1994: 495, 499).

Similarly, studies on the projection of women in Indian advertisements in the past have shown that women were mostly projected as glamorous or enticing, whether they were used to sell cosmetics, fabrics, jewellery, domestic appliances, suitcases, scooters or stationery. Men's clothing advertisements invariably used admiring women by the side of the male models, creating the impression that 'all a woman desired was a man dressed in sophisticated garments' (Strategic Marketing Website Editorial, 2004). Such advertisements, which have been described as portraying 'fashion model poses,' share the characteristics of depicting women as 'sights' to be looked at, as passive and inviting, and as welcoming the gaze of the anonymous (male) viewer (Griffin et al., 1994: 497). In fact, the study by Griffin and others found that the greatest similarities between US and Indian magazine advertisements involved the 'conventions of Western fashion pose,' including the portrayal of women next to men as subordinate and/or decorative objects, lying provocatively on beds, sofas, or the ground, revealing a feminine touch or engaging gaze (ibid.: 501).

In addition to their general objectification, images of women are often sexualized, which sends the message that men may 'possess' women's bodies (see Frederickson and Roberts, 1997). Evidence that women are more sexually objectified than men has been found in many media realms, including fashion and fitness magazines (Rudman and Verdi, 1993), MTV (music television) commercials (Signorielli, McLeod and Healy, 1994), and prime-time television commercials (Lin, 1998; Murnen et al., 2003). Although sexual images have been used to sell products since the very beginning of the industry, in recent decades, the prevalence of sexual imagery has become more common, explicit, exploitative and violent. Researchers concluded that female nudity and erotic content had become quite commonplace in contemporary US advertising by the mid-1980s (Frith et al., 2004: 2).

One significant difference between Indian and American advertising is that the display of female anatomy is much more explicit and frequent in American advertisements than in Indian ones (ibid.). Similarly, while depictions of 'sexual pursuit' in both Indian and American advertisements almost always portray men as the pursuers and women as the pursued, such depictions occur three times more often in American advertisements than in Indian ones (Griffin et al., 1994: 496). Indian advertisements are more likely to portray women in 'neutral/other' ways than to portray them as sex objects. Nonetheless, although, some stereotypical portrayals of women in Indian advertisements decreased in the nineties (e.g., 'housewives, concerned with looks'), they were more likely to be portrayed as sex objects in the nineties (Das, 2000).

The findings that Indian women are less sexually objectified in advertisements than western women are consistent with other studies of the use of western and Asian models in Asian advertising. For example, one study found that Asian magazines used western female models more frequently in clothing advertisements whereas Asian female models were used more in advertisements for beauty products. In addition, Asian magazine advertising reflects that a higher proportion of western models are of sensual or sexy beauty types (i.e., the model is posed in a sexual way, usually wearing sexy attire or tight-fitting, revealing clothes) whereas a higher proportion of Asian models is either of the 'classical' or the 'cute' or 'girl next door' beauty type. These differences may indicate that the objectification of women's bodies is racially or culturally-based, as western models are more often featured in advertisements for body-related products – even in Asian magazines, whereas Asian models are used more often in advertisements for facial beauty (Frith et al., 2004: 7).

A number of scholars have made connections between the objectification and sexualization of women in media imagery and tacit cultural understandings that women are appropriate objects of physical and sexual violence and abuse. For example, Kilbourne opines that 'men would not oppress what they see as equal,' but advertisements that objectify women encourage men to think of women as unequal and inferior. She explains how advertisements that eroticize rape and sexualize women contribute to creating a society that has less trouble digesting violence against women.

Kilbourne gives an example of such objectification, describing how some advertisements show young women with their mouths covered. This depiction might seem harmless, such as a turtleneck sweater pulled up over the young woman's mouth or an advertisement for nail polish with her hand across her mouth. Or, it might be much more sinister, such as an advertisement for a CD featuring a young woman with her lips sewn shut. Kilbourne explains that on the surface these advertisements sell sweaters and nail polish and CDs, but they are also selling the idea that women should be silent. This may not be intentional on the part of the advertisers, but we get the message whether it is intended or not (Bryant, 2004).

This technique of objectifying women as sex objects is evident in an Indian advertisement for Motorola phones with digital photo capability. The photography conveys the same message that women are objects who should be silent by cutting off the heads and necks of the two presumably young women who are dressed in school uniforms and standing on bleachers, leaving their objectified lower limbs to be ogled by a male who is peeking up at their legs from below where they are standing on the bleachers. Thus, the objectification and sexualization of women's bodies is by no means only an American phenomenon, but has infiltrated the magazine advertisements of other countries, including India, despite significantly different cultural contexts with different standards of modesty for explicit portrayals of sex.

Promotion of Negative Stereotypes

A second problem area related to gender images in advertising is that they promote negative stereotypes. Past research indicates that both men and women are portrayed in stereotypical ways in magazine advertisements in most parts of the world. However, most scholars agree that these stereotypes are more negative, and thus more damaging, for women than for men. Although it is important to be sensitive to cultural differences, which certainly do exist, especially between the US and India, for example, studies have shown that 'sex-role stereotyping tends to be surprisingly consistent across different countries' (Furnham and Mak, 1999: 431).

Scholars have pointed to four primary stereotypes of women that are prevalent in advertising:

1. sexual objects,
2. homemakers,
3. dependent on men, and
4. ornamental or decorative objects seldom shown as making important decisions or doing important things (Das, 2000).

These four types of stereotypes are remarkably similar across US and Indian cultures, due in large part to a significant extent, perhaps, to the effects of globalization, and the adoption of western advertising conventions by Indian advertisers. A study of TV commercials, for example, found that commonalities included the greater use of men as authoritative central figures, with women more often depicted as users of products; frequent portrayals of men as interviewers or professionals while women are given dependent or secondary roles; men more often portrayed during leisure/outdoor or business occupations while women are more frequently shown at home, confined to a domestic setting; males more often older than the females; and males depicted in association with pleasurable rewards, whereas females more often used to advertise products oriented to social or self-enhancement (Furnham and Mak, 1999: 432–33).

Until very recently, Indian magazine advertisements portrayed women primarily in their stereotypical roles. Women were shown either in the kitchen cooking food, washing a bucketful of clothes, bandaging wounds or feeding their husbands and children. In addition, women are more often depicted in domestic settings in Indian magazine advertisements than in American ones. Authors of the study making this finding in fact observe that 'Indian ads showing mothers in the kitchen or serving meals to the family appear more similar to American ads from the 1950s or 1960s than they do to American ads in our 1985–87 sample' (Griffin et al., 1994: 496).

However, during and since the 1990s, the image of the 'new Indian woman' is explicitly cultivated in Indian advertising. Women are shown less frequently as dependent upon men while men are less likely to be depicted in themes of sex appeal, dominance over women and as authority figures (Strategic Marketing Website Editorial, 2004). Advertisements have also started portraying women more frequently as career-oriented and in non-traditional activities and are constructing the persona of the 'new Indian woman'. Nonetheless, while it is harder to find images in recent magazine advertisements that depict women as only homemakers, depictions of women in professional roles continue to be limited. A study of television commercials conducted as recently as 1999 confirmed that available evidence shows that women are usually depicted at home, and they most commonly appeared in commercials for domestic products (Frith et al., 2004: 3; Furnham and Mak, 1999: 432–33).

In both US and Indian advertisements, women are used to sell different types of products than men. Following traditional stereotypes, advertisements selling home and body products are female dominated, whereas advertisements for automobiles and sports products are male dominated (Singh and Schoenbachler, 2002: 23; Furnham and Mak, 1999: 433). While the percentage of neutral or non-traditional product advertisements in Indian magazines with a female in them increased from 38.7 per cent in 1987 to 62.6 per cent in 1994, the opposite was true in the case of men, who were less likely to appear in advertisements for non-traditional products (i.e., female-oriented and neutral products) in 1994 than in 1990 or in 1987 (Das, 2000).

However, women were also portrayed in traditional ways in advertisements for neutral products. Some of the common stereotypical portrayals of women seem less prevalent in Indian advertisements, however. For example, Indian advertisements are more likely to portray women in 'neutral/other' ways and less likely to portray them as sex objects. This is consistent with research on advertisements in other parts of Asia, which show statistically significant differences in western models more frequently being posed in sexy dress than are Asian models (Frith et al., 2004: 5). However, the softening of stereotyped female role portrayals in more recent Indian advertisements seems to be primarily due to increases in neutral portrayals rather than increases in portrayals of women engaged in non-traditional activities.

Further, there are still a number of Indian advertisements which convey the message, more and less subtly, that women are dependent on men. An advertisement, for example, conveys this message through showing the man using his visa card to pay the bill following dinner with his female companion at a fancy restaurant. Standing alone, this is not worthy of comment, but when it is not accompanied by similar depictions of the female in a couple paying, it sends the message that men continue to be the primary breadwinners, on whom women are financially dependent. Similarly, advertisements illustrating the point that women are shown engaging in activities that are not important continue to be fairly common. An example is an Indian advertisement for Nitco tile, portraying a young Indian women in blue jeans and sleeveless sweater lying happily on a bare floor (presumably newly tiled). The advertisement suggests that women lives of leisure with nothing better to do but lie around and admire their floors!

One other way that gender stereotypes operate in advertising is in relation to the informational content about the products being sold. The findings of a study of Indian advertising suggest that while most advertisements in general contain information, more advertisements targeted at women contained no information at all. This indicates that Indian advertising targeting women tends to contain less and different types of information than does advertising directed at men (Singh and Schoenbachler, 2002: 23). In addition, this study found that advertising directed at women included significantly more hedonistic themes and less themes such as achievement and success. Interestingly, although sex is used far less often to sell projects in India than in the US, this study found that sex was more likely to be used in advertisements targeting women. Whether this stereotyping is due to the influence of western advertising strategies or indigenous ones, it seems to have a negative impact on India women.

Promotion of Impossible (and Harmful) Ideals

A third problem with the way gender is depicted in advertising is the creation of impossible ideals for appearance. These ideals include what have been or can be called 'the beauty myth,' the 'eternal youth myth,' and the 'ability to buy perfection myth' – all of which may result in unhealthy behaviours, even addictions. Far greater pressure placed on women to conform to these ideals than is imposed on men.

The Beauty Myth

The term 'beauty myth' was coined by Naomi Wolf as the title of her book *The Beauty Myth: How Images of Beauty are Used Against Women* (1992) to describe how the images of women in advertisements create impossible standards of beauty and thinness for 'real' women to live up to. One study of American advertising found that one of every 11 commercials has a direct message about beauty (this is not counting the indirect ones) (Dittrich, 2004). In America, at least, the image of the ideal beauty typically is a model less than 25 years old, over five feet nine inches tall, weighing less than one hundred twenty pounds, and without wrinkles, blemishes, or pores. In America, the ideal beauty has typically been blonde, and certainly white skinned.

That Caucasian ideal seems to be prevalent in India today as well, as suggested by the actresses, models and music stars who typically adorn the front pages and style sections of the national newspapers and many advertisements that appear in Indian magazines. For example, a L'Oreal advertisement on the inside-front cover of the Indian edition of *Cosmopolitan* shows a very young looking, light skinned, blue eyed woman with flawless skin and wide lips. Women of colour, when they do appear in magazine advertisements, are usually exoticized and marked by their 'Otherness', as an Indian magazine's advertisement for Louis Vitton handbags featuring an African woman dressed in gold lame shorts and top and high heels in the middle of the desert clearly illustrates.

Advertising also promotes unrealistical ideals for women's weight and body size. A study conducted in 1984 found that the average size of idealized woman (as portrayed by models) has become progressively thinner over the years, and has stabilized at 13–19 per cent below physically average weight. It is then not surprising to learn that women generally are less satisfied with their bodies than men (Hornor, 1998; American Association of University Women, 1990; Dittrich, 2004).

Wolf criticizes the media for disseminating such narrowly defined and unrealistic illusions of unobtainable perfection because of how they negatively affect women. Researchers have found that repeated exposure to the thin beauty myth ideal through various media renders these images seemingly achievable and real. By inviting women to compare their unimproved reality with the air-brushed, 'beauty myth' models, such advertising images work to erode women's self-esteem and satisfaction with their bodies. The term 'beauty' is reduced to a mere decorative quality, which makes women appear ornamental and valued only for their appearance.

The 'Eternally Young' Myth

A second harmful consequence of female-gendered images in advertising is the promotion of an obsession with youth. 'If little girls are presented as sex objects, grown women are depicted as children' (Jacobsen and Mazur, 1995: 80). Images of women used in advertisements in women's magazines have become progressively younger in the past thirty years. Cultural and aesthetic trends apparent in examining advertisements over time, as well, indicate a trend towards using models who look girlish and waif-like, with feline or child-like features, as opposed to top models of the 1980s, who had square jaws and broad shoulders, which emphasized a powerful, mature look.

The media also uses female teen celebrities to sell products, ideas and values. Models in their 20s are used to market anti-ageing products. When models or actresses known to be in their late 30s and early 40s are hired for anti-wrinkle product campaigns, their faces are airbrushed to appear a decade younger. The beauty myth is especially harmful to young women who, from their early teenage years, are bombarded by images on how to look, how to dress, and how to attain an ideal body. Through 'ideal body' advertising and programming, these images play an indirect role in the promotion of body image distortions. This role starts with the mass media's influence on young women's development of the internalized ideal body. Unfortunately, adolescent girls not only turn to advertising for image guidance, but often maintain this ideal image no matter the consequences.

Studies reveal how advertising and other media encourage young girls to compare their own bodies to what they see in the media and, inevitably find their own bodies lacking. It is the norm for young girls in the United States to feel dissatisfied with their bodies and how they are willing to go to any length to turn their bodies into ones similar to those they see in the media. The pressure to look like a model makes it difficult for children and youth to accept and love their bodies as they are, which can lead to a negative body image, less confidence and decreased self-esteem (Snow, 2000). These problems are also evident in Indian magazine advertising. For example, an advertisement for 'Ever Youth' clear skin complexion mask depicts a young woman's face with a caption telling her how she can attain and preserve a clear and youthful complexion.

The 'Ability to Buy Love' (or Perfection) Myth

Advertisements promise us instant happiness through buying products. The 'Ever Youth' advertisement just mentioned is one example of how products are packaged to promote this idea that beauty (and thus happiness) are just a bottle away. By promising the fast solution of every problem, instant gratification as something you can buy, something you can take that will make you feel better instantly, something that will end boredom, advertising also feeds addiction.

Kilbourne explains that advertising creates dissatisfaction with our unembellished selves. 'And at some level, Kilbourne says, when the accumulated stuff doesn't do the trick [to make us happy], we feel there's something wrong with us. We don't think that the ideal image of beauty that is put in front of us is impossible; we think we just haven't learned how to put the eyeliner on right, or we didn't buy the right kind. It works for Cindy Crawford, so why doesn't it work for me?' (Bryant, 1998). One disturbing consequence of girls' and women's exposure to advertisements is the lengths to which they are willing go to achieve the beauty myth ideal, including unhealthy weight loss regimens using harmful weight loss medications, liposuction, breast augmentation and other forms of cosmetic surgery, taking up or not quitting cigarette smoking, spending inordinate amounts of money on clothing and cosmetics, and so on.

One study concludes that 'women who internalize the thinness-as-beauty ideal may engage in extreme and often pathological behaviours in order to achieve and maintain a slim figure' (Hornor, 1998). In addition to concern about thinness, the beauty myth has propelled some women and even girls into considering or actually undergoing cosmetic surgery, especially breast implants that have been promoted by the media and plastic surgeons as a way to increase the psychological and social well-being of females (Jacobson, 2000). While such advertising promoting diet and weight loss, health and fitness, and cosmetic surgeries, is not yet pervasive in Indian advertising, though there are signs that the trend is in that directions. For example, an advertisement appearing in *India Today* promises 'permanent fat reduction' illustrated only by the thin, muscularly sculpted torso of a woman.

According to Kilbourne, one reason that magazine advertisements that objectify women and use sexual images are so successful is because they attract attention. 'Just saying the word "sex" or showing a woman's breast is an effective way to get people's attention. These sexual images yoke the product with our basic desires, as if by buying the product, we were going to get, not just sex, but love. We know that isn't really true but it's hard not to believe it on some level. By now we have all seen so many of these images all through our lives that there is an immediate connection and reaction. Buying the product=sex=love" (Bryant, 2004).

This sales strategy has become increasingly prevalent in Indian magazine advertisements as well. As women have made significant progress in education and employment over the past 40 years, and have become more self-reliant and independent, advertisers have targeted women as the primary market for products and services in India. Indeed, extensive market research has resulted in a trend to address many advertisements for goods and services to a growing class of urban middle class women who have independent salaries or an increasing control in purchase decisions.

Although some advertisers have been careful to avoid a 'westernized' image of the 'new' Indian woman, but have instead attempted to construct a cognate, pan-Indian gender identity, thereby maintaining India's distinctive cultural markers despite increased economic globalization and further development of an open market system (Strategic Marketing Website Editorial, 2004), other advertisers have clearly adopted western models, techniques and stylistic conventions. While the advertising techniques may be similar, the consequences are undoubtedly not the same, given the different cultural contexts into which these advertisements are being disseminated.

This contributes to the promotion of western images as the ideal standard by which beauty as well as all other markers of value and worth are measured – a message that is especially problematic when articulated in advertising in non-western societies. In the Indian context, the proliferation of images of westernized women can be viewed as part of a larger trend towards cultural 'homogenization' which many fear is the inevitable outcome of globalization. Through the various media, the west is having an increasing influence upon the more affluent sector of the Indian economy – a trend that is especially prominent in Indian women's fashion magazines.

Even though Indian advertisements use Indian models with traditional dresses, they are being increasingly replaced with western models, models in western outfits or models with other western attributes. According to one commentator, 'this osmosis of traditional culture with western culture not only reflects the metamorphosis of women in society but also reveals the new Indian market – a revolutionized consumer marketplace' (ibid.). In addition, a comparative study of images of women in weekly US news magazines (*Time* and *Life*) and weekly Indian magazines (*India Today* and *Illustrated Weekly of India*) found that many of the western advertising conventions and poses for women were being transferred across cultures and that female models in India were adopting poses and displays that conformed closely to gender portrayals in the advertising of the industrialized western nations (Griffin et al., 1994). The authors of this study note that the proliferation of branded advertising in the increasingly open markets of nations such as India and China has provided standardized images of gender (and what it means to appear 'attractive') (ibid.). The effect of this new trend on gender ideals in India has yet to be fully revealed, but initial indications are not promising.

Summary and Conclusions

There are numerous similarities between gender advertisements in American and Indian magazines. Nonetheless, significant differences remain. One comparative study of western and Indian magazine advertisements observed that there are several factors that should have led to even more liberal portrayals of women in Indian magazine advertisements, such as the increasing number of middle class consumers and their higher levels of education and decision-making. Yet it found that women for the most part are still portrayed in very traditional ways in Indian magazine advertisements. Although Indian society is changing, it is still a patriarchal society. Consequently, portraying Indian women in non-traditional ways may not be accepted as easily in Indian society as in western society.

One area which needs further research is the impact of western female models and beauty myth ideals on Indian women. As John argues:

> We clearly and urgently need to have a better appreciation of how women are addressed by the beauty business: in what ways they consent to the new and impossible standards of sexual attractiveness beamed at them, what levels of consumption are now considered normal if not necessary, or what aspirations lead so many to hone their skills and their bodies in the hope of a modeling career. (2000: 374)

To what extent are these western images replacing indigenous aesthetics of female beauty? To what extent are such images viewed as foreign and thus not representative of normative standards for Indian women? What is the impact of the proliferation of these western images on the Indian advertising industry as well as on Indian women's own understandings of their beauty and attractiveness?

Overall, similar kinds of depictions of men and women in Indian and western advertisements suggests that the problems with gender advertising in the United States are also prevalent in India. The ways that gender advertising objectifies women, depicts them as sex objects, promotes the beauty myth, and encourages unhealthy behaviours suggests the gender advertising in India, as the US and elsewhere in the world, has negative consequences for the status of women in both cultures. In addition, the predominance of magazine advertisements featuring western or westernized women is also potentially harmful to the self-esteem and self-acceptance of Indian women whose appearance is markedly different. Since economic liberalization and globalization make it more difficult to eliminate or even reduce the powerful effects of these advertisements, the impact of western ideals and norms on Indian cultural understandings of gender and how they are manifested in advertising must also be seriously assessed.

References

Bryant, Erica (2004) 'Can't Buy My Love: Jean Kilbourne Takes on the World of Advertising', Blue Jean Online, http://www.bluejean online.com/ features/features_archives/features0301b.html

Curties, Mandi and Corina MacKay (1991) 'Interview with Naomi Wolf', online at Greeenleft Website, http://www.greenleft.org.au/back/1991/33/33–24.htm.

Das, Mallika (2000) 'Men and Women in Indian Magazine Advertisements: A Preliminary Report', *Sex Roles: A Journal of Research*, 43 (9–10) (November): 699–717, online at http://www.findarticles.com

Dittrich, Liz (2004) 'About-Face Facts on Body Image', online at About-Face Website, http://www.about-face.org/r/refs/media.shtml

—— (2004) 'About-Face Facts on the Media', online at About-Face Website, http://www.about-face.org/r/refs/media.shtml

Faludi, Susan (1991) *Backlash: The Undeclared War Against American Women*, New York: Crown.

Frith, Katherine Toland, Hong Cheng and Ping Shaw (2004) 'Race and Beauty: A Comparison of Asian and Western Models in Women's Magazine Advertisements', *Sex Roles: A Journal of Research*, 50 (1–2): 53–61.

Furnham, Adrian and Twiggy Mak (1999) 'Sex-role Stereotyping in Television Commercials: A Review and Comparison of Fourteen Studies Done on Five Continents over 25 Years', *Sex Roles: A Journal of Research*, 41 (5–6): 413–37.

Gallagher, Margaret (2001) *Gender Settings: New Agendas for Media Monitoring and Advocacy*, London: Zed Books.

Griffin, Michael, K. Viswanath and Dona Schwartz (1994) 'Gender Advertising in the US and India: Exporting Cultural Stereotypes', *Media, Culture, and Society*, 16: 487–507.

Hornor, Marianne (1998) 'The "Who", "What", "When", "Where" and "Why" of "How" Advertising Works', online at http://www.ciadvertising.org/studies/student/98_fall/theory/hornor/who.htm.

Jacobsen, Michael and Laurie Mazur (1995) 'Sexism and Sexuality in Advertising', in M.F. Jacobson and L.A. Mazur (eds), *Marketing Madness: A Survival Guide for a Consumer Society*, Boulder, CO: Westview Press, pp. 74–87, online at Media, Power, and Culture, School of Journalism and Mass Communications, Kent-State University Website, http://www.personal.kent.edu/~glhanson/readings/ advertising/womeninads.htm (accessed on 3 May 2004).

John, Mary (2000) 'Globalisation, Sexuality and the Visual Field: Issues and Non-issues for Cultural Critique', in Mary John and Janaki Nair (eds), *A Question of Silence? The Sexual Economies of Modern India*, New Delhi: Kali for Women, pp. 368–96.

Kilbourne, Jean (1999) *Deadly Persuasion: Why Women and Girls Must Fight the Addictive Power of Advertising*, New York: Free Press.

—— (1999) *Can't Buy My Love*, New York: Simon and Schuster, excerpted on her websites: http://www.jeankilbourne.com and http://www.cant-buymylove.com

—— (2000) *Killing Us Softly: Advertising's Image of Women*, Northampton, MA: Media Education Foundation (video documentary).

—— (1995) *Slim Hopes: Advertising and the Obsession with Thinness*, Northampton, MA: Media Education Foundation (video recording).

—— (1987) *Still Killing Us Softly: Advertising's Image of Women*, Cambridge, MA: Cambridge Documentary Films (video recording).

Murnen, Sarah, Linda Smolak, J. Andrew Mills and Lindsey Good (2003) 'Thin, Sexy Women and Strong, Muscular Men: Grade-School Children's Responses to Objectified Images of Women and Men', *Sex Roles: A Journal of Research*, 49 (9–10) (November): 427–37, online at http://www.findarticles.com/p/articles/mi_m2294/is_9-10_49/ai_110813265

Reading, Anna (1997) 'Women, Men and the Mass Media', online at World YWCA Website, http://www.worldywca.org/common_concern/sept1997/ wm_media.html.

Rohlinger, D. Andrea (2002) 'Eroticizing Men: Cultural Influences on Advertising and Male Objectification', *Sex Roles: A Journal of Research*, 46 (3–4): 61–74, online at http://www. findarticles.com

Singh, Tanuja and Denise Schoenbachler (2002) 'Women's Advertising in Developing Nations: An Analysis of the Thematic and Information Content of Indian Magazine Advertisements', *Journal of Asia-Pacific Business*, 4 (2): 3–28.

Strategic Marketing Website Editorial (2004) 'Perspectives: Female Role Portrayals in Women's Magazines', online at Strategic Marketing Website, http://www.etstrategicmarketing.com/smNov-Dec1/persp_women.htm.

Verma, Manish, 'Gender Roles in Advertising', PhD dissertation research, unpublished, on file with the author at Himachal Pradesh University, Shimla, Himachal Pradesh, India.

Wolf, Naomi (1992) *The Beauty Myth: How Images of Beauty are Used Against Women*, New York: Anchor Books.

Wysocki, Diane Kholos (2002) 'Using Film to Teach Women's Studies Courses: A Teaching Aid Recommendation', *Journal of International Women's Studies*, 3 (2): 70–74.

14

Reframing Globalization and Internationalism

Feminisms in India and the Question of Asia

Mary E. John

My central focus in this paper – drawing from the history of feminism – concerns globalization and its pre-eminence in contemporary reflections, both theoretical and political. It is broadly divided into two parts. The first part interrogates current frameworks for approaching globalization and internationalism, while part two reframes the issue from the perspective of the recent 'rise of Asia'.

Across India, globalization has become the decisive mark, if not horizon of our time. The fact that globalization is open-ended and fuzzy has done little to diminish its power, gauging the way the concept is retrospectively restructuring not just our relationship to space but to time itself. Thus, India's post-independence history has now been narrativized as a shift, a transition from the 'national' phase (when the newly created nation–state embarked on its path of Nehruvian development) to the current globalizing one, with a period of crisis in between.

The problem I am trying to address concerns the extent to which this narrative – and the hegemony accorded to globalization in particular – is crowding out alternate accounts of our present. My point is not to deny the depth of contemporary transformations, or indeed the power of 'global' forces at different levels. Rather, I wish to draw attention to the political and methodological fallout of *already presuming* 'globalization' to be the prime mover of the present in contrast to that of the nation before. The danger here is that we are left with a uni-dimensional relationship to our present and our immediate past – one that obscures a host of questions and challenges. While it is obviously true that the nation no longer occupies the pre-eminent position that it once did, this is because of multiple pressures and transformations, simultaneously within and beyond its boundaries. I would like to argue that it is imperative today to seek out such multiple accounts of recent processes, especially from the perspectives of long-standing social movements such as the women's movement. Without such accounts, current problems and crises are reduced to the 'effects' of globalization, which can be more or less mechanically read off in a relation of direct causality, such as for instance, the negative impact on women and others of the new economic policies, or the co-option of once autonomous social movements and struggles through internationally funded NGOs.

What changes, then, if one were to narrativize recent processes from the perspectives of feminist struggles, as an example of a long-standing social movement? This section attempts to locate some of the strands for such a narrative, beginning with current responses to globalization, before touching on the relationships between nationalism and the women's movement, other recent developments as well as more direct challenges confronting feminism and the women's movement today. To anticipate my subsequent arguments, drawing these strands together calls for a conjunctural analysis of the present that would be better described as 'post-national' rather than simply 'global'.

First of all, a closer look at current responses by feminists would reveal a surprising degree of diversity characterizing feminist engagements with 'globalization' itself. This diversity not only indicates conflicting political positions, but also points to deep differences in conceptualizing the term itself – globalization – then, is a far from settled question. Not enough attention has been paid to the conceptual and political underpinnings of these varied approaches, each of which raises further questions of its own. Let me offer a few examples.[1]

The most prominent feminist voices in the Indian context are those that have opposed the coming of globalization, and for reasons well rehearsed in the literature. In this view, globalization can only result in deepening processes of impoverishment and insecurity for the majority, with women suffering the most. In an effort to combat the dominant image of the 'irreversibility' of the new economic order, a common strategy adopted by this perspective is to claim that globalization is really nothing more than a bundle of policies undertaken at the behest of international pressure by a willing Indian state. Being the product of deliberate choices, this policy bundle can indeed be reversed by a differently oriented nation–state prepared to resist and counter the new imperialism.

In sum, leftist critiques of 'globalization as economic policy' remain pinned to state-led welfare and socialist planning. The problems with this critique are then transferred to the alternative policy prescriptions offered. Since political-ideological frameworks centred on economic nationalism have lost much of their authority in the current climate, and since the state itself has changed with globalization, they require much more careful justification. Ever since the landmark *Towards Equality* report (on the status of women produced for the UN International Women's Year of 1975) it has been common knowledge that the condition of women deteriorated sharply in the very era of socialistically-oriented, import-substituting planned development – precisely the era that leftist critiques of globalization hark back to today. How can we be confident that a resurrected version of this state – in the adverse market-dominated conditions of today – will be more accountable to its women?

A more fundamental oppositional critique has been offered by eco-feminists such as Vandana Shiva. Her critique extends well beyond the latest form of globalization to cover the entire period of modernity, colonialism and capitalism, and in such a manner that 'decentralized agricultural communities' are the only alternative (Shiva, 1998). Here, too, one is left with a host of unanswered questions, especially when it is claimed that women farmers already possess a non-hierarchical relation to production, nature, and to gender.

From a perspective that is very different from other left-oriented critiques, the Marxist-feminist Rohini Hensman argues against reducing globalization to a set of policies. For her, globalization is nothing short of the unfolding of a new phase in the evolution of world capitalism, one that demands a correspondingly international level of intervention and struggle (this includes taking advantage of controversial WTO directives to link trade with labour standards). The anti-globalization agenda, in her view, does not make sense for Third World women workers, with its defence of national boundaries which foster nationalisms that, in turn, promote imperialism, fascism and war (Hensman, 2004). While there is much that is cogent in this account, where are the signs, however nascent, of such an international working class? Indeed, has it not become that much easier – in the era of global outsourcing – to pit workers against each other?

Yet others like Gail Omvedt have made the case that the new economic order could actually help those very groups whom the prior era of developmentalism had marginalized. Thus, the unviable monopolies and inefficient bureaucracies led by Hindu upper castes may well lose out to new multinational corporations employing the cheap labour of women or lower castes (Omvedt and Gala, 1993). But why – asks Omvedt polemically – should this be seen a problem? While this argument has something in common with the feminization of labour arguments made elsewhere, it too begs many questions like, on what basis can one expect that hitherto marginalized groups will be in a position to take advantage of the new situation, or that dominant groups would lose out?

Finally, we have positions advocating what I would call a 'people's capitalism' in the SEWA mould. The central argument of this perspective is that providing economic and financial security to poor women workers in the informal sector is the proper pragmatic response to a world where both the public and private sectors – in short, almost the entire formal sector which has been the backbone of India's mixed economy – are facing erosion (Jhabvala and Subrahmanya, 2000). The irony here is that it is international agencies such as the World Bank that were the first and keenest votaries of this way of responding to globalization.

These are doubtless highly schematic, if not reductive accounts. My simple aim is to show that very divergent pictures are being painted, even though we are dealing with only one dimension of globalization – and the best known one, at that – namely, its economic aspect. And, this diversity exists in spite of the fact that all the views presented above are held by feminists committed to social justice or seasoned members of the women's movement – and are not the responses of the neo-liberal or fundamentalist right wing. There has been far too much reluctance, in my view, to recognize and therefore engage with such differences; nor has there been enough effort to tackle the many issues that each of these positions leaves unaddressed. A recent polemic by Gail Omvedt (2005) in favour of being 'politically incorrect' by arguing against the 'anti-globalizers' demonstrates how much more debate is needed. In the context of this essay, however, I wish to emphasize what these diverse perspectives have in common. In spite of being incommensurable on many counts, the above mentioned responses share an important feature, i.e., they serve to destabilize the 'nation to globalization' narrative that is otherwise routinely seen as being beyond question.

In fact, and this is my second point, even a cursory examination of the women's movement would demonstrate to what extent it has been pervasively structured by local and global forces from its very inception in the 19th century to the present. One would be hard pressed to find any period when women's issues emerged autonomously or authentically 'in their own right', so deeply mired have they been in the complex histories of colonialism and nationalism. And yet, this heteronomy and even subjection to more powerful others has not stopped us from marking the contours of a movement, including the evolution of women's rights. The ebb and flow of the campaigns and debates that have come to be associated with the women's movement bear a particularly difficult relationship with the history of nationalism and the nation–state. During the period of social reform, for instance, it has been argued that the emergence of cultural nationalism in the late 19th century in colonial Bengal resulted in the virtual disappearance of the women's question from public debate, whether the nationalist strategy be interpreted as having resolved the issue (Chatterjee, 1993) or rather, of having failed to do so (Sarkar, 2001). During the early 20th century, moreover, when women's organizations came into their own for the first time in several parts of the country, at a time when political nationalism was expanding, their own agendas were often universalist and international in scope. Once again, different accounts have been offered (Nair, 1996; John, 2000; Roy, 2005; Sinha, 2006) of this particular period. It is not for nothing that the 1950s and 60s – the very years when the nation enjoyed a hegemonic status among most of its citizens and in the eyes of the world – were first called 'the silent period' of the women's movement. Even though this is no longer an accurate description, the 1970s still mark a new beginning for many movements, including the women's movement, and in large part because these years witnessed the first major national crisis after independence.

Accounts of the rebirth of the women's movement in the 1970s focus almost exclusively on the range of local struggles that defined it – dowry deaths and custodial rape, mass organizing for better wages, and so on. Far too little is said about how this moment was part of a larger conjuncture that witnessed movements for women's liberation in many parts of the world. There are reasons for such an aversion – the identification of feminism with the West, in particular. In retrospect we can discern a conflation of the desire for local accountability with that for authenticity. But rather than stick with a national narrative alone, we need accounts that are able to situate the rise of the women's movement in relation to developments elsewhere, including all the problematic claims of universal sisterhood that were in currency at the time. Moreover, the International Women's Year of 1975 had significant effects on the movement here as well. Interestingly, the role of the nation–state in this process was remarkably contradictory. We are more familiar with the state's repressive arm during the Emergency years, which forced many radical groups, including women, to go underground or face imprisonment for their beliefs and activities. Less is publicly known about how the Indian State in 1972 did little in response to the United Nations' call for an in-depth examination of the 'status of women' in its member-nations, and how ultimately the Department of Women and Family Welfare sponsored the study and publication of the path-breaking *Towards Equality* report on its own. This report shocked many with its evidence of widespread state failure, and subsequently became a 'founding text' for the women's movement.

Indeed, if we take a step back from the 'nation to globalization' narrative, and look instead at the trajectory of movements, the story would, if anything, be the reverse. Feminism was a much stronger force internationally in the 1970s and 80s than it is today. It is hard even to speak of the presence of movements such as the women's movement in many parts of the contemporary western world. What we do have are international organizations which have taken on 'our' concerns in various ways, which are significantly different. Or again, there are pedagogic responses, whereby 'third world feminism' has entered the first world classroom – again a somewhat different development. Even though globalization is certainly aiding the traffic in people and ideas unthinkable a generation ago, the pre-globalization years witnessed a much more intense international feminist ferment, including combating false universalisms and highlighting local differences.

My third counter to the univocal emphasis being placed on globalization today is that the challenges before the women's movement are irreducibly plural. The very years from the late 1980s and 90s that witnessed the official abandonment of the regimes of state-led development, have also seen the (re)emergence of communalism, the rise of caste and, more recently, the challenges of non-normative sexualities. Each of these has disturbed the grounds of the women's movement in fundamental ways, and need to be looked at in their own right, regardless of whether they are related to global processes. There is no way, for instance, that the wave of backward caste politics of the 1980s, culminating in the pathological backlash of the anti-Mandal agitation of 1990, can be laid at the door of globalization. Links would have to be drawn in the opposite direction, as upper caste elites kicked away the welfare state – as the ladder they no longer needed – with greater ferocity after the move to implement reservations in government services and higher education. It was only in the 1990s that significant sections of an identifiably upper caste women's movement developed caste-based critiques of gender, rediscovered the forgotten legacies of Periyar, Phule and Ambedkar, and responded to the demands of Dalit women for a separate political space. We have just begun to historicize this hugely significant moment in the making of the movement (e.g., Tharu and Niranjana, 1994; Chakravarti, 2003; Rao, 2003; Rege, 2006).

Issues of sexuality are equally far-reaching and contentious. Unfortunately, it has been possible for a number of feminists to evade the newer languages and challenges of sexuality movements – such as the gay and lesbian movement or struggles over sex work – precisely by seeing them as off-shoots of globalization. Thus, heavily financed AIDS awareness campaigns among sex workers have been viewed with considerable unease, as have LGBT NGOs dependent on foreign funding. Sexuality campaigns against the sodomy laws, or in favour of sex workers rights – not to speak of questions of normative sexuality – are just beginning to find some space for debate and recognition, whether among major women's organizations or in women's studies (e.g., Menon, 2007).

Finally, of course, we must have fuller narratives of the recent trajectories of the women's movement as a movement in its own right. No one would deny that much has changed in the intervening years, and the heightened institutionalization and professionalization of feminism is one of the hallmarks of our present (is this uniquely true of the women's movement, and, if so, why?). Feminism now has a marginal presence in the syllabi of different disciplines in the social sciences and humanities, while women's studies centres are proliferating across the country under the fiat of the University Grants Commission (UGC). Institutionalization has congealed around the term 'gender,' as state, NGOs and women's organizations take on various tasks in its name. These include: the collection of gender disaggregated data, gender sensitization and training of a range of personnel, from high ranking officials to activists, the provision of gender-related services, legal awareness and research, and they all require expertise and funding. This means that a certain presence if not power, however contradictory, attaches to the subject 'women'.

But the question remains – how exactly should we contrast this situation with yesteryears, without claiming a unique autonomy for an earlier time? Equally critically, if the future of the women's movement occupies an uncertain place today, compared to the buoyant energies of the 1970s and 80s, then these current challenges must be described, at least to some minimum degree, with the vocabulary of feminist politics. In what ways, then, have patriarchies and gender relations changed in recent decades? In spite of the greater institutional visibility of feminism today, what are the experiences of a younger generation, such as metropolitan students (who spearheaded the women's movement a generation ago) that appear to be generating expressions of disavowal towards feminism? A teacher in a Mumbai college recently described her disappointment when, barring a few exceptions, most women students did not relate positively to issues concerning the women's movement and feminist theorizing. For some – English-speaking, upwardly mobile and with strong professional ambitions of their own – feminism was rejected because it seemed to block or mock their desires; for others, particularly lower-middle class students, unsure of any future outside of marriage, feminism appeared alienating, unable to touch their destinies (Phadke, n.d.).

We need many more 'thick descriptions' of such situated experiences – and not only from major cities – in order to better understand the current trajectories of women and the women's movement. It is only by synthesizing analyses drawn from a range of contemporary locations, especially those that have been marginal in most accounts so far, that we can see at what points a movement like feminism is overdetermined by other developments such as 'globalization'. But such accounts are hard to come by.

Drawing these strands together clearly calls for a conjunctural analysis of the distinct moments structuring the period from the 1970s into these first years of the 21st century. Moreover, in order to produce urgently needed – and less insular – 'big pictures', we must look towards comparative accounts of multiple feminisms and their diverse destinies – within South Asia, across Asia, and in relation to other regions.[2] As I have been claiming throughout, the women's movement has never simply been a local phenomenon but one whose history has been characterized by profound mutual influences, contestations, commonalities and differences. Where do feminisms stand in relation to 'globalization' (howsoever construed) in other spaces – Pakistan or Sri Lanka, China or Korea, the US or France?

II

This brings me to the question of Asia. If any continent has emerged as a power to reckon with in recent times, it is Asia. The 'rise of Asia' evokes not just the economic ferment of accelerated production, trade and financial flows, but a pervasive cultural sensibility, a potent source of meaning and structure of feeling. Asia has also fundamentally restructured, overused and often careless references to globalization. Feminists have been at the forefront of drubbing claims that nations (in general) are giving way to a (single) borderless global world, pointing instead to the deepening of inequalities across and within them. Less noticed, however, are signs of new patterns of regionalization, and Asia has become a prime representative. Asia today is, therefore, something more than an arbitrary collection of territorially contiguous nations on the world map. Different nation–states in the region are both more globally integrated and more interdependent than ever before, which was the reason why the major financial crisis a decade ago was called 'Asian' – not global, and certainly not western. Many aspects of life and its institutions are also being called Asian – such as the Asian family, for example – implying thereby both something we Asians supposedly share and have in common, and a mark of difference from the rest of the world.

What changes when questions of feminism are refracted through accounts of this region in particular? Historically speaking, of course, there are much deeper roots to these issues. Due to the impact of women's movements worldwide, it should be remembered, the destinies of many non-western nations had already been changed by the early 20th century, as Kumari Jayawardena's classic study *Feminism and Nationalism in the Third World* demonstrated two decades ago (notice that her study focuses almost exclusively on countries in Asia).[3] My earlier claims about the *simultaneously* local, national and international quality of the new questions that attached to women from the 19th century onwards are well illustrated here. Current scholarship has most effectively captured this conflicted simultaneity within the dynamics of histories of imperialism and colonialism, and the nationalisms they spawned – *both* in the West and elsewhere.

Much of the pre-history of Asia as a cultural idea and geo-political force is, of course, well-known. As Edward Said argued in his path-breaking study on Orientalism, the naming of Asia was intrinsic to the Orientalist project, so much so that he characterized it as an idea and concern for western intellectuals alone. But as many have pointed out, such a view has effectively blocked other histories of Asia, such as the prolonged involvement of Japanese intellectuals with Asia and its regional history. In her fascinating and meticulous reading, the Chinese scholar Sun Ge has emphasized the problematic mode in which these Japanese intellectuals sought 'to lift Asia as a principle into the context of world history'. It rested on an over simple opposition between East and West, failing to 'notice the regional historical tensions inherent in Asia contained in the very idea of Asia' (Sun, 2000: 336). One must also add the further problem that, in the work of these writers, Asia invariably reduced to the conflicted relationships between Japan and China. A more inclusive effort would be the Indian scholar-diplomat K.M. Panikkar's classic *Asia and Western Dominance,* first published in 1953. Spanning five centuries and a host of (in his words) 'greater' and 'lesser' Asian countries – notably also the special case of Russia's historical relationship to Asia – Panikkar's erudition remained nonetheless somewhat constricted by his limited frame. Against those writers who were maintaining the superficiality of European influence in this part of the world, his treatise sought to demonstrate the extent and depth of the relationship. In his conclusion, Panikkar claimed that it was the very solidarity with which European nations emphasized their '*European-ness* in dealing with Asian countries, (that) gave rise to a common feeling of Asian-ness … . From 1880 to 1914 – during the period of imperialism – the Europeans were united against Asia, and this attitude, in its turn, gave birth to a sense of Asianism, which even the aggressive actions of Japan and its proclaimed policy "of standing in with the West" did not seriously undermine' (Panikkar, 1969: 322–23, emphasis original). None of these writers touch upon the significance of the subject of women in the making of Asia during the period of colonization. Further, the primacy of the East-West relationship has ensured that most accounts to date have focused on the extraordinary travels of people and ideas between Euro-America and countries of Asia – be they Indonesia, Sri Lanka or Japan. Given the focus on the colonizer by a founding generation of feminists in colonial India, for instance, much less is known about how imperialism also made possible complex interactions and links between many countries in the region, which were by no means confined to Britain or the United States. Women's universities in Japan became the preferred model for the social reformer Dhonde Keshav Karve's first women's university in the city of Poona, founded in 1916. In his autobiography *Looking Back*, Karve discusses his conception of the status of women – different yet equal – which he believed was embodied in Japanese women's universities rather than western co-educational institutions (Karve, 1936). It is also surely not accidental that at the high point of raising demands for women's equality within the Indian National Congress, the first Asian gathering on women's rights – the All-Asian Women's Conference – was held in Lahore (now Pakistan) in 1931.

In the wake of widespread trans-continental decolonization and independence movements from the mid-20th century onwards, however, an alternate collective identity – at once economic and political – took the stage, namely, that of the 'third world'. With its connotations of political autonomy, on the one hand, but also of exploitation and revolutionary potential, on the other, the concept of the third world held considerable appeal, and extended from the newly independent nations of Asia and Africa to South America as well. From the 1970s, the third world also entered the political vocabulary of numerous social movements, so much so, that many non-western women's groups came to identify with 'third world feminism'.

Today, we tend to forget that we not only live in the wake of the collapse of the 'second world', but also that of the 'third'. Not only has the era of state-led non-alignment clearly exhausted itself, the rise of Asia in recent years simultaneously occupies a similar discursive space to that of yesteryear's third world, and also marks a radical rupture with it. Like its predecessor, Asia is something of an oppositional category, set up in contrast to the West. But there is also another level where Asia means something radically new, especially after the end of the three worlds, the most recent transformations of capitalism – neo-liberalism and economic restructuring – and the rise of a uni-polar political order. In an important essay 'Asian Women in Reregionalization', Tani Barlow (2008) begins by emphasizing the central role of US capitalism in the reregionalization of Asia: I wish to draw attention to how the global ascent of Asia itself has been intrinsic to the demise of the third world, since the latter depended both on the politics of non-alignment as well as the perception of a shared condition of economic deprivation at the hands of the exploitative structures of capitalism and neo-colonialism. The economic 'miracles' of East and South-East Asia, not to speak of the aggressive market socialism of China, the prior petrodollar-boom of West Asia, or the creation of new Central Asian states with the break-up of the Soviet Union – in contrast to the sense of deep and pervasive crisis emanating from regions such as sub-Saharan Africa – represent developments that have robbed the third world of its earlier meanings. It is true that these meanings were never closely examined for the degree to which they were in fact shared across the disparate nations and regions of the third world. But, however woolly or wishful the term might have been as a description that included Asia, at least it did not seem implausible then. Today, it is clearly a non-starter. All too frequently, in fact, Asia refers only to the swathe of successful newly industrialized countries, from South Korea to Singapore. Broader conceptions of Asia effectively carve it into distinct zones – of success and affluence, of failure and endemic poverty, of conflict and Islamic fundamentalism. India now increasingly believes that it must look East rather than West in the development race, not just to China, but also to Korea, Thailand, Malaysia and Indonesia, in their ability to combat financial crises and the world market.

This historical background to the trajectories of Asia, however, while certainly creating the conditions for new connections, can only partly account for the desires fuelling the building and rebuilding of relationships among feminists and women's organizations in the region today. One kind of overarching framework is being provided by the global 'gender and governance' discourses that, as Barlow (ibid.) acutely points out, are large-scale ideological formations that hardly anyone can escape today. But they, too, only tell a partial story, however dominant and deft at annexing feminist agendas. For one thing, the most significant cross-border movements to challenge India and the Indian nation–state came from pioneering feminists in Pakistan, Sri Lanka, Bangladesh and even India, who changed the face of South Asia for its citizens. Their efforts prised open the sealed boundaries between India and Pakistan, underscored the potent dangers of militaristic nationalisms spreading throughout the region, and broke the hegemonic habit whereby India could so easily stand in for South Asia as a whole.[4] But if meetings with South Asian feminists in Colombo, Lahore, Delhi and Dhaka presented India in a different light, interactions with Asian feminists in Lucknow, Bangkok, Bangalore, Manila, Dalian, Shanghai, Seoul, Tokyo and Taipei have offered fresh perspectives on Asia.[5]

If, then, we were to reframe histories of women and feminism by paying more attention to comparisons and connections across Asia, rather than work with the more common default comparison with the West, at least two sites of exploration suggest themselves – the first historical and the other more contemporary.

Historically, I already had occasion to remark on the significance of the period of the late 19th and early 20th centuries in any account of the emergence of histories of the women's question and feminism. As I have argued elsewhere, when we look at the problems that attached to early debates on women's rights and feminism in contexts like that of colonial India, questions of 'culture' occupy a critical position. As bearers of Indian culture, women have had to contend with the selective association of feminism with the West (in an earlier article I contrasted this situation with the discursive and institutional role of 'nature'/biology in the construction of the subject of women and feminism in western contexts). Tejaswini Niranjana has gone on to argue that given the antithetical relationship between modernity and culture, the alignment of women and national culture, women and tradition, in a number of contexts across Asia, in spite of differences among them, has resulted in a selective displacement of the problematic of modernity onto feminist work. The critical emergence of the 'new woman' in many locations in the early 20th century is one indication of the significance of this. Inter-Asian comparisons here, therefore, can bring into the picture critical perspectives on gender and culture – and indicate how much more is needed for comparative histories of modernities outside the West.

The second example I would like to consider concerns the new visibility of international migration. As many social scientists have noted, migration in Asia has undergone major and dramatic changes in the last few decades. As the result of a number of developments, not the least of which is the complex rise of Asia as a heterogeneous and globally integrated region referred to earlier, movements within the region have come to predominate over movement out of the region towards the West. Even more interesting, however, is that it is not just the direction of migration that has changed, but their gender composition. A deep earlier assumption that the migrating worker was male has been belatedly exposed. Both statistics and accounts of movements make it evident that this changing composition was by no means confined to one location – West Asia (what we call the Gulf), Japan and Korea, Hongkong and Singapore, not to mention new migration patterns within countries like India and China. Even more significant is that these new migrants did not always fit into customary definitions of work – carework, domestic labour of various kinds, sex work and, yes, marriage migrations are part of an emerging international division of labour that is restructuring the most intimate spheres of the family, sexuality and reproduction.

It is in all these ways that the simultaneity of local, national and international feminisms needs to be thought through in each instance. The project of envisaging new comparative work across these complex histories and locations has barely begun. By way of a provisional conclusion, I would like to suggest that – at least in India – we are better served using the notion of the 'post-national' as a marker of our present. The 'post-national' acknowledges that the nation no longer occupies the sovereign position or horizon of intelligibility that it once did. Its most constructive function would be to provide some critical distance from the 'nation to globalization' narrative dominating India's post-independence history. The ruptures and disorientations of the last decade or so should also be seen as an invaluable opportunity, enabling us to look back from different subaltern locations at the makings of 'India'. By virtue of its own remarkable history and entanglements in a range of processes – from the most local to the most international – and its closeness to centres of power along with its presence at the margins, the women's movement offers a unique vantage point for retelling the story of contemporary India.

Notes

1. The following section is drawn from an earlier discussion in John (2005).
2. For an example of recent work within Asia, see John (2007).

3. Jayawardena (1986: 1). The countries she included for comparative study were Egypt, Iran, Turkey, India, Sri Lanka, China, Japan, the Philippines, Vietnam and Indonesia, chosen she says, both for their 'parallels' and 'differences of strategy'.
4. Given the enormous 'industry' on the partition of British India that has emerged in recent years, it may be worth remembering the very first explorations undertaken by feminists at a time when there were no models to look to. See the women's studies special issue of *EPW* in Butalia (1993). The first major volume to emerge out of South Asian feminist networks is edited by Kumari Jayawardena and Malathi de Alwis (1996), *Embodied Violence: Communalising Women's Sexuality in South Asia*, whose title is broadly indicative of the kinds of questions that were being collectively responded to.
5. See, in particular, the article 'Feminisms in Asia' in the special issue of *Inter-Asia Cultural Studies* edited by Tejaswini Niranjana and Mary E. John (2002), which was the outcome of a workshop that brought together feminists from as many as nine different countries, probably for the first time in India. See also the eight country study hosted by the Women's Studies Centre of Ewha Women's University in Seoul, Korea, for the production of textbooks on women's studies in Korea, China, Japan, Indonesia, the Philippines, Thailand, Taiwan and India. The Women's Studies Centre has been pioneering the creation of academic networks in Asia, including their now ten year old journal *Asian Journal of Women's Studies*.

References

Barlow, Tani E. (2008) 'Asian Women in Reregionalisation', Special Issue, *What's Left of Asia? Positions: East Asia Cultures Critique*, Hairong Yan and Dan Volkavitch (eds).

Butalia, Urvashi (1993) 'Community, State and Gender: On Women's Agency during Partition', Women's Studies Special Issue, *Economic and Political Weekly*, 28 (17): WS 2–11, 12–21.

Chakravarti, Uma (2003) *Gendering Caste: Through a Feminist Lens*, Kolkata: Stree.

Chatterjee, Partha (1993) *The Nation and its Fragments: Colonial and Postcolonial Histories*, Delhi: OUP.

Ding, Naifei (2005) 'Comment: Subjects of Feminisms in Question', *Asian Journal of Women's Studies*, 11 (2): 89–97.

Hensman, Rohini (2004) 'Globalisation, Women and Work', *Economic and Political Weekly*, 6 March.

Jayawardena, Kumari. (1986) *Feminism and Nationalism in the Third World*, London: Zed Books.

Jayawardena, Kumari and Malathi de Alwis (eds) (1996) *Embodied Violence: Communalising Women's Sexuality in South Asia*, New Delhi: Kali for Women.

Jhabvala, Renana and R.K.A. Subrahmanya (eds) (2000) *The Unorganised Sector: Work, Security and Social Protection*, New Delhi: Sage Publications.

John, Mary E. (1996) *Discrepant Dislocations: Feminism, Theory and Postcolonial Histories*, Berkeley: UC Press and Delhi: OUP.

—— (1999) 'Feminisms and Internationalisms: A Response from India', in Mrinalini Sinha and Angela Woolacott (eds), *Feminisms and Internationalism*, Oxford: Basil Blackwell.

—— (2000) 'Alternate Modernities? Reservations and the Women's Movement in India', *Economic and Political Weekly*, 31 October.

—— (2005) 'Feminism, Poverty and the Emergent Social Order', in Raka Ray and Mary F. Katzenstein (eds), *Poverty, Power, Politics: Social Movements in India*, Delhi: OUP.

—— (2005) 'Women and Feminism in China and India: A Conversation with Li Xiaojiang', *Economic and Political Weekly*, 16 April, pp. 1594–97.

John, Mary E. (ed.) (2007) 'Women and Feminisms in Asia', Special Issue, *Interventions: International Journal of Postcolonial Studies*, 9 (2).

Karve, Dhonde Keshav (1936) *Looking Back*, Poona: Hingne Stree Shikshan Samstha.

Kim, Eunshil (2004) 'Republic of Korea', in Philip Bergstrom (ed.), *History of Women's/Gender Studies in Asia-Pacific*, Bangkok: UNESCO, Regional Unit for Social and Human Sciences in Asia and the Pacific, pp. 49–77.

Menon, Nivedita (2007) *Sexualities*, New Delhi: Women Unlimited.

Nair, Janaki (1996) *Women and Law in Colonial India: A Social History*, New Delhi: Kali for Women.

Niranjana, Tejaswini (2000) 'Alternative Frames?', *Inter-Asia Cultural Studies*, 1 (1).

Niranjana, Tejaswini and Mary E. John (eds) (2002) 'Feminisms in Asia', *Inter-Asia Cultural Studies*, 3 (2).

Nyamdorj, Anaraa (2004) 'Mongolia', in Philip Bergstrom (ed.), *History of Women's/Gender Studies in Asia-Pacific*, Bangkok: UNESCO,

Regional Unit for Social and Human Sciences in Asia and the Pacific, pp. 317–20.

Omvedt, Gail and Chetna Gala (1993) 'The New Economic Policy and Women: A Rural Perspective', *Economic Review*, October.

Panikkar, K.M. (1969) *Asia and Western Dominance*, New York: Collier Books.

Phadke, Shilpa (n.d.) 'Sexing Up Feminism: The Space-Time Politics of the Classroom', paper presented at the workshop on 'Gender and Critical Pedagogies', Women's Studies Programme, JNU, 19–20 March 2004.

Rao, Anupama (ed.) (2003) *Gender and Caste: Issues in Contemporary Indian Feminism*, New Delhi: Kali for Women.

Rege, Sharmila (2006) *Writing Caste, Writing Gender: Dalit Women's Testimonies*, New Delhi: Zubaan.

Roy, Anupama (2005) *Gendered Citizenship: Historical and Conceptual Approaches*, New Delhi: Orient Longman.

Sarkar, Tanika (2001) *Hindu Wife, Hindu Nation: Community, Religion and Cultural Nationalism*, New Delhi: Permanent Black.

Shiva, Vandana (1998) *Globalisation of Agriculture, Food Security and Sustainability*, New Delhi: Research Foundation for Science, Technology and Ecology.

Sinha, Mrinalini (2006) *Specters of Mother India: The Global Restructuring of an Empire*, Durham: Duke University Press.

Sinha, Mrinalini, Donna J. Guy and Angela Woolacott (eds) (1999) *Feminisms and Internationalism*, Oxford: Basil Blackwell.

Sobritchea, Carolyn I. (2005) 'Representations of Gender Inequality and Women's Issues in Philippine Feminist Discourses', *Asian Journal of Women's Studies*, 11 (2): 67–88.

Sun, Ge (2000) 'How does Asia Mean?', *Inter-Asia Cultural Studies*, 1 (1): 13–47 and 1 (2): 319–41.

Tharu, Susie and Niranjana, Tejaswini. (1994). 'Problems for a Contemporary Theory of Gender', *Social Scientist*, 22(3/4): 93–117.

UNESCO (2004) Regional Unit for Social and Human Sciences in Asia and the Pacific, Women's and Gender Studies in Asia and the Pacific, Bangkok.

15

Dalit Feminism and the Question of Violence[1]

Krishna Menon

Modern India and Caste

When India became independent in 1947, the fond hope in the hearts of the Nehruvian elite was that India would embark upon an obvious journey towards modernity. This journey would entail the relegation of all 'archaic' and obscure identities such as caste and religion into the private sphere. Modern India, based on an aggressive programme of industrialization, would create modern, secular, unmarked citizens. However, this project failed even before it gathered steam; ethnic, linguistic and religious identities remained stubborn in their presence in modern India. Many a slogan were coined extorting Indians to sink their differences and remain united. The nation, based on undifferentiated citizenship, was suggested as the possible way out from communal and caste ghettos that separated Indian citizens. Forces of modernity, however, have not been able to offer adequate resistance to caste- and religion-based identities in the social life and for that matter even in the political life.

The nature of this modernity has today become the subject of much academic and political debate (Chatterjee, 1997; Eisenstadt, 2000; Menon and Nigam, 2007). For the mainstream national movement, as well as the nationalist elite, caste remained one of the most embarrassing facets of Indian society. The resolution offered was to quietly sweep it into the inner recesses of the private sphere, and thereby, create a caste-free public sphere (Chakravarti, 2003; Rege, 2006). This manner of resolving the caste question was challenged by Ambedkar, Phule and a host of others who saw the possibility of a new and free India emerging only on the debris of the caste system.

Opposition to caste was thus restricted to pious platitudes against caste in the public sphere, and a retreat into the secure caste marked private sphere (Rege, 2006). This fractured modernity[2] – which is comfortable with caste in the private sphere but speaks the language of universality in the public sphere – was understood rightly by Ambedkar and others as nothing but an attempt to continue with caste-based privileges in the private sphere, while denouncing it in public. Viewed from this vantage point, Dalit-bahujan[3] activists who insist on raising the bogey of caste in public appear casteist, non-modern and sectarian (ibid.). Ambedkar, on the other hand, posited a different kind of modernity – a modernity that would be characterized by its challenge to caste-based exploitation and oppression.

Very early on in his political journey, Ambedkar established an insightful relationship between independence for India, the overthrow of the oppressive caste system and eventually freedom for women. He identified the domination and control of women, through the practice of closely regulated marriage norms as the foundational principle of caste and its perpetuation. Hence, he advocated inter-caste marriage as the only way out to challenge caste and in the process free women. Thus, for Ambedkar, caste was the lens through which he theorized India's quest for freedom and indeed the nature of the post-independence Indian state.

In the euphoric years following independence, it was believed that the problem of caste had been adequately addressed by the detailed provisions in the Constitution. Hence, it was assumed that caste would quietly fade. But caste proved to be recalcitrant and raised its 'ugly' head at all kinds of inopportune moments (Menon and Nigam, 2007). Had caste ever gone away? By the end of the 1980s decade, and especially in the 1990s decade, it became apparent that caste had not gone away and indeed it held the national imagination like never before. The early 1990s witnessed turbulence in north Indian cities over the issue of extension of caste-based reservations to other backward castes.[4]

The reaction to the report and in particular the unleashing of upper caste fury startled all those who believed that modernity was a successful work in progress. Caste was out in the open and one could see skirmishes on the streets of the capital of India around the issue of caste. The secular, modern and universal language of citizenship, it seems, was being challenged by the particularistic and primitive discourse of caste. The nation had to be rescued from this, it was claimed. Merit and efficiency would be the casualty, and young women students of the University of Delhi protested the prospects of not finding employed husbands. And thereby hangs a tale!!

Caste and Gender

In 1990, the then Prime Minister of India, Vishwanath Pratap Singh announced the government's decision to implement the Mandal Commission's recommendations. Amidst a series of protests that finally brought the government down, particularly noteworthy was the enthusiastic participation of 'even' women. Middle class localities and educational institutions were the nerve centre of these protests. Upper caste fury knew no bounds, and women protesters ironically had taken to the streets on behalf of their brothers, sons and would-be husbands. Young women carried placards saying that they did not want unemployed husbands, implying that with reservations all the jobs and opportunities would be cornered by backward caste men whom of course they could not conceive of marrying (Tharu and Niranjana, 1999).

The fact that these women did not see themselves in the reckoning for government jobs and higher education is disturbing enough, additionally, the assumption that they would marry only upper caste men vindicates the argument made in the earlier section. Those who were speaking about caste were portrayed as sectarian and backward, as in a secular modern nation–state the language should be of merit and efficiency, it was argued. On the other hand, when it came to the question of marriage none of the placard carrying young women thought it was regressive to assume that they would marry only upper caste men. Thus I would like to restate my argument that the nature of modernity in India is such that one could uphold virtues of merit and efficiency in the public sphere, while comfortably upholding caste-based endogamy in marriage and other social and cultural practices.

Caste and gender were thus at crossroads, as upper caste women came out against caste-based reservations that were specifically aimed at opening up opportunities for the socially and educationally backward communities.

This is the backdrop of renewed discussion about caste-based exploitation and marginalization. By the 1980s, secularism was being openly challenged and so was the need for caste-based reservation. The response of the Dalit and backward communities was to reassert and restate the need for democratic rights while pointing to the essentially hierarchical and exploitative nature of the caste structure.

The Mandir-Mandal movements in the last two decades of the 20th century threw up new challenges for Indian politics in general and the women's movement in particular. The Mandir movement sought a re-definition of the idea of the universal Indian citizen drawing heavily from upper caste Hindu discourses on the nation and its citizens. The Mandal movement, on the other hand, questioned the possibility of such a re-definition, and indeed wanted to rewrite the meaning of Indian democracy to include groups that had hitherto been excluded. Both the Mandal and the Mandir movements exposed the fragility of the idea of an Indian sisterhood, divided as it was so sharply along the lines of caste and religion.

It was no longer possible to speak in terms of an Indian women's movement; it became apparent that women are divided along lines of religious identity and indeed caste. The idea of a universal Indian woman was discretely abandoned, for the pursuit of such an idea in the changed political context of the 1990s could mean only one thing – privileging the voice of the most powerful group, i.e., Hindu upper caste women.

Caste and the Challenge to Indian Feminism

By 1995, the National Federation of Dalit Women (NFDW) had been formed. The basis for the formation of the NFDW and many similar organizations was the sentiment that Indian feminism had been unable to address the issue of caste and its inseparable links with patriarchy. Feminist theorization was unable to see the caste-based inequality. Indian feminism was seen as hegemonic and the formation of the NFDW was a challenge to what came to be described as Brahminical feminism.[5] The reluctance of the existing Dalit groups to address issues specific to Dalit women and the feminist movement's Brahminical orientation were the reasons cited for setting up the NFDW.

Today, Dalit-bahujan feminists are re-thinking feminism based on the unmarked Indian woman as the ideal subject of feminist theory and politics. In the process Dalit-bahujan feminists are keen to demonstrate the limited nature of the feminist enterprise as it has existed in India (Rao, 2003). Dalit-bahujan feminism states forcefully that caste is not just a matter of identity or difference but indeed it is an entire matrix of power and privilege on the one hand, and exploitation and humiliation on the other hand (ibid.). The unmarked woman can no longer be the ideal subject of feminism.

The Dalit Women's Voice

Around the same time as the formation of the NFDW, a significant debate began to unfold about Dalit women's voices, the issue was whether 'Dalit women speak differently' (Guru, 1995). Guru's argument is that Dalit women's voices need to be heard, recorded and understood differently given the fact that Dalit women experienced patriarchy very differently from the women of the Brahminical castes.

The specific nature of patriarchy experienced by Dalit women consists of two distinct strands: on the one hand, Brahminical patriarchy that considered despised Dalit women as unclean and polluting (however good enough to have sex with), and a more intimate form of patriarchical control over work and sexuality exercised by the Dalit men on 'their' women. This view is echoed by an emerging body of academic and political insight that expresses its discomfort with mainstream Indian feminism. The claims of 'Indian feminism' to speak on behalf of 'Indian' women came to be questioned aggressively. Guru's argument is that social location determines the perception of reality and hence any attempt by non-Dalit women to represent Dalit women's lives appears less authentic and valid, indeed it appears to be homogenizing (Rao, 2003).

The caste mediated nature of patriarchy produces different worlds for different women depending upon their caste. Gopal Guru illustrates this argument with the example of rape. Instances of rape are typically explained by feminists as the expression of male aggression, and/or as a symbol of patriarchal control and regulation of women. Such an explanation misses out on a very important dimension of most incidents of rape in India. The woman's body is seen as marked by caste and the instance of rape is a message to her caste, it cannot be understood fully by describing it as merely an exercise of male power. The caste calculus lends to the account of rape a completely different dimension. Let us illustrate with one of the most horrific incidents in recent times which went unreported by mainstream media for a very long time.

The Bhotmanges were an upwardly mobile Dalit family in Khairlanji village in Maharashtra. Forty-four-year-old Surekha and her nineteen-year-old daughter Priyanka were gangraped and sexually abused in full public view because they refused to yield to the plans of the local land grab mafia. The mainstream media began to report this incident a full one month after it had taken place on 29 September 2006 (Rao, 2009). This and other similar incidents all over India cannot be simply understood as rape and murder, rather the entangled nature of caste and gender needs to be underscored in such instances, and hegemonic Indian feminism is accused of being insensitive to this aspect.

Priyanka and her mother Surekha were raped not just to assert male authority, but as a message to all Dalits who try to challenge upper caste privileges. The public nature of such incidents is to shame not only the women who are being raped but the community itself. It subscribes to the quintessential patriarchical idea that honour, dignity and privacy of a community's women is a marker of the community's power and prestige in society. Public rape and stripping reinforces the powerlessness of the caste to which the women belong.

Rape, public stripping and other forms of gendered humiliation that Dalit women are subjected to have to be seen as an enactment of upper caste men's privilege of sexual access to Dalit women. Often the violent sexual act is punishment for the Dalit family or community's assertion of its rights. The sexual dimension of this supposed upper caste male privilege needs to be understood as a specific form of patriarchy entrenched in the caste structure.

Dalit feminists have argued that caste itself is the result of sexual regulation – a fact that Ambedkar was acutely aware of and hence campaigned for inter-caste marriages as the only way of challenging caste oppression and hierarchy. Caste determines who one can have sex with; it determines who one can desire sexually. The ideology of power on which the caste system is based normalizes upper caste men's unique privilege of sexual access to Dalit and other lower caste women, and is experienced as a shameful secret by the lower and Dalit castes. This is a constant reminder of the inability of Dalit and lower caste men to 'protect' 'their' women and hence of their lower status in society in general. It is generally understood that higher the caste, the greater the mechanisms for the 'protection' of women who belong to that caste. Caste purity is maintained by strict regulation of the sexual conduct of upper caste women and the lower status of other castes is demonstrated by the easy availability of women of these castes for upper caste men to have sex with. Thus, sex with Dalit and lower caste women is an enactment of caste privilege as well as assertion of patriarchy coded in caste language (ibid.).

Dalit feminists are arguing that upper caste feminists have been unable to see the expression of caste power and the reinforcement of Dalit stigmatization in the instances of sexual violence against Dalit women. Dalit feminism argues that such incidents are in response to the growing assertion by Dalit-bahujan citizens asserting their citizenship.

In view of this discussion over the understanding of rape, Gopal Guru might argue that rape as understood by mainstream feminists is not able to capture the unique caste dynamics that determine it. Resistance to sexual violence is not just that, but it is also about resistance to caste domination and hence an assertion of Dalit-bahujan identities.

We cannot turn our attention towards the more intimate form of patriarchy experienced by Dalit women vis-à-vis the men of their community. Dalit women have also been consistently raising their voices against their marginalization by Dalit men who fear the uncontrolled sexuality of their women as a disruptive influence (Margaret, 2005).

This underscores the importance of a distinct platform for Dalit women from where it becomes possible for them to express a unique epistemological standpoint. This formulation implies that those who are marginalized by society and rendered powerless are nevertheless endowed with the ability to have a more all-encompassing view of social reality this gives them a unique epistemic privilege. This unique epistemic privilege endows the Dalit women with a different voice. I would like to quote Swathy Margaret defending the need for Dalit women to speak differently: 'I, as a Dalit woman, primarily write for Dalit women to uphold our interests. This statement of mine is necessary because if we do not define ourselves for ourselves, we will be defined by others – for their use and to our detriment. This voice is not representative of all Dalit women. However, I know that my voice is important because it is the voice of a socially denigrated category, suppressed and silenced' (ibid.).

This statement of Swathy Margaret's captures the spirit of standpoint theories in social science. Marx, Engels and subsequently Lukacs have deliberated upon this idea and held up the proletariat as the only universal class, capable therefore of a universal vision (because of their marginalization and powerlessness the proletariat does not have any stake in the existing social structures), and hence capable of initiating universal politics, and not class-specific politics. If we replace the proletariat with Dalit women in the above formulation, we would get a sense of what Gopal Guru is trying to suggest.

This position assumes that those having privilege in society are unable to engage in any kind of critical interrogation of the social structures in general and of their own privileges in particular. Standpoint theory's application to the caste-gender tangle would yield us the following formulation: upper caste feminists because of their privilege position in society are unable to engage in a critical interrogation of their privileges and thus would be insensitive to the privileges that they have because of the caste position they occupy. Dalit feminism on the contrary begins from the lived, daily lives of Dalit women, having the valuable insight given by individual experiences and claims a unique authenticity of voice.

Sharmila Rege, in sharp contrast, states that while Dalit women definitely need a space and platform that is distinct, however it cannot flourish if it remains isolated from the experiences and challenges faced by other marginalized groups (Rege, 2006). She contends that subjectivities can indeed be transformed, not to suggest that non-Dalit feminists can speak on behalf of Dalit women but that they can surely 'reinvent' themselves as Dalit feminists. She believes that such a position will help narrow identity-based theorization and politics. In fact, in her opinion, such a Dalit feminist standpoint (DFS) is more emancipatory, because it involves a critical re-statement of the existing feminist voices, a conscious interrogation of the received feminist discourse. This would have profound transformative impact on both the individual feminist as well as the broader feminist programme which is to say that they can *transcend* their non-Dalitness (ibid.).

S. Anand believes that Sharmila Rege's logic, which seeks to divorce *experience* from knowledge formation, can eventually be used to claim that non-Dalits can produce Dalit writing and in doing so it challenges the claims of epistemic privilege by Dalits, in the process once again enabling non-Dalits to theorize the subjectivity of Dalits.

Sharmila Rege is obviously suggesting the possibilities of existing feminist movements coming together with Dalit groups, and on this it would be interesting to hear Swathy Margaret stating that 'Dalit feminists share a definite sense of identification with many basic articulations raised by both these movements. We have gained a lot from them. While it is important and strategically wise to form coalitions and build solidarity with other marginalized groups, it should be considered only when a movement is armed with a clear understanding of its own historicity based on the experience of oppression and discrimination. It is productive to have in mind the historical dialogue between different marginalized sections of people. Otherwise, there is the danger of Dalit women, their self-definition and their peculiar positioning in the society being rendered invisible.'

Caste, Gender and the Subject of Feminist Theory and Politics

Dalit-bahujan women and their specific caste-based experiences of oppression, as well as the specific experiences of women belonging to religious minorities, mounted a serious challenge to the hitherto neat world of Indian feminist politics. By the end of the 1980s, it was obvious to women's groups to find no uncomplicated 'woman' as the subject of feminist politics or of the pursuit of gender justice in India. Nivedita Menon has argued that these developments have brought the realization that 'woman' as a ready-made subject of feminist politics does not exist, instead women are located within a grid of identities ranging from caste, class and religion among other possible identities. Menon further argues that people in democracies are mobilized along the grid of multiple identities, at different times and in different political conditions, different identities are foregrounded. In other words, just because many women have come together it does not imply that they have indeed come together as 'women', they could have gathered together because they are upper caste or because they are Tamil. Subjecthood to put it differently has to be the conscious result of deliberate political mobilization (Menon, 2004).

Creation of specific subjecthood, it is feared, could constitute a challenge to the language of universalism – the fundamental principle of modern democracies. Talking of Dalit women, Muslim women, Brahmin women and so it is being argued weakens the cause of democracy. The response to this fear of a particularistic position is to argue that unproblematized universalism can well turn into a kind of undemocratic imposition of identities. Menon has argued that a democracy is indeed not possible without a conception of the universal, however democratic politics should guard and struggle against any attempts to attach a permanent content and definition of democracy. The continuous challenge to the meaning of the universal and the temporary appropriation of the same is what politics in democracies is about (ibid.).

I find this argument rather persuasive and would like to employ it to respond to the debates around Dalit women speaking differently. We need to see democratic politics as a space that is always getting reconstituted, as a space that is always contested and not as a space with defined permanent meanings. The specific articulation by Dalit-bahujan women or by Muslim women has forced the feminist movement in India to revisit the universal claims that it made on behalf of Indian women. Similar challenges are being mounted rather persistently by lesbian women and by women with disabilities. These challenges have to be seen in my opinion not as cracks or fissures in the feminist movement but as democratic attempts at re-articulating the somewhat frozen definitions of feminism.

Notes

1. 'Dalit Women Speak Differently' is the title of a very well-known and rather a landmark essay by Gopal Guru (1995).
2. Sanjay Joshi's book *Fractured Modernity: Making of a Middle Class in Colonial India* (2001) looks at his phenomenon.
3. The Dalit-Bahujans make up what is known as the Scheduled Castes, the Scheduled Tribes and the Backward Castes (the Other Backward Classes?). 'Scheduled' means that they are listed in a special 'index' appended to the Constitution. 'Backward Castes' are those whose rank and occupational status are above the Dalits, but who still remain socially and economically depressed. The Scheduled Castes were until recently also known as the 'Untouchables' because they were deemed literally untouchable by the upper castes. The word 'Dalit' means 'broken' or 'crushed' and the word 'bahujan' indicates membership in the majority people or the larger population. Combined, these groups make up 67 per cent of the population of India.
4. The Mandal Commission was established in 1979 by the Janata Party government under Prime Minister Morarji Desai with a mandate to 'identify the socially or educationally backward'. It was headed by Parliamentarian Bindheshwari Prasad Mandal to consider the question of seat reservations and quotas for people to redress caste discrimination, and used eleven social, economic and educational indicators to determine 'backwardness'. In 1980, the Commission's report affirmed the affirmative action practice under law whereby members of lower castes [known as Other Backward Classes (OBCs) and Scheduled Castes and Scheduled Tribes] were given exclusive access to a certain portion of government jobs and slots in public universities, and recommended changes to these quotas, increasing them from 27 per cent to 49.5 per cent.
5. Brahminical feminism has been described by Anupama Rao (2003) as a kind of feminist position that denies caste as a problem for gender.

References

Basu, Amrita (ed.) (1998) *The Challenge of Local Feminisms: Women's Movements in Global Perspective*, New Delhi: Kali for Women.

Chakravarti, Uma (1993) 'Conceptualizing Brahminical Patriarchy in Early India: Gender, Caste, Class and State', *Economic and Political Weekly*, 3 April.

—— (2003) *Gendering Caste*, Kolkata: Stree.

Chatterjee, Partha (1997) *The Partha Chatterjee Omnibus*, Delhi: OUP.

Eisenstadt, S.N. (2000) 'Multiple Modernities', *Daedalus*, Vol. 129, No. 1, Winter, pp. 137–62.

Guru, Gopal (1995) 'Dalit Women Speak Differently', *Economic and Political Weekly*, Vol. 30, No. 42, p. 2548.

Joshi, Sanjay (2001) *Fractured Modernity: Making of a Middle Class in Colonial India*, New Delhi: OUP.

Kothari, Rajni (1988) *State Against Democracy*, New Delhi: Ajanta.

Margaret, M. Swathy (2005) *Insight*, 3 June.

Menon, Nivedita (2004) *Recovering Subversion*, New Delhi: Permanent Black.

Menon, Nivedita and Aditya Nigam (2007) *Power and Contestation: India Since 1989*, New Delhi: Orient Longman.

Rao, Anupama (ed.) (2003) *Gender and Caste*, New Delhi: Kali for Women.

—— (2009) *The Caste Question*, New Delhi: Permanent Black.

Rege, Sharmila (2006) *Writing Caste/Writing Gender*, New Delhi: Zubaan.

Sarkar, Tanika (1991) 'Woman as a Communal Subject: Rashtra Sewika Samiti and the Ram Janma Bhoomi Movement', *Economic and Political Weekly*, 31 August.

Tharu, Susie and Tejaswini Niranjana (1999) 'Problems for a Contemporary Theory of Gender', in Nivedita Menon (ed.), *Gender and Politics in India*, New Delhi: OUP.

16

Can the Feminists qua Feminists be Allies of M.C.?

Shefali Moitra

Professor Mihir Chakraborty (M.C. for short), former Professor of Mathematics, Calcutta University was the founding member of the *Calcutta Logic Circle* and is still a very active member of this Circle. He is interested in Pure Mathematics. His approach has been non-conventional. Many of the basic concepts of mathematics are intrinsically vague and many mathematical definitions keep changing according to him. He is well acquainted with the feminist debates on rationality, more specifically, with the debates in feminist logic. On many occasions M.C. and I have exchanged views on issues relating to abstract thinking. During these discussions, my stance was one of a feminist philosopher, and his was of a non-conformist mathematician. M.C. has always been concerned with meta-mathematical questions as well as meta-logical questions.

Many of these questions are relevant to the theoretical enterprise that preoccupies feminists as well. Due to his somewhat non-conformist position in mathematics he would be more acceptable to the radical feminists than to the liberal feminists. At the outset, let me clarify why I regard M.C. a non-conformist in mathematics. I shall then move to state in brief the difference between the liberal feminist and the radical feminist positions in relation to theory construction and logic. This should clearly bring out the relationship between M.C. and the liberal feminist on the one hand and M.C. and the radical feminist on the other. In this context, when I refer to M.C. I am referring to a representative individual and not to an individual mathematician.

According to the mainstream accounts, mathematics as a subject is equated with rationality. For these thinkers, the other name for mathematics is rationality, just as the other name for rationality is mathematics. M.C. characterizes the mainstream position by saying, 'for the mainstream "understanding means understanding through mathematics".'[1] Mathematics is often referred to as an exact science. One of the reasons why mathematics has been given a coveted position in the history of knowledge is that it is perceived as an instrument of success. (This continues to be the case in spite of the fact that predictability is not an epistemic virtue.) M.C. finds an echo of this perception in the words of William F. Taylor, who during an interview in 1977, stated, 'Quantitative science – that is science with mathematics – has proved successful in controlling nature. The majority of the society backs it for this reason. At the present moment, they want nature to be altered and controlled – to the extent, of course, that we can do it and the results are felicitous.'[2] The mainstream refer to mathematics as the queen of science. M.C. reminds us that this status is granted to mathematics as long as it delivers the desired results. Thus mathematics is not seen as an end-in-itself; all that it offers is an instrumental value. This is the majority view.

Things are however changing. Even Taylor in the above-mentioned interview goes on to say, 'The humanist point of view (regarding mathematics) is a minority point of view. But it is influential – one sees this among young people'. The assessment of mathematics as an exact science has been constantly changing over the past hundred years. M.C., quoting Bertrand Russell in his favour, says, 'Mathematics is the subject in which we never know what we are talking about nor about whether what we are saying is true.'[3] This 'not being certain' is a recurring theme in M.C.'s writings. He keeps saying that the aim of mathematics is not to establish the truth. He does not believe that there is any such thing as the correct position in mathematics. He quotes Morris Kline who says, 'The major fact that emerges from the several conflicting approaches to mathematics is that there is no one body of mathematics but many.'[4] M.C. also denies the possibility of a unique logic. Till today, many think that the Aristotelian laws of thought are sacrosanct. M.C. does not subscribe to this view. He quotes Rudolf Carnap in this context, who says, 'In logic there are no morals. Everyone is at liberty to build up his own logic, his own form of language.'[5]

The acceptance of pluralism and open-endedness in logic and also in mathematics would be very close to the heart of the radical feminist. But the question is: who are the protagonists of this view? In other words, does this view carry any authority? When it comes to the operative part, we find that we are still guided by monolithic systems of logic and mathematics. In his article on when there will be no further question (*'Jakhan Ar Kono Jijnasa Thakbe Na'*) M.C. wonders why this mainstream version of mathematics continues to prevail in the syllabus of the teaching institutions, especially at the primary level. M.C. envisages the urgency of looking into the social, cultural and commercial basis for this trend.[6]

M.C. repeatedly refers to the cultural and commercial influences on the selection of theories and on their dominance in the field of knowledge, including mathematics. In his article on the right to fantasy (*'Akashkusum-er Adhikar'*) he makes a passionate appeal. He says mathematics must free itself from the clutches of such dominance. This is the dominance of advertisements, the market, commerce and utility. Mathematics must return to its pristine realm of beauty. We should enter this realm with a kind of wonder *'mugdhata'*.[7] We should not expect to receive a criterion for demarcating truth from falsity. That is not the task of mathematics. The relevant question to be asked of mathematics is, 'how did you like it?' (*kemon lagche eke?*). It is the 'beauty' of mathematics that is to be appreciated and enjoyed. Perhaps M.C. would be willing to use the word *'rasa'* in this context. Once we delve deep into the intricacies of pure mathematics we delve into its *rasa* as well. M.C. believes mathematics comes closer to poetry.[8]

The call to save mathematics from all forms of external influences and allow it to establish its autonomy is an attractive proposition especially for those of us who are mired in all sorts of power politics and are yearning to break away. It is like finding 'a room of my own'. The question is: Has this ever been possible? Will this ever be possible? Or, is this a dream that some beleaguered mathematicians like to cherish? Did mathematics have a golden past when it had an intrinsic value? If so then what caused its enslavement, its co-option? M.C. gives a clue. He says the eulogy showered on mathematics by the sciences especially physics has led mathematics to believe that it is the queen of sciences. It fails to realize that it is being praised for its 'use' value and not for its intrinsic value. M.C. says mathematics must come out of this orbit of sycophancy.[9] For him the question is not so much whether such autonomy was enjoyed by mathematics in the past or not. From the layman's point of view one may ask whether men and women have the right to create a subject like mathematics in M.C.'s sense; is such a move legitimate in the name of mathematics? The question is one of rights or *adhikar*. I would say, of course, one has the right to think of a situation where mathematics is interested in the creation of beauty alone, or a situation that accommodates mathematical pluralism. It is also plausible to approximate such a goal. But approximation and achievement are not synonymous. The possibility of the achievement of such a goal is problematic. The autonomy of mathematics may be maximized but can absolute autonomy ever be achieved? The radical feminist would say the goal of absolute autonomy (absolute freedom from history) is a fantasy, some kind of absurdity or *akashkusum*.

The way M.C. argues in his article 'Akashkusumer Adhikar' it appears that the power-utility-market nexus is an avoidable evil.[10] Its influence on mathematics is to be seen as a fault-line which is to be got rid of. The liberal feminists would agree with him. They have a great faith in the autonomy of reason. They accept the fact that reason has been used for various vested interests, including power politics. For them the only way to escape from this unholy alliance between rationality on the one hand and power-market-utility on the other is to be more and more rational, more and more logical, and more and more objective. The liberal feminists believe in the autonomy of reason, in the possibility of pure reason as well as in the possibility of aperspectivity. For them a paradigm example of reason is to be found in Aristotelian logic. This logic was later incorporated by Kant. Liberal feminists believe in the existence of absolute binaries such as reason/emotion, subjective/objective, logical/illogical.

Thus, we find that though the liberal feminists would agree with M.C. on one major point (the point of escaping from a mundane context) they would not entirely endorse his position. Their point of agreement would be on the possibility of the autonomy of logic and mathematics. They would further state that human beings could achieve pure freedom only in the domain of pure rationality. Their allegiance to a rigid logical system would, however, distance them from M.C. They would not agree with him in ratifying Carnap's view stated above, 'in logic there are no morals. Everyone is at liberty to build up his own logic, his own form of language.'[11]

M.C. agrees that there was a time when rationality had a pivotal role in emancipating man. Many say this about the Age of Enlightenment. Reason facilitated the rupture with the Dark Age of dogmatism. M.C. suggests the time has come now to free ourselves from the domination of reason as well.[12] He does not intend to give up reason. He merely wants to dethrone reason from its seat of domination. Not allowing reason to dominate implies the possibility of questioning reason itself and allowing multiple reasons to flourish.

By questioning rationalism alternatives to the mainstream dominant trend in reason may emerge. For instance, classical two-valued logic would demand a clear yes or no, true or false, right or wrong answer to every problem amenable to logical explanation. M.C. does not subscribe to this requirement. He is a radical on this account. He says if he is asked which is true, the axiom of choice or its oppositional positions, he would prefer to remain silent on this issue. Not because he is undecided, but because his answer cannot be judged by clear-cut true or false categories. He thinks the classical notion of truth was too arrogant, too self-confident, too self-promoting. Today, we are willing to accept concepts like partial truth, mutually inconsistent truth, contingent truth, soft truth and so on.[13] This would sound like music to radical feminist ears. They are comfortable with a considerable amount of vagueness and ad hocism in theory construction.

The major difference between liberal feminism and radical feminism is that the liberals are pro-status quo. They are comfortable with the existing systems of science and justice. According to them, what is at fault is the application of the system; therefore, the fault is extrinsic to the system. In places the fault lies in the non-inclusion of women into the system. The liberal feminists primarily follow an agenda for inclusion into the mainstream. The radical feminists, on the other hand, feel that the existing systems are themselves faulty and intrinsically biased against women. What is needed is a systemic change – a change in the very structure of thought, a change in concepts.

It seems that the distinction between an extrinsic fault and an intrinsic fault of a system will be acceptable to M.C. He has spoken of the power-market-utility nexus that manipulates a system from outside. The intrinsic fault is caused by the arrogance of reason and its claim to exactitude. According to the radical feminists, this fault is closely related to reason's denial of any association with feelings and emotions. For the radical feminists emotions are inalienable parts of woman's lived experience. Therefore, it should find its place in every human endeavour including theory construction. Since emotion carries an element of fuzziness the liberal feminists would like to keep reason and emotion in separate watertight compartments. I am not sure whether M.C. will be willing to give emotion a constitutive role in mathematics. He talks about enjoyment in the encounter with mathematical systems; he also speaks of the beauty of the system. Needless to say, these need not be constitutive components of mathematics. I think he may admit the role of intuition in mathematics and that would take him away from pure reason, but it need not bring him close to emotion. It may merely bring him close to a more nuanced form of reason. M.C., however, grants an important role to imagination.

Moving away from pure reason does not necessarily imply some form of methodological anarchy. M.C. tells us so far whenever mathematics has changed it has replaced one consistent system by another consistent system. Metaphorically speaking, one cage is introduced to replace another cage. For instance, non-Euclidian geometry replaced Euclidian geometry. The choice between the two was always based on pragmatic considerations. The replacing of one cage by another is the procedure followed by mainstream mathematics, which M.C. does not subscribe to. He is not enamoured by a fully consistent mathematical system. He proposes a system that accommodates some amount of inconsistency or makes room for partial consistency. These proposed systems will have a constructed structure. That does not mean that the structure will be flawless. M.C. extends the cage metaphor and says his cage may have some vulnerable bars, it may also have some broken bars and there will be gaps. There will be room for light as well as for darkness in this cage. Clearly, this alternative standpoint aims at avoiding hegemony by welcoming different voices and admitting that all is not crystal clear nor will it ever be.[14] Now, we understand why M.C. stands against the mainstream position of clarity and certainty.

Having spoken in favour of extreme non-conformism in mathematics M.C. wonders why feminists insist on clubbing all abstractionists under one rubric. He wonders what could be the ground for holding all forms of abstraction responsible for gender bias. I had the privilege of receiving pre-publication comments from M.C. on my book *Feminist Thought* (2002). I admit that the feminist literature on the basis of which I made my observations in *Feminist Thought* were a reaction to mainstream mathematics and logic and not to the non-conformist position adopted by M.C. and others. In the mainstream position, it is believed, science has a universal mode of understanding based on mathematics. It is also believed that mathematics is based on logic – Aristotelian two-valued logic. They further claim that there is a unity between rationality, science and mathematics. There is no room for pluralism in this way of looking at abstraction. This point is explicitly elaborated by M.C.[15] Having followed the radical feminists, I had made the statement that abstraction is a male-gendered virtue and, therefore, necessarily associated with authority and power.

M.C. had read the typescript and he commented that abstraction and formalism need not be associated with authority and power and, therefore, it could distance itself from all forms of gender politics. Abstraction could be a way to escape from mundane power politics. M.C. argued, authority is often very much part of our concrete lived experience, it pressurizes us to the extent that we become numb. When the human condition gets so oppressive that we feel that there is no exit, then, the world of mathematics, logic, and other forms of abstraction like music and art may offer some respite. Abstraction then offers an alternative to the coercion of our day-to-day concrete existence. I conceded to this point made by M.C. and added a note to the original text of *Feminist Thought*. In the note I wrote, 'The notions of the abstract and concrete are commonly contrasted in women's studies to establish the fact that abstraction is a male-gendered virtue, and therefore associated with authority and power. Such an association is a historical contingency. Power and authority could have been associated with an allegiance to the concrete. The dualism between the abstract and the concrete with the related privileging of one member of the pair must always be investigated for the detection of power games.'[16] This implies that all abstraction is not associated with oppression. Abstraction could at times be non-oppressive. Each case of abstraction has to be evaluated separately *in situ*.

Looking back at my book *Feminist Thought* almost after a decade I would like to formulate my response somewhat differently. The context of the remark 'abstraction is a male-gendered virtue and therefore necessarily associated with authority and power' needs clarification. In patriarchy the male-gender virtues are generally paired in the manner so that the former member of the pair stands for male-gender virtues and the latter for female-gender virtues. The list commonly includes the following pairs of virtues: reason/emotion, abstract/concrete, assertive/submissive. Subsequently, the former characteristic of each pair is not only forwarded as a male-gender virtue, it is also touted as a human virtue. Since the former members of the pairs are foregrounded and the latter backgrounded a clear preference is indicated for male-gender virtues. The former virtues are associated with positive values and power and the latter members of the pair are associated with weakness and disvalue. I believe this gendered explanation of the relation between abstraction and power will be conceded by M.C. Here, the relationship between male-gender virtues and abstraction is a stipulated relationship.

M.C.'s entry point and my entry point into the discussion of abstraction are very different. M.C. is looking at abstraction from the perspective of hope. The radical feminists and I are looking at abstraction from the standpoint of suspicion. If asked, 'why is abstraction to be suspected?', the radical feminists will say that in the past abstraction has been projected as a guarantor of neutrality but on further analysis it has been shown that abstraction serves as a wonderful camouflage for partiality, more specifically for gender bias. The fact that various vested interests do perpetuate their hidden agenda under the garb of abstraction is a well-known fact. The liberal feminists will argue that these vested interests cannot only be exposed given the time and effort, they can also be eliminated. In this way, a biased abstract theory can be sanitized. This may be M.C.'s position as well. He admits the involvement of mathematics in power politics. In 'A Conversation with Helen Longino on Feminist Epistemology' published in *Margins,* M.C. remarks, 'Set theory to me always appears to be a code of capitalist nations where only individuals and states remain, everything in between is wiped out. It seems to me very much political in that way.'[17] Why does M.C. say this? Is it not an admission of covert politics being encoded in theory? M.C.'s remarks on set theory seem to support the presence of politics that is intrinsic to mathematics. Earlier we had mentioned that M.C. accepts the political pressure on mathematics generated by the nexus of power, market and utility. This was an instance of external politics. Thus, we find M.C. at times admits the presence of internal politics and at times he also accepts the presence of external politics in relation to mathematics. He speaks of the possibility of extricating oneself from politics, both of the intrinsic and the extrinsic types.

The feminists accept the possibility of the presence of gender politics at every level of cognition. Gender politics is unique because it causes a mindset where gender discrimination is internalized. Subsequently, the patriarchal mindset is reflected in every individual action – be it mental or physical. M.C. will perhaps agree with this possibility. The liberal feminists argue, with an effort one can transcend this mindset and acquire a gender-neutral/gender-transcendent mindset. They refer to this new mindset as the 'human' mindset. The liberal feminists propose to go beyond gender politics with the help of reason. In that case abstraction will facilitate the movement beyond mundane politics. For the liberal feminists reason is regimented and not loosely structured as M.C. would like it to be. The radical feminists do not accept the possibility of a future when gender will be transcended, and a neutral context will be achieved. The radical feminists understand politics in terms of distribution of power. Power could be distributed in a top-down fashion as in patriarchy. This could be replaced by a feminist distribution of power; the structure could be one of power-sharing.

The liberal feminist agenda seems to be one of moving from patriarchy to some form of 'neutered humanism'. In that case women's studies would only be a transitory phase to be transcended by humanism. For the radical feminists 'feminist thought' always has a political dimension. Politics is not necessarily bad. There can be good politics and there can be bad politics, but there cannot be any escape from it. Those who say they have got away from politics, and are engaged in pure abstraction, are also engaged with politics. The only difference is that the presence of politics is not openly admitted.

Does the presence of politics crush M.C.'s dream of unconditional free knowledge.[18] When politics is thrust upon a researcher, then it is oppressive, but when a researcher chooses a political paradigm it may not be oppressive. M.C.'s remark that mathematical activity is a part of human activity, emboldens me to infer that he does not subscribe to the possibility of a view from nowhere.[19] Moreover, he clearly says that the mathematician has to create his or her own parameters, even though these parameters are temporary and relative.[20] M.C. agrees that the artist and the mathematician have to begin with some axiom. These axioms need not be derived from a factual basis; rather, they come from convention or imagination. Of these alternative possible grounds of an axiom imagination seems to be the most autonomous and the most unencumbered by context. To push the feminist critique a little further, we may ask: 'can imagination be free from context, from political context?' The radical feminists will say 'NO'. M.C. seems to have a similar proclivity. M.C. says in mathematics the days of Plato seem to have come to an end. Now, we can state our preferences and decide which logic, which mathematics, we would like to accept. Wittgenstein held that the growth of mathematics depends on our form of life. M.C. says though he cannot give any final opinion on this issue, but he acknowledges the importance of these debates.[21] The feminists take a stand in this ongoing debate. The liberal feminists think they can step out of the grid constituted by the 'form of life' and walk into a neutral zone, whereas the radical feminists believe that all our activities are circumscribed by some 'form of life'. I think M.C. would be more comfortable with radical feminists.

Notes

1. 'Akashkusumer Adhikar', in *Ganiter Dharapat O Galpasalpa*, p. 13.
2. Ibid., p. 14.
3. 'Sukumar Rayer Logic', p. 73.
4. 'Khela Bhangar Khela, p. 24.
5. 'Sukumar Rayer Logic', p. 75.
6. 'Jakhanar Kono Jijnasa Thakbe Na', p. 87.
7. 'Akashkusumer Adhikar', p. 14.
8. 'Sundarer Satya Ganiter Satya', in *Amimamsar Alo Andhari*, p. 112.
9. 'Akashkusumer Adhikar', p. 14.
10. 'Sundarer Stya Ganiter Satya', p. 111.
11. 'Sukumar Rayer Logic', p. 75.
12. 'Kaler Jatrar Dhvani', p. 64.
13. 'Ganitjagate Parbaparibartan', p. 60.
14. 'Achin Pakhir Ghar', p. 94.
15. 'Kaler Jatrar Dhvani', p. 62.
16. Shefali Moitra, *Feminist Thought*, New Delhi: Munshiram Manoharlal, p. 144.
17. *Margins*, p. 11.
18. 'Khela Bhangar Khela', p. 25.
19. Ibid., p. 19.
20. 'Achin Pakhir Ghar', p. 93.
21. 'Khela Bhangar Khela', p. 26.

17

Microfinance and Gender Equality

A Myth or a Reality

Madhu Vij

Microfinance initiatives have grown rapidly across the country in the last decade. Professor Mohammad Yunus is credited with starting the Grameen Bank in 1976 in Bangladesh. Microfinance programmes (in developing countries) offer financial services to low income households and specifically target women. This is based on the premise that women in poor households are more likely to be credit constrained (Swain and Wallentin, 2009). Group-based microfinance also brings together millions of women and men worldwide and is potentially a significant force for equality and empowerment, then, in turn, also contributing to economic growth, pro-poor development and civil society strengthening (Mayoux, 2010).

Microfinance is fast emerging as a powerful instrument in transforming women's empowerment. Women's empowerment takes place when women challenge the existing norms and culture, to effectively improve their well-being (Swain and Wallentin, 2009). Since microfinance initiatives have started targeting women, the discussion has been whether microfinance has actually been a critical aspect of women's empowerment (Skarlatos, 2004; Jyotish, 2006; SIDA, 2009; and Gobezie, 2010).

Women's empowerment is an important development objective for microfinance programmes. However, not enough empirical research exists on the link between microfinance and women's empowerment. Given the complexity of defining women's empowerment, it is not surprising that only a few empirical studies have tried to examine the impact of microfinance on women's empowerment (Goetz and Sengupta, 1996; Swain and Wallentin, 2009). Kabeer (1999) stresses that women's empowerment is about the process by which those who have been denied the ability to make strategic life choices acquire such ability. The World Bank defines empowerment as 'the process of increasing the capacity of individuals or groups to make choices and to transform those choices into desired actions and outcomes'.

A list of the most commonly used dimensions of women's empowerment was constructed by Malhotra et al. (2002) drawing from the frameworks developed by various authors in different fields of social sciences. Allowing for overlap, these frameworks suggest that women's empowerment needs to occur along multiple dimensions including economic, socio-cultural, familial/interpersonal, legal, political and psychological. Empowerment signifies increased participation in decision-making and it is this process through which people feel themselves to be capable of making decisions and the right to do so (Kabeer, 2001).

According to Mayoux (1997), the loans received by women are sometimes used to set up enterprises by men or they end up being employed as unpaid family workers with little benefit. The result is that the impact of microfinance programmes on women is not always positive. Similarly, Guerin and Palier (2006) are of the view that there is no reason why this financial service should automatically lead to a process of empowerment. Microfinance is simply a financial tool allowing families – and especially women – to better manage family cash flow.

The present study would help us to provide some empirical evidence of the current trends regarding the microfinance sector with a special focus on empowering women. The empowerment potential of microfinancing has been articulated very forcefully in recent years, primarily because the key actors are women (Kulkarni,

2011). Microfinance has helped to transform the role of women and has also caused a shift in values and expectations that affects women's roles in society. Women involved in microfinance are not only empowered to make decisions but they are also instrumental in changing their own roles and the roles of others in their families and communities.

The remainder of the paper is organized as follows: After studying the literature examining the link between microfinance and women's empowerment, the research methodology is discussed. The research findings for the questionnaire study are presented next. And, lastly, the conclusions and suggestions are provided.

Review of Empirical Studies

Have women benefited from easy access to credit? Has it impacted their lives? Various empirical studies have investigated the role of women in microfinance and does microfinance contribute to gender equality? WAM believes that microfinance not only contributes to gender equality, but that it benefits from it. Gender equality is good for business (ADA Dialogue, 2007). According to Susy Cheston (2007), it appears that not only are women good for microfinance, but also that microfinance could be even better for women with a little more focus on gender differences.

Kabeer (1999) in her work attempts to measure women's empowerment due to microfinance. She contends that the presence of low-cost microcredit can act as a trigger of change for a woman. An increase in woman's resources acts as a catalyst on her ability to make strategic choices in her life, especially for the children, which she did not have before. The paper describes three interrelated dimensions as a measure of women's empowerment, namely, resources, agency and achievement. The paper contends that these three dimensions of choices are indivisible in determining the meaning of an indicator and hence its validity as a measure of an empowerment.

Studies by Mayoux (1997) emphasize that women's empowerment needs to be an integral part of planning of policies and promoting microfinance programmes does not automatically lead to the development of an innovative and diversified microfinance sector which makes a real contribution to women's empowerment. A much more commitment from donors than has been the case to date is required. Mayoux (1997) further discusses that the impact within a programme also varies from woman to woman due to differences in their social and economic status. Some microfinance programmes have changed the lives of many women, increasing their independence, and improving their status, both within their families and broader communities. However, in other cases, there are challenges facing poor and rural women – they are either neglected by the programmes or are least able to benefit because of their low resource base, low health and literacy levels, lack of skills and market contacts.

Funding for microfinance programmes is set to increase further in the years to come, also with the intention to promote gender policies (Mayoux, 1997). Literature has also recognized microfinance to be a powerful instrument of social change, particularly for women. Research by Swain (2006) stresses that increased access to financial services represents an opportunity for greater empowerment. Such organizations explicitly perceive microfinance as a tool in the fight for the women's rights and independence. This has helped not only in improving their status both within the family and in the community but also contributed significantly in increasing their self-confidence and independent thinking.

According to Sen and Baltimore (2000), empowerment brings greater self-confidence and increased capability to overcome barriers to resource access as well as implementing the changing ideology, i.e., changing role of women in education, income and participation in the labour force. Hashemi et al. (1996) investigated whether women's access to credit has any impact on their lives, irrespective of who had the managerial control. Their results suggest that women's access to credit contributes significantly by increasing their independence, giving them additional income earning opportunities and an increase in asset holdings in their own names.

Research Methodology

In order to get an idea about the impact of the microfinance sector on gender and highlight the practices adopted, a questionnaire survey was conducted. The advantage of the questionnaire technique is that it allows information to be collected from the respondents in both a structured and semi-structured format.

Sample Characteristics and Data Collection

A questionnaire consisting of two sections was mailed to 30 people to gather responses of professionals involved across sectors like PSUs, NBFCs and private organizations regarding their outlook about microfinance sector and the advantages and threats posed in this sector. In addition, the survey also focused on the perceived benefits of microfinance on women empowerment and independence. Care was taken to ensure that we have a fair representation from different levels in the managerial hierarchy as well as their duration with the organization. A covering letter to the respondents explained that the purpose of the survey was academic and that all responses would be kept anonymous and confidential. Online surveys and interviews were also carried out with the respondents.

The questionnaire consisted of two sections – Section 1 had 10 questions which gave insights into the scale of agreement with respect to various options (all the questions were so worded that it could be measured using a 5-point Likert scale; 1 = strongly agree, 5 = strongly disagree). Section 2 had four subjective questions on the sector to examine, among others, the link between microfinance and women empowerment.

Research Findings

Analysis of Results – Section 1

The analysis in this section considers each issue individually and derives inferences based on the overall implications and evidence regarding the microfinance sector. Annexure Tables 1 and 2 present the tabulated results of our survey. In the following analysis respondents strongly agreeing or agreeing with the statements have been clubbed together for the purpose of analysis.

Question 1 asked the respondents if microfinance needs to recognize the specific needs and constraints for marginalized groups. Approximately 97 per cent of the respondents strongly agreed or agreed with this statement. Question 2 asked the respondents if they think their organization has benefited from its association with microfinance institutions, 53 per cent of the respondents agreed with the statement.

Questions 3 sought information on the contribution by microfinance on women empowerment. 100 per cent of the respondents agreed with this statement. Almost all the respondents (96.7%) were of the opinion that microfinance lending is good for women (Question 7). However, 3.3 per cent respondents strongly disagreed with this statement.

Only 33 per cent of the respondents believed that microfinance programmes, when done well, demonstrate the dynamic coherence between the practical and spiritual requirements of life. The next question (Question 5) was regarding microfinance being a powerful tool for social transformation. For our survey, 100 per cent of the respondents agreed with the statement.

Question 6 enquired whether microfinance can play a positive role by helping young men move out of forced labour without leaving their village. A majority of the respondents (83%) acknowledged that this is indeed true. The majority also agreed with the next two statements. While 96 per cent of the respondents agreed that microfinance is not just about giving micro credit to the poor but is an economic development tool, 100 per cent were of the view that one of the major hindrances in the growth of the microfinance sector is the financial illiteracy of the people. Finally, 90 per cent of the respondents agreed that the growth and profitability of the microfinance sector is constrained by poor regulations.

Microfinance and Gender – Section 2

In the second part of our questionnaire study, four open-ended questions were asked which the respondents had to answer. A summary view of the responses is presented below.

Microfinance has played a very positive role in women empowerment in the last few years. Swain and Wallentin (2009) emphasize that the empowerment level of women is determined by their behavioural reactions to situations that reflect their well-being and the indirect empowerment that they attain due to participation in the labour market.

Microfinance has carried many promises of social and economic transformation, with the shift towards targeting women being seen as a major strategic move through which the promise of social development could be most effectively delivered (Minh-Phuong and Wahhaj, 2009).

The first question was: 'How have women benefited from microfinance?' Most of the respondents strongly felt that the emergence of women entrepreneurs and their contribution to the national economy is quite visible in India, especially after the 1990s.

The respondents agreed that the main aim of microfinance is to empower women since women make up a large proportion of microfinance beneficiaries. Microfinance institutions contribute to women's empowerment in several ways. It gives them the confidence that can only come from having financial success. In addition, women experience an increased participation in decision-making in their day-to-day life because of their improved financial status. Buying and selling property, education of the children, poverty reduction, greater respect from their husbands and children, avoiding family quarrels over financial issues are some of the benefits linking microfinance lending and women empowerment.

More recently, the feminist paradigm – where the central concern lies in promoting gender equality and human rights – has been emphasized as an effective route to women's empowerment through microfinance institutions (Kulkarni, 2011). The empowerment dimension of microfinancing has been emphasized very strongly in recent years as gender inequalities act as a deterrent to economic growth and development of a nation.

The second question was, 'What should be done to mitigate the microfinance risks that organizations face and what has your organization done in this context?'

From the survey, we found that that every organization should have a risk management framework for microfinance institutions in order to mitigate potential risks and poor quality loans that have been a problem for all of them. Since microfinance involves lending to customers who are not highly credit worthy, it is necessary for organizations to protect themselves. So, guidelines have been set to place a ceiling on the quantum of loans to be lent to microfinance institutions that make such loans.

In addition, some of the other risks mentioned were:

- Inappropriate regulation
- Cost control
- Political interference
- Management having different opinion

In most of the organizations surveyed, respondents said that they have tried to mitigate these risks by having a continuous discussion at all levels with all the stakeholders to enable them realize the importance of microfinance and the reputation which it will provide to the organization by virtue of its enabling of empowerment to rural and poor people.

The next question was, 'What material market changes and trends do you anticipate within the microfinance sector in your organization?' Most of respondents believed that given the worsening economic outlook in India, it is possible that the sector growth could be quite sluggish. As more regulations emerge in the microfinance world, the returns that companies can expect to make in this sector could decline. In the wake of poor economic climate, loans to microfinance institutions will be more strictly watched and action will be quickly taken on defaulters. Organizations are also trying to provide financial literacy to the poor people to make them understand the relevance of microfinance.

The last question was regarding the key priorities and threats that the microfinance sector will face in the coming years. The respondents were of the opinion that though the programme is spreading rapidly there is slow progress in targeting the poorest households. Two important dimensions mentioned here were:

- Avoiding exposure to clients who are overdrawn with other banks.
- Evaluate risk adjusted return given government caps on lending rates.

In addition, the threats that microfinance sector needs to address in the coming years are as follows:

- Political interference
- Credit risk
- Interest rates
- Government regulations
- Management quality
- Financial illiteracy

Conclusions and Suggestions

The present study examined some issues facing the microfinance sector with a special focus on women's empowerment. A small but intensive survey was done on the various dimensions of the microfinance sector in India. As indicated by the analysis, all the major organizations agreed on the social transformational role that microfinance plays, at least in the Indian context. It is believed to be a strong economic development tool affecting the poor and helping the cause of women's empowerment. The key deterrents to this sector as indicated by the survey were poor regulations and financial illiteracy. To mitigate the effects of this, some organizations have gone out of their ways to educate rural people about the advantages of microfinancing and how it would be helpful for their living.

Regarding women's empowerment, all agreed that microfinance has played a very positive role. Microfinance institutions contribute to women's empowerment. The benefits of microfinance for women are life changing and extend beyond finances to the provision of education and training, economic opportunities, and female empowerment, leading to an improved standard of living for poor families including children. One important result is increased self-confidence and self-esteem. Another is increased participation in decision-making.

References

Cheston, S. and L. Kuhn (2002) "Empowering Women Through Microfinance". In S. Daley-Harris (ed.) *Pathways Out of Poverty: Innovations in Microfinance for the Poorest Families*, Bloomfield, CT, USA: Kumarian Press, pp. 167–228.

Cheston, Susy (2007) Opportunity International, *ADA Dialouge*, NE37, May.

Gaiha, R. and M. Nandhi (2005) *Microfinance, Self-help Groups and Empowerment in Maharashtra*, Rome: International Fund for Agricultural Development.

Gobezie, Getaneh (2010) Empowerment of Women in Rural Ethiopia: A Review of Two Microfinance Models, PRAXIS, *The Fletcher Journal of Human Security*, Volume XXV, pp. 23–37.

Goetz, A.M. and R. Sengupta (1996) Who Takes the Credit? Gender, Power and Control Over Loan Use in Rural Credit Programmes in Bangladesh, *World Development* 24: 45–63.

Harvard Business Review, September, 2013.

Isabelle Guérin and Jane Palier (ed.) (2006) Microfinance Challenges: Empowerment or Disempowerment of the Poor? http://www.persee.fr/web/revues/home/prescript/revue/tiers/

Jyotish, Prakash Basu (2006) "Microfinance and Women Empowerment: An Empirical Study with Special Reference to West Bengal".

Kabeer, N. (1999) The Conditions and Consequences of Choice: Reflections on the Measurement of Women's Empowerment, UNRISD.

Kabeer, N. (2001) "Conflicts Over Credit: Re-Evaluating the Empowerment Potential of Loans to Women in Rural Bangladesh, *World Development* 29 (1): 63–84.

Kulkarni, Vani S. (2011) Women's Empowerment and Microfinance: An Asian Perspective Study, Occasional Paper, IFAD.

Lakshmi Kumar, "Illusions of Women Empowerment in Microfinance: A Case Study", *Economic and Political Weekly*, April 13, 2009, Vol. XLV111 No. 15.

Malhotra, A., Schuler S.R. and Boender, Carol (2002) Measuring Women's Empowerment as a Variable in International Development, Background Paper for World Bank Workshop on Poverty and Gender: New Perspectives.

Mayoux, Linda (1997) 'Impact Assessment and Women's Empowerment in Micro-Finance Programmes: Issues for a Participatory Action and Learning Approach', mimeo, Consultative Group to Assist the Poorest (CGAP), Washington DC.

—— (1998a) Women's Empowerment and Microfinance Programmes: Approaches, Evidence and Ways Forward, The Open University Working Paper No. 41.

—— (1998b) Participatory Programme Learning for Women's Empowerment in Microfinance Programmes: Negotiating Complexity, Conflict and Change, *IDS Bulletin* 29: 39–50.

—— (1999) Questioning Virtuous Spirals: Microfinance and Women's Empowerment.

—— (2002) "Microfinance and Women's Empowerment: Rethinking 'Best Practice'', *Development Bulletin*, No. 57, pp. 76-81.

—— (2006) Women's Empowerment and Microfinance: A 'Think Piece' for the Microfinance Field, http://www.genfinance.info/

Ngo, Thi Minh-Phuong and Zaki Wahhaj (2009) "Microfinance and Gender Empowerment".

Schuler, S., S. Hashemi, A. Riley and A. Akhter (1996) Credit Programs, Patriarchy and Men's Violence Against Women in Rural Bangladesh. *Social Science and Medicine* 43 (12): 1729-42.

SIDA (2009) Women's Economic Empowerment: Scope for Sida's, Engagement, Working Paper, December 30, 2009.

Skarlatos, Katy (2004) Microfinance and Women's Economic Empowerment: Bridging the Gap, Redesigning the Future, Working Paper Series No. 1, Wisconsin Coordinating Council in Nicaragua.

Swain, Ranjula Bali and Wallentin, Fan Yang (2009) "Does Microfinance Empower Women? Evidence from Self-help Groups in India, *International Review of Applied Economics*, Vol. 23, No. 5, September 2009, pp. 541–56.

ANNEXURE

Table 1 *An Overview of the Microfinance Sector*

		Strongly Agree	*Agree*	*Can't Say*	*Disagree*
1.	Microfinance needs to recognize the specific needs and constraints for marginalized groups	56.7%	40.0%	3.3%	0
2.	Do you think your organization has benefitted from its association with microfinance institutions?	6.6%	46.7%	26.7%	20.0%
3.	Microfinance can contribute to female empowerment	70%	30%	0	0
4.	Microfinance programmes, when done well, demonstrate the dynamic coherence between the practical and spiritual requirements of life	6.7%	26.7%	60%	6.6%
5.	Microfinance is a powerful tool for social transformation	83.3%	16.7%	0	0
6.	Microfinance can play a positive role by helping young men move out of forced labour without having to leave their village	50%	33.3%	16.7%	0
7.	Is microfinance lending good for women?	46.7%	50%	0	3.3%
8.	Microfinance is not just about giving micro credit to the poor rather it is an economic development tool	73.3%	23.3%	3.3%	0
9.	One of the major hindrances in the growth of the microfinance sector is the financial illiteracy of the people	50%	50%	0	0
10.	Could the microfinance sector growth and profitability be constrained by poor regulations?	36.7%	53.3%	6.7%	3.3%

Table 2 *Statistics for the Questionnaire Study*

		Mean	*Median*	*Standard Deviation*
1.	Microfinance needs to recognize the specific needs and constraints for marginalized groups	1.466	1.000	0.571
2.	Do you think your organization has benefited from its association with microfinance institutions	2.667	2.000	1.154
3.	Microfinance can contribute to female empowerment	1.300	1.000	0.466
4.	Microfinance programmes, when done well, demonstrate the dynamic coherence between the practical and spiritual requirements of life	2.667	3.000	0.711
5.	Microfinance is a powerful tool for social transformation	1.167	1.000	0.379
6.	Microfinance can play a positive role by helping young men way out of forced labour without having to leave their village	1.667	1.500	0.758
7.	Is microfinance lending good for Women?	1.600	2.000	0.674
8.	Microfinance is not just about giving micro credit to the poor rather it is an economic development tool	1.300	1.000	0.535
9.	One of the major hindrances in the growth of the microfinance sector is the financial illiteracy of the people	1.500	1.500	0.508
10.	Could the microfinance sector growth and profitability be constrained by poor regulations?	1.766	2.000	0.728

18

Private Space in Public Transport

Locating Gender in the Delhi Metro*

Shelly Pandey

A young girl wearing short pants and a T-shirt, lots of junk jewellery, carrying a big casual bag, enters the metro station, gets herself frisked at the ladies security check, crosses another check with the use of a smart card (a plastic magnetic strip card used as a prepaid swipe card by frequent travellers of the metro services), waits at the 'women only' side of the platform and enters the ladies coach of the Delhi Metro.

This is how most of the middle class women are experiencing public transport in Delhi. The metro train which has brought unprecedented comfort to public transport has further added to this comfort by introducing an exclusive ladies coach. The ladies coach has become a phenomenon in the Delhi Metro, promising a safer journey to its women passengers. Experiences of the space provided by the ladies coach in public transport remain unexplored.

Based on an ethnographic study, the aim of this article is to locate gender in the Delhi Metro and the kind of space it has

---

* This paper was published in *Economic and Political Weekly*, XLVI (51), December 2011.

provided to its women passengers. It is based on the participant observation on the Delhi Metro over one year during which the informal interviews were conducted with women passengers.

Public Transport and Gender

In policy making the transport concerns are mainly about how transport infrastructure could be efficiently and cost-effectively constructed and maintained. Fernando and Porter's (2002) work on gender and transport, using a gender perspective to look at a range of transport issues in a variety of locations, maintains that gender has not been fully integrated into the mainstream of either the infrastructure debate or the debate on transport services. However, this work mainly focuses on rural areas and highlights that while transport professionals have taken little account of gender, the issues of access and mobility have also been marginalized in the discourse on gender and development (Fernando and Porter, 2002). Some studies in this work (Iga, 2002) suggest that the influence of culture should not be ignored in the usage of transport.

> The cultural rules which are rarely unfavourable to men reinforce the unequal gender power in the transport as well. Men can usually travel as they wish, by whatever means available. However, women may be constrained by restrictions on where, how and with whom they travel (ibid.).

The experiences of urban women are remarkably different from that of their rural counterparts for the need of transport, as urban women mostly need to travel for work or education on a daily basis. Urban women travel long distances to reach offices or commercial areas and for that they have to depend on public transport. Woman's access to the economic, social and cultural life of a city has always been constrained as she could never circulate freely. In addition, 'because a woman's spatial range is kept limited, she is often anxious about travelling alone to a new place or unknown areas even in her own city. Thus, the physical structure of a city reflects and reinforces inequalities of its social structure through not being equally accessible to both the genders' (Desai, 2007).

Before the advent of Delhi Metro, public transport in Delhi relied primarily on the Delhi Transport Corporation (DTC) buses and private bus service which used to be called the Blue Line buses.

The experiences of women in these buses comprised narratives of harassment by men, which occurred mostly silently and sometimes verbally. The only space for women in these buses was around six to eight reserved seats. However, the experiences of boarding and de-boarding the buses hijack the whole purpose of having reserved seats as women feel that they would not mind standing in the bus if the journey is harassment-free.

There have been initiatives to address these issues. For example, DTC welcomed the partnership with a Delhi-based non-governmental organization (NGO) Jagori for holding workshops to sensitize bus drivers and conductors on issues of gender and sexual harassment and to not tolerate harassment in their buses. The training programme was inaugurated by the Chief Minister, Sheila Dikshit on 3 September 2007 (Jagori, 2007).

Some of the findings of a survey conducted by Jagori during these workshops show that if women commuters confront the harassers, support from co-passengers and bus staff is difficult to get. The seats reserved for women are often occupied by men who do not vacate them even when requested to do so. The harassers most often are not intimidated by the presence of bus drivers and conductors and they usually get away without much protest by the bus staff or the public. Women have also reported the presence of drunken men around bus stops after dark which gives them an acute sense of insecurity (Unifem, 2011).

The understanding of gendered experiences in public transport in Delhi before the metro confirms that in the buses there is no sense of secure space, as women share the space with anonymous men. Hence travelling in the buses has always been reported as a struggle by women passengers. It curtailed their field of opportunity and dimmed their sense of secured travel in the city.

Here Comes the Metro

The Delhi Metro was inaugurated on 24 December 2002. The initial days of metro journey were reported safer than the bus travel by women. However, the increasing connectivity of the metro on different routes resulted in it getting overcrowded. Especially, after its connectivity to prime stations like Rajeev Chowk, Kashmiri Gate and NOIDA, special security personnel have to handle the crowd on the platforms and help maintain queues of the passengers for the convenience of those passengers who have to de-board the metro.

Women's experiences started getting closer to the earlier experiences of the bus journeys because of the increasing population in the metro train. In October 2010, Delhi Metro Rail Corporation (DMRC) decided to reserve the first coach of the train for women passengers in view of increasing number of passengers in general and women passengers in particular.

The ladies coach is the first coach of every train. Unlike the ladies coach of the Mumbai local trains, the coach does not have picture or figure of a woman outside the coach, neither does it have 'ladies' inscribed on it. The ladies coach can be recognized by its placement on the platform because the platform has specific space where the ladies coach stops. 'Women only' in pink colour is written on that part of the floor of the platform where the first coach/woman's coach is designated to stop. However, inside the coach some differences can be found which demarcate it from the rest of the train. These are marked by the advertisements about contraceptive pills or beauty products and sometimes awareness about health issues faced by women like breast cancer or cervical cancer. The ladies coach accommodates about 361 commuters (43 seating and 318 standing). However, one can find more than 43 women sitting, as they do not mind sitting in congested way and the coach accommodates more women as they do not have to mind the body distance in the absence of men. In other instances of public transport women always have to be alert in public areas to protect their physical as well as visual boundaries. There is no barrier to separate the ladies coach from the rest of the train as the emergency exit is at the end of the ladies coach. However, the barrier is in the form of a penalty of ₹ 250, which deters men from boarding it.

Gender and Delhi Metro

Gender exploration in public transport has been done in earlier studies (Phadke, 2007), where women's presence and usage of public transport has been explored. Nevertheless, as far as the Delhi Metro is concerned, Sadana's (2010) work on it has explained women's better access to the city and their emancipation from the dependency on male family members for mobility in the city. Apart from the increasing number of women passengers in the Delhi Metro, there are quite a number of instances where gender can be located. It starts with the entry gate, where the security is divided along gender lines, with women security police, who frisk women passengers entering the metro station. At the customer care and token selling counters the presence of women staff is quite evident, which brings women employees in a noticeable number, in the realms of the public transport for the first time in Delhi. The Delhi Metro employed three women drivers in 2002 and the number has increased to 25 in 2011 (*The Times of India*, 2011). After this initiative DTC decided to hire women conductors for the DTC buses (Pandey, 2010), which gradually would result into rendering a new face to the public transport in Delhi. Women guards are also employed on the metro's platforms to restrict men from boarding the ladies coach. This illustrates how these women guards, who come from lower middle class families, exercise authority in the public realm which they might not claim in the private realm of their homes. This reinforces one of the claims of gender and space discourse that people and social identities are determined by the physical or spatial environment (Desai, 2007).

Private within Public

The ladies coach provides a private space for women. Apart from the safety aspect, women's physical interaction with men is almost absent during travel in the metro. Many women reported that they hire a cycle rickshaw to reach the metro station, get themselves frisked at the women's security check counter and most of them use the smart card to travel in the metro, so they do not need to even stand in the queue with men to buy the token. At the platform they have a separate space to stand while waiting for the train's arrival and which separates them from the male passengers even on the platform. In the initial days a lady guard used to stand on the platform to instruct men not to stand on the space which is reserved for the women.

Many women reported that they do not mind the crowded platforms now as they have a separate space to stand. Even male passengers reported that when they travel with women family members on crowded routes, they ask them to travel in the women's coach. Women travelling with men also prefer to travel in the ladies coach and on the platform stand at the space reserved for them.

Even in the night women feel safe in the ladies coach. The metro trains run from 6 am till about 11 pm. Many women who travel to faraway stations like NOIDA or Gurgaon (cities at the periphery of Delhi) have to travel by metro after dark as well. But these women reported that the ladies coach provides them a secure space to travel and a male family member picks them up at the metro station near their homes. Many women are found to be waiting for a male family member, outside the metro station (in the daytime). However, in the night hours, women prefer to wait at the 'women only' section of the platform as they find this space safer than that outside the metro station. The 'women only' section of the platform has been reported as a waiting point by many women. Sometimes, even in daytime, many women are found to be waiting there.

Inside the ladies coach, the observations reinforce the sense of space and freedom among women in many ways. A group of women is often found to be sitting on the floor of the train and chatting with each other. They feel less conscious in the ladies coach than in the other coaches with men. Women passengers reported that they can talk, sit and laugh without being conscious of the male presence. The studies on women's access to public space attach the discourse of respectability with their presence in public space. In this discourse women moderate their behaviour in public to avoid being labelled as unrespectable. This moderation involves tone, volume of voice along with body language. These body politics have been discussed in detail in the studies on social construction of gender (Dube, 2001).

One important finding that came out during the study was about their agency in dressing. There are many young female students who travel by metro to the Delhi University wearing short pants and skirts.

Many of these students explained their limited agency earlier as far as their dressing was concerned (when they used to travel by bus). However, due to the ladies coach of the Delhi Metro the threat of physical proximity with men in the public transport is absent thus allowing them the freedom to wear clothes of their choice.

In the gender and space discourse, the public space is the site for exchanging ideas, values and a platform for leisure activities for men. However, for women, public spaces are often regarded as transit ways to other regions. A woman is supposed to use public spaces as a transit between one private space to another (Gardner, 1990). Her negotiation of the public spaces is more likely to be governed by some markers stipulated for the woman like physical look, proper decorum, non-verbal communication, proper attire and so on (Paul, 2001).

Women's claim to the freedom of body language and choice of clothes reflect how space and spatial considerations contribute in the constitution of femininity (Niranjana, 2001). Many geography scholars maintain that it is important to understand that there is a difference between the metaphorical (or cultural) space and material space. This understanding particularly becomes imperative, if we consider how certain cultural ideas of space have an impact upon the bodily practices of women, conceptualizing and embodying the socio-spatial matrix (Soja, 1989). The understanding of bodily practices in the ladies coach of the metro emphasizes the spatial perspective to women's experiences showing that spatiality itself participates in the production of gendered bodies. On a parallel note, Bourdieu's work (1977) also demonstrates how space enters into the very constitution of social life and identities. His concept of habitus reveals how a spatial classification is fundamental to one's social and cognitive map, providing individuals with a set of parameters within which to deal with everyday lives and situations. In Bourdieu's conceptual scheme, the habitus not only plays a major role in shaping and orienting our practical acts, but is also renewed along this course.

The new notion of expressivity in the public transport (provided by the ladies coach) also puts forth an understanding of how the ladies coach has come up as a resource for 'doing gender'. Doing gender means constructing the differences between men and women and using them in actions and interactions to reinforce the essentialness of gender (West and Zimmerman, 1987). The creation of separate public washrooms in North America has been recognized as the earliest resource of doing gender (Goffman, 1977). In the Indian context the ladies coach of Delhi Metro is the latest example of such resource. In the feminist studies of social construction of gender and doing gender, gender itself is constituted through interactions (West and Zimmerman, 1987), which explain that in Indian society girls internalize the use of space and behaviour including posture, dress and speech. The freedom of conduct and clothing in the public space provided by the ladies coach reveals, first, how a private space is created for women in a public transport while transiting from one space to another, second, how gender is reproduced in a new environment, and third, how women conduct themselves to fit their own notion of expressivity.

Policing the Space Invaders

Apart from the sense of freedom and protection, the ladies coach also provides a sense of authority among women passengers. Many women confirmed that they feel a sense of belongingness with the ladies coach and protect the purpose of the same by not allowing men to travel in it. Many women protest and generally do not let the men enter. The DMRC has a special squad for the metro train for the same purpose. Women passengers claim that they sometimes inform the male passengers about the fine which they will have to pay if they travel in the ladies coach, which works to stop them from travelling in ladies coach. This, however, reveals that the ladies coach does not only provide a sense of private space to women but also accords an unprecedented authority to them in the public place to protest. Women explained that, while travelling by bus, it is difficult to protest in case of any assault as co-passengers who are mostly men do not support the woman victim. The protest in the bus becomes more of an embarrassment rather than being an effective means to redressal. Feminist scholars and geographers have posited access to and control over space as key elements in power dynamics (Paul, 2001). Power relations demarcate the boundaries of spaces and determine the legitimacy of users who enter these spaces as well as their identities, discourses and interests (Gaventa, 2006).

> The physical space is frequently utilised as strategy to reproduce self which, embody and sometimes naturalise such behavioural strategies with passage of time. It is through replication of such identities that specific spaces come to be associated with either masculine or feminine that strongly influence men's and women's actual behavior and power within them. (Kilde, 1999)

The experiences of women passengers in policing men in Delhi Metro brings forth an understanding about the gender relations in public space that the power equation of every space involves the question of majority. In the gender and space discourse, the subjugated position of women in public space has a lot to do with their minority status and where a space like ladies coach brings them together and provides them with a sense of majority which makes them feel empowered and renders them the capacity to protest vocally. Second, the space of metro train is a controlled space where it is difficult for the offender to run away unlike the bus journeys of earlier days, however, it may be added that with the inclusion of Tata buses of the Marcopolo make in the fleet of the DTC, the entry and exit in DTC buses have become relatively controlled. The doors of the metro train open only at the station and in between the two stations the security can be contacted to complaint against the offender. Hence, the space of ladies coach, providing a sense of majority to women and the special security attached with it (penalty of ₹ 250 and special squad) facilitate an unusual kind of power relation in the public space.

This power relation can be understood by Bourdieu's work (1989) on symbolic power, where the space of the ladies coach can be analysed as a space of symbolic power. Symbolic power is the power, according to Bourdieu, 'to conserve or to transform the current classification in matters of gender, nation, region, age and social status'. It is used through words to describe individuals, groups or institutions. But to understand how women get this symbolic power in the ladies coach, it is important to understand that symbolic power has to be based on symbolic capital. Bourdieu has recognized symbolic capital as a 'credit', 'which grants power to those who have obtained sufficient recognition to be in the position to impose recognition' (ibid.). The separate ladies coach is a symbolic capital for women, which helps them to recognize themselves as a group and to look upon men in this public space as the other group. Within the space of their own group they exercise power to impose the recognition that has been provided to them.

Now, we can understand that women's capacity to police men in the ladies coach comes through the symbolic power provided to them in the space of the ladies coach. To make them exercise their symbolic power they are given symbolic capital (in form of punishment and penalty to the invaders). Public space has always been a no-authority space for women and women were always expected to negotiate with the power relations, which are tilted towards men. However, the ladies coach of the Delhi Metro, representing symbolic power and symbolic capital to women, has brought a transformation of power relations in the public space. The space of the ladies coach as a part of public transport has provided certain amount of agency as well as power to women which has manifested in making their negotiation with the public space smoother.

Conclusions

Although there are continuous shifts and transformations in how public and private spaces are characterized, as the meanings they acquire are always contingent upon their contexts, the dichotomy of public-private space can get blurred when one space can become part of another. The ladies coach of Delhi Metro has provided a little private space to women in the vast public space. The meaning of a public space can be beyond its physical boundaries and there can be an emotional meaning of the space (i.e., space that is mentally inhabited) which creates an attachment with the space inhibited. The ladies coach has provided a private space in a public transport to women for the first time in Delhi. There is a visible transformation in their conduct, decorum and even in physical looks including the attire, to fit their own notion of expressivity in this new space.

The space of the ladies coach also highlights a distinct power dynamics in public transport which is tilted in favour of women and reproduced or transformed the internalized meaning of public space for women.

References

Bourdieu, Pierre (1977) *Outline of a Theory of Practice*, Cambridge: Cambridge University Press.

—— (1989) 'Social Space and Symbolic Power', *Sociological Theory*, 7 (1): 14–25.

Desai, M. (2007) 'Introduction', in Madhavi Desai (ed.), *Gender and the Built Environment in India*, Delhi: Zubaan, pp. 1–29.

Dube, Leela (2001) *Anthropological Exploration in Gender: Intersecting Fields*, New Delhi: Sage Publications.

Fernando, P. and G. Porter (2002) 'Introduction', in P. Fernando and G. Porter (eds), *Balancing the Load: Women Gender and Transport*, New York: Zed Books, pp. 1–14.

Gardner, Carol Brooks (1990) 'Safe Conduct: Women Crime and Self in Public Places', *Social Problems*, 37 (3): 311–28.

Gaventa, John (2006) 'Finding the Spaces for Change: A Power Analysis', *IDS Bulletin*, 37 (6): 26–33.

Goffman, Erving (1977) 'The Arrangements between the Sexes', *Theory and Society*, 4: 301–31.

Iga, Harriet (2002) 'Bicycles, Boda Boda and Women's Travel Needs', in P. Fernando and G. Porter (eds), *Balancing the Load: Women Gender and Transport*, New York: Zed Books, pp. 50–56.

Jagori (2007) 'DTC Partners with Jagori on the Safe Delhi Campaign', viewed on 26 June 2011 (http://safedelhi.jagori.org/news/dtc-partners-with-jagori-on-the-safe-delhi-campaign/).

Kilde, Jeanne Halgren (1999) 'The Predominance of the Feminine at Chautauqua: Rethinking the Gender-Space Relationship in Victorian America', *Signs*, 24 (2): 449–86.

Niranjana, Seemanthini (2001) *Gender and Space: Feminity, Sexualisation and the Female Body*, New Delhi: Sage Publications.

Pandey, Neelam (2010) 'DTC Hires Women Conductors', *Hindustan Times*, viewed on 30 June 2011 (http://www.hindustantimes.com/DTC-hires-women-conductors/Article1-615197.aspx).

Paul, Tanushree (2001) 'Public Spaces and Everyday Lives: Gendered Encounters in the Metro City of Kolkata', in S. Raju and K. Lahiri-Dutt (eds), *Doing Gender, Doing Geography: Emerging Research in India*, New Delhi: Routledge.

Phadke, S. (2007) 'Re-Mapping the Public: Gendered Spaces in Mumbai', in Madhavi Desai (ed.), *Gender and the Built Environment in India*, Delhi: Zubaan, pp. 53–73.

Sadana, Rashmi (2010) 'On the Delhi Metro: An Ethnographic View', *Economic and Political Weekly*, XLV (46): 77–83.

Soja, Edward (1989) *Postmodern Geographies: The Reassertion of Space in Critical Social Theory*, London: Verso.

The Times of India (2011) 'DMRC Marks 100 Months of Operations', *The Times of India*, viewed on 25 June (http://articles.timesofindia.indiatimes.com/2011-04-24/delhi/29468392_1_delhi-metro-rail-corporation-metro-today-metro-train-operations).

Unifem (2011) 'Initiative to Make Delhi Safe for Women Takes Off with Training of DTC Instructors', viewed on 27 June (http://www.unifem.org.in/DTC%20Story.htm).

West, C. and D.H. Zimmerman (1987) 'Doing Gender', *Gender and Society*, 1 (2): 1–25.

19

Feminist Perspectives on Honour Killings and Domestic Violence

The Case of Indo-Canadian Communities

Chantal Maillé

This text relates to the ongoing debates about the use of the term 'honour killings' in Canada. We look at the arguments given by those who support using the term as well as those made by opponents to the term. If honour killings are a very specific form of violence against women, in Canada, media have used the term in ways that have been seen as offensive and exclusionary by many. Beyond the semantic aspect of naming crimes committed against women, we want to uncover how this debate is a reflection of power dynamics between different visions of cultural differences in Canadian society. Using texts and materials from different sources, we look at the implications of the term 'honour killings' for Indo-Canadian communities in terms of stigmatization. In our conclusion, we propose recommendations to address the problem in the Canadian and international contexts.

What do we know about the struggle against honour killings? Two United Nations (UN) documents have called for the elimination of this form of violence against women; the call of 'elimination' appears first in the 1993 'Declaration on the Elimination of Violence Against Women' (Mojab, 2004: 22). In a more recent UN report, *Working Towards the Elimination of Crimes Against Women Committed in the Name of Honour*, released in 2002, the Canadian situation with regard to honour killings is assessed in these terms: 'Canada indicated that honour crimes, including killings, were extremely rare in Canada, but such crimes would be investigated and prosecuted as offences under the Criminal Code, and such crimes as assault, aggravated assault or sexual assault and murder, which could occur in the execution of an honour crime, were covered by that Code' (United Nations, 2002: 3).

Canada has signed UN declarations on the elimination of violence against women. It is a country where men and women are legally equal. The Canadian Charter of Rights and Freedoms, adopted in 1982, enabled Canadians to move aggressively in the areas of gender and sexual equality. As a result, some would say that Canada's experience with landmark equality decisions and human rights cases is formidable (L'Heureux-Dubé, 2003). But if equality between the two genders has been, to a great extent, achieved, yet inequality and violence go on (Mojab, 2004: 23).

In Canada, since 2002, the murders of 12 women were identified as honour killings (Papp, 2010: 4). In 2003, in British Columbia, a province of Canada, Amandeep Singh Atwal, 17, was stabbed to death by her father, because she wanted to date a non-Sikh classmate. In 2006, in the city of Ottawa, Khatera Sadiqi and her 23-year old boyfriend, were killed by her brother. In 2009, in Ontario, near Toronto, Amandeep Kaur Dhillion, an immigrant from Punjab, was driven by her father-in-law to and from the family-owned-and-run grocery store, where she worked long hours, was killed by him when she threatened to leave his son (ibid.).

How is the issue of honour killings within Indo-Canadian communities understood and conceptualized? In 2010, the Canadian government was looking to making honour killing a separate charge in the Canadian Criminal Code. The Canadian Minister for the Status of Women Rona Ambrose said publicly that honour killings are a form of heinous cultural violence that has no place in Canadian society. She said:

> There is a small minority in some communities who use violence against women as a method of avenging their so-called honour. Let

> me be explicit: this type of violence, the most extreme of which is often known as 'honour killing', has no place in Canadian society. Killing or mutilating anyone, least of all a family member, is utterly unacceptable under all circumstances, and will be prosecuted to the full extent of the law. So-called honour crimes are an extreme and brutal violation of the values we hold dear, and it is shameful that there are those who encourage or tolerate them. Being a member of Canadian society comes with the responsibility of upholding Canadian laws and values. (cited in Galloway, 2010)

The minister's announcement was prompted by the release of the Papp report focusing on the growing problem of the abuse of girls and women in Canada's immigrant communities. The report outlined recommendations such as mandatory orientation sessions for male sponsors and sponsored women regarding gender equality in Canada. However, Indian immigrant women who are claiming the risk of being victims of honour killing if they are deported to India can hardly get the protection of the Immigration and Refugee Board of Canada.

Another question emerged in relation to the discussion of the issue in the Canadian context is should there be a distinction for honour-based crimes – for example, special provisions in the criminal code, or should they be understood as cases of domestic abuse? What are the implications of honour-related violence to be recognized as a distinct form of violence against women in the western and more particularly Canadian context?

Arguments in Favour of the Term 'Honour Killings'

American feminist writer Phyllis Chesler argues that honour killings are distinct from domestic violence and that they need to be recognized by governments and communities so that society can begin to tackle the problem. She writes:

> When a husband murders a wife or daughter in the United States and Canada, too often law enforcement chalks the matter up to domestic violence. Murder is murder; religion is irrelevant. Honor killings are, however, distinct from wife battering and child abuse. Analysis of more than fifty reported honor killings shows they differ significantly from more common domestic violence. The frequent arguments made by Muslim advocacy organizations that

> honor killings have nothing to do with Islam and that it is discriminatory to differentiate between honor killings and domestic violence is wrong. (Chesler, 2009: 61)

If Chesler's arguments point to the need for an explicit term, she also locates her arguments in the specific religious configuration of these crimes. Chesler identifies at least eight differing characteristics of honour killings and domestic violence, the first one being that honour killings are, she writes, committed mainly by Muslims against Muslim young adult women, while domestic violence is committed by men of all faiths usually against adult women. Among the other differences, Chesler identifies the reason given for honour killing being that the woman has dishonoured the family while in other cases of domestic violence the abuser does not claim any family concept of honour (ibid.: 62).

The application of the phrase 'honour killing' can be contentious, particularly for minority communities that fear being collectively targeted by the violence of a small number of people. Anver Emon, a University of Toronto law professor who specializes in Islamic law, said that he sympathizes with such concerns but supports the employment of the phrase when justified by the facts: 'From a social perspective, you don't want to criminalize a community by associating them with a particular, heinous act of violence, Emon said. 'On the other hand, from a legal perspective ... why "honour killing" can be useful is that it captures the idea of a kind of premeditation – that this wasn't an in-the-moment, spur-of-the-moment crime of passion but something that may have been planned. It speaks to a kind of evil and hideousness that we must at all times prevent' (Thestar.com).

Aruna Papp, in her report on honour killings in Canada, writes: 'In patriarchal societies that are comprised of the self-appointed and more authentic non-Westernized bulk of the South Asian community, where honour/shame codes are rife, men are found to exercise rigid control over women. The result is a higher incidence of violence against women as compared with the mainstream Western host communities' (Papp, 2010: 5). Papp further argues that immigrant, refugee and non-status immigrant women in Canada are more vulnerable to violence from both men and women because they have less control over their lives than Canadian women whose ancestors came to Canada long ago or who come from European backgrounds. South-Asian immigrant women living in Canada have to compose with traditional values and community leaders who point to cultural traditions and who consciously exploit multiculturalism-inspired fears amongst Canadians of appearing racist or perpetuating cultural stereotypes (ibid.: 8). The author is also in favour of using the term honour killings in the Canadian context because she sees these crimes as distinct from other domestic crimes. According to the Papp report, when women are killed due to reasons of honour and family shame, they had been threatened over such issues as refusing to cover their heads, wearing makeup, wearing Western clothes, dating, going to parties, choosing friends the family disapproved of, refusing to marry a man chosen by the family, seeking a divorce from a violent husband and marrying against the families' wishes.

For Papp, honour killings in Canada have to be understood in relation to the South Asian family structure, which sanctions the domination of women through different mechanisms:

> Research suggests that traditional patriarchal power imbalances are even more strongly maintained in the South Asian immigrant communities in the hope of ensuring cultural continuity. Like other patriarchal systems, the South Asian culture is characterized by deep-rooted inequalities in male-female roles and legitimized by social and cultural norms that place men in controlling positions over the lives of women. (ibid.: 9)

A second mechanism of control present in the South Asian family structure is sexuality:

> The South Asian patriarchal structure controls female sexuality not only in a physical manner but also in a psychological one, by making explicit the link between family honour and the sexual purity of the women within the family. (ibid.)

Papp also identifies family structures and a distinct conception of honour in the construction of the specificity of honour killings:

> The complexity of gender domination is much more apparent in the concepts of honour and shame. Honour killings are carried out in order to cleanse the family name and to restore the family honour. Unlike Western domestic violence, typically perpetrated bilaterally by one intimate partner on another, honour

> violence is perpetrated unilaterally within the family: against girls and women by male relatives – such as fathers, fathers-in-law, brothers, brothers-in-law, husbands and occasionally sons – often with the complicity of older females. Killing is not the only crime committed in the name of honour, simply the most violent. (ibid.: 9)

This being said, Papp discusses the malaise in the media with regard to the treatment given to crimes that correspond to the description of honour killing. She reports that when honour killings occur, the media are not generally very helpful in identifying the problem: 'The events are filtered through a reflexive, multiculturalism-inspired reluctance to racialize the crime. All too often, the killing becomes subsumed under the heading of domestic violence or the global problem of patriarchy' (ibid.). She argues that this does a disservice both to the South Asian immigrant community and to Canadian society in that the media wilfully ignores a cultural problem in dire need of acknowledgement and reform, while indicting Canadian men for attitudes the overwhelming majority of them do not hold.

Richelle Wiseman, Executive Director of the Centre for Faith and the Media, a Canadian independent, non-profit organization to inform, advise and help media and the general public achieve a stronger understanding of spiritual history, practices and values in Canadian society, is also a defendant of the term 'honour killing'. For her, honour killing is about a set of patriarchal cultural values that must be named, condemned and confronted and the claim that there is nothing special about honour crimes is a mistake as she sees distinctive features of an honour killing, such as a background obsession with female purity, pre-planning, family approval of complicity, and often broader community approval for forcing an errant woman to toe the line according to culturally-sanctioned norms (Wiseman, 2010). Like Chesler, Wiseman disagrees with those who worry that if we give this kind of violence a special name, we risk smearing whole ethnic communities with women-led hating stereotypes that they do not deserve. For Wiseman, we have to single out cultural practices which violate women's right to equality without condemning entire cultural groups. There is a problem with specific cultures, as 'not all cultures embrace gender equality. It is not racist to name those practices which deny women's dignity in the name of "honour", entire cultures are not being condemned, just the aspects of them incompatible with women's humanity' (ibid.).

Chesler, Papp and Wiseman share a common perspective on the need for a term such as 'honour killings' to designate crimes that they see as grounded in specific cultural and religious practices. In the next section, we will review arguments developed by those who oppose to the term 'honour killings' in the Canadian context.

Arguments Against the Term 'Honour Killings'

For most people who live in Canada, the term 'honour killings' is known through sensasionalistic media coverage of crimes committed in South Asian communities. It is exotic in a postcolonial sense as it defines a sense of marginalization and exclusion for some communities perceived as outsiders in the West. Canadian feminist scholar Shahrzad Mojab argues against the use of the term 'honour killings' in Western countries. She writes, 'the extreme right and racists explain honour killings as a part of what they call the "barbaric culture" of immigrants from the non-Western world. (...) Racist culturalization of honour killing ignores the fact that killing women is a universal phenomenon in patriarchal cultures in both the East and the West' (Mojab, 2004: 29).

Alia Hogben, Executive Director of the Canadian Council of Muslim Women shared similar concerns at the panel on Honour Killings in Canada held in 2010[1] and she called for the rejection of the term 'honour killings' in the Canadian context. For Hogben, the argument taking place in Canada is whether some crimes are violence against women or something very different. Some are insisting that these murders are distinct and unlike other domestic violence; while others, including Hogben, are unwilling to label these as anything but violence against women. Hogben writes: 'By our refusal in Canada to label any murder as "honour killing" we are stating unequivocally that we reject the whole context and rationale for any murder of women. We do not want to be apart of any world movement to acquiesce to such violence' (Hogben, 2010).

In addition to the argument that these crimes belong to a broader category labeled as violence against women, Hogben sees in the term 'honour killing' an expression of racism:

> For us to label these murders as honour killings is both divisive and dangerous. It makes these murders exotic and foreign, alien

> to our Canadian culture. It encourages blatant racism for some as it gives them permission to blame those people and demand their ousting from Canada. It makes others defensive or apologetic about their culture or religion, and blocks any acknowledgement that these murders do irreparable harm to religion or culture. For others who differentiate these women's killings as part of their culture, it gives them reasons for using cultural relativism as the argument to lessen the horror of the crimes, and to make these women's lives less valued. (ibid.)

Hogben wonders if some people want considerations such as culture or religion to mitigate the punishment of these murders and she reaffirms that naming this kind of murder of women honour killing and laying the blame on specific cultures ignores the fundamental issues of patriarchy, control and power over women. She concludes that Canadians must uphold the UN's recommendation that there be no invocation of custom, tradition or religion to justify violence against women and girls.

The Canadian Laws

In Canada, every time, when the word 'honour killing' is used in the media, it contributes to increase racism and marginalization for some communities. It reinforces the message that there are huge cultural differences between white settler communities living in Canada and some other communities such as South Asian communities. It is often presented as an argument proving cultural inferiority and that is the first reason to think that the term 'honour killing' serves to maintain hierarchy between the different communities living on the Canadian territory. A second problem with the use of the term 'honour killing' in Canada is that it is often used to legitimize these crimes and make them more acceptable than if they were simply represented as domestic violence homicides. In a context where journalists in the media are looking for sensationalist coverage of the news, crimes that are presented as honour killings get a lot of attention.

Do Canadian criminal laws need amendments to better take issue of specific crimes against women? Janet Keeping, president of the Sheldon Chumir Foundation for Ethics in Leadership, based in Canada, argues that honour killings are not just another form of domestic violence but instead represent the acting out of a sharply regressive view of women. There are practical consequences to pretending otherwise and thus it is wrong to avoid identifying these killings for what they are, says Keeping. She defends the existing Candian laws and writes that the current Canadian criminal law – which does not contain specific provisions on honour killings – is probably adequate to cope with all crimes against women and thus does not need amendment. Keeping points to the kind of leadership that is needed among communities concerned with honour killings and she argues that leadership of all types of organizations and at all levels should acknowledge that there are people in Canada who hold the poisonous beliefs that motivate honour killings and commit to working towards change of those attitudes and effective protection of those vulnerable to this kind of violence.

According to Keeping, the question has been raised as to whether the Criminal Code of Canada should be amended to make specific reference to honour killings. For her, there is no need of such a change: 'Canadian court seem well able to deal with honour killings under existing law. So the issue is not for the most part a legal one, but rather a question of how well Canadians understand the whole phenomenon of "honour" motivated violence and intimidation and what ultimately can be done to minimize the impact in Canada of the attitude that family honour trumps the right of girls and women to full equality' (Keeping, 2010: 6).

Instead of focusing on the need to categorize violence against women, Keeping proposes that in addressing honour-related violence, Canada needs to acknowledge the scope of violence against women and the magnitude of their oppression in the country, where human rights protections are relatively advanced. As Keeping suggests, there is violence against women in Canada and most of this violence has nothing to do with notions of honour. So is it necessary to distinguish honour-based violence from other types of domestic violence against women? Is it different to kill by jealousy or to kill to satisfy a sense of family honour? Keeping also asks the question: Why do some people resist the identification of honour-motivated violence? Among the reasons to resist the identification of honour-motivated violence, she fears that by using the label 'honour killings', law and policy makers might draw the wrong conclusion and treat those killings less seriously than other forms of violence against women.

Some Canadian women's organizations, such as the Canadian Council of Muslim Women, oppose to the use of the term 'honour killings' in Canada because they reject the whole context and rationale for any murder of women. They also fear that openly talking about an honour killing will somewhat undermine the seriousness of those murders. Another reason why some argue that honour killing should be discussed as ordinary domestic violence is the way that by naming the violence an honour crime we feed into the stereotyping of the cultures in which honour plays such a role. For example, this might contribute to representing Muslim or Sikh Canadians as barbarians. The use of the term 'honour killings' can contribute to a general aversion of cultures in which specific forms of violence against women are found and Canadian media are good at stereotyping entire communities when presenting stories of violence against women located in South Asian communities.

Without special provisions for honour killings, the Canadian Criminal Code allows a judge to hand down a more serious penalty for crimes where there is evidence that the offense was motivated by bias, prejudice or hate based on race, national or ethnic origin, religion, sex, age, mental or physical disability, sexual orientation or any other similar factor. Such evidence shall be deemed to be aggravating circumstances and thus would warrant more, not less, severe punishment than would otherwise be the case (ibid.: 16). So is there a need to change the Canadian Criminal Code? Evidence suggests that there is no need to do so.

Conclusion: Plan of Action

Canadian feminist scholar Shahrzad Mojad is critical of the use of the term 'honour killings' in the West and in Canada. She opposes reducing these crimes to a cultural or religious problem, but she recognizes the relevance of the term for other contexts. She proposes to read and understand crimes of honour in relation of the broader framework of patriarchy:

> In order to achieve the goal of eliminating honour killing, we need to move out of the prevalent range of debate, which reduces violence against women to questions of culture, religion, psychology, ignorance, practice, and law breaking. One alternative is to see patriarchy as a system of gender relations, which, much like the state, exercises political power. This system, much like capitalism or feudalism, has to survive through unceasing

reproduction. It produces male domination, and uses culture, language, religion, education, the economic and every other social formation on order to reproduce itself. Violence is one means of reproducing male rule. Eliminating honour killing means denying patriarchy one of the means of its reproduction, that is, killing women.' (Mojab, 2004: 36)

In terms of actions, what can be done to address the multiple forms of violence against women? Mojab's plan of action on this includes the promotion of the idea of the right to life for women, and its actualization through law and law enforcement, feminist education in all levels of schooling, the creation of publicly supported feminist media, print and broadcast, and the financing of women's advocacy groups and shelters (ibid.: 37).

This paper has thus identified arguments both in favour and against the term 'honour killings' in the Canadian context. In conclusion, it appears that Canada needs to move away from stereotypical representations of cultures, mostly when approaching issues of violence against women.

Note

1. Panel on Honour Killings in Canada, Symposium on Ethical Leadership and Gender Responsibility, Alberta (Canada), 2010.

References

Caplan, G. (2010) 'Honour Killings in Canada: Even Worse than We Believe', *Globe and Mail*. Retrieved from http://www.ccmw.com/documents/WHIG/201010_speech.pdf on 23 July 2010.

Chesler, P. (2009) 'Are Honor Killings Simply Domestic Violence?', *Middle East Quarterly*, Spring, pp. 61–69.

Galloway, G. (2010) 'Women's Minister Warns Against "Honour Killings"', *Globe and Mail*. Retrieved from http:/m.theglobeandmail.com/news/politics/ottawa-notebook/womens-minister-wars-against-honour-killings/article1390510/?service=mobile on 12 July 2010.

Hogben, A. (2010) 'Gender, Culture and Religion: Tackling Some Difficult Questions', Speech, Sheldon Chumir Foundation Conference, Calgary, 1–2 October. Retrieved from http://www.ccmw.com/documents/WHIG/201010_speech.pdf on 21 January 2011.

Keeping, J. (2010) 'Honour Killings in Canada: What Needs to be Said? What Needs to be Done?', A Discussion Paper from the Sheldon Chumir Foundation for Ethics in Leadership, Prepared for the 'Gender, Culture and Religion: Tackling Some Difficult Questions' Symposium on 1–2 October. Retrieved from http://www.chumirethicsfoundation.ca/files/pdf/HonourKillingsPaper_rw_20100827_web.pdf on 21 January 2011.

L'Heureux-Dubé, C. (2003) *Equality and the Canadian Charter of Rights*, LSE Human Rights. Retrieved from http://www 2.lse.ac.uk/humanRights/events/Equality_Canadian_Charter.aspx on 25 January 2011.

Mojab, S. (2004) 'The Particularity of "Honour" and the Universality of "Killing": From Early Warning Signs to Feminist Pedagogy', in S. Mojab and N. Ablo (eds), *Violence in the Name of Honour: Theoretical and Political Challenges*, Istanbul, Turkey: Istanbul Bilgi Universitesi Yayinlari, pp. 15–37.

O'Neill, J. (2011) 'Muslim Women's Group Opposes Addition of Honour Killings to Criminal Code', *Postmedia News*. Retrieved from http://www.canada.com/life/Muslim+women+group+opposes+addition+honour+killings+Criminal+Code/3275824/story.html on 21 January 2011.

Papp, A. (2010) *Culturally Driven Violence Against Women: A Growing Problem in Canada's Immigrant Communities*, Report for the Frontier Centre for Public Policy, No. 92.

United Nations (2002) *Working Towards the Elimination of Crimes Against Women Committed in the Name of Honour*, Report of the Secretary-General.

'Were Deaths of 4 Women a Matter of "Honour"?', *Toronto Star*, 24 July 2009. Retrieved from http://www.thestar.com/News/Ontario/article/671148 on 21 January 2011.

Wiseman, R. (2010) 'Naming "Honour Killings" Necessary to Prevent Further Violence Against Women', *Troy Media*, 14 September. Retrieved from http://www.ccmw.com/documents/WHIG/201010_speech.pdf on 21 January 2011.

—— (2010) 'The Honour Killing Debate in Canada', A Discussion Paper from the Sheldon Chumir Foundation for Ethics in Leadership, Prepared for the 'Gender, Culture and Religion: Tackling Some Difficult Questions' Symposium on 1–2 October. Retrieved from http://www.chumirethicsfoundation.ca/files/pdf/HonourKillingsPaper_rw_20100827_web.pdf on 21 January 2011.

Celebrating the Global Concern

Research: Discovering Women Priests at Rudraprayag, Uttarakhand

Quantum Jump of Women's Studies with Introduction of UGC Refresher Course in Women's Studies

Academic Links Far and Wide

Finding Foothold

Scholars Interacting with Students

Women's Studies: Coming Together

Contributors

Amrit Kaur Basra is Associate Professor in History, Delhi College of Arts and Commerce. Presently, she is on deputation in the Institute of Lifelong Learning, since March 2012, as a fellow and academic secretary. Her education from B.A. through M.A., M.Phil. and Ph.D. is from the University of Delhi. Her areas of research are Communalism and Communal Riots in Colonial Punjab, Identity Formation among Sikhs, Sikhism and Interfaith, Gender and Violence, History of Canada and the Historiography.

Ann Stewart, specializes in the area of gender and the law, particularly in the context of international development, has worked collaboratively in a number of jurisdictions, particularly in southern and eastern Africa, South East Asia and in South Asia. She was Ford Visiting Professorial Fellow at the Centre for Law and Governance at Jawaharlal Nehru University, New Delhi in 2010. At present, she teaches courses on gender and law at undergraduate and postgraduate levels. She has also been research supervisor to scholars working on gender issues from many jurisdictions in particular with collaborative ventures in Ethiopia and with the Southern and Eastern African Regional Centre for Women's Law at the University of Zimbabwe. She is also member of the Centre for the Study of Women and Gender at Warwick. Her areas of particular academic interest are postcolonial feminist theory, feminism and globalization, affective labour/care/body work.

Chantal Maillé is Associate Professor in the Women's Studies Programmes at the Simone de Beauvoir Institute. She received her Ph.D. in 1989 from Université du Québec à Montréal. Her research has focused on Feminisms and Political Representation, Postcolonial Theories and Women's Movements in Quebec, Canada and within Francophonie. She is the author of *Les Québécoises et la conquête du pouvoir politique* (Montreal, St-Martin, 1990), *Primed for Power* (Ottawa, Canadian Advisory Council on the Status of Women, 1990), *Cherchez la femme Trente ans de débats constitutionnels au Québec* (Montreal, éditions du remue-ménage, 2002), and co-editor with feminist political scientists Diane Lamoureux and Micheline de Sève of *Malaises identitaires échanges féministes autour d'un Québec uncertain* (Montreal, éditions du remue-ménage, 1999). She has published articles in journals such as *Women: a Cultural Review, Québec Studies, Globe, Revue internationale d'études québécoises, Journal of Canadian Studies, Politique et Sociétés, Cahiers du CEDREF, Recherches féministes, Zeitschrift für Kanada-Studien, Estudios Feministas, The Gerontologist, Journal of the Gerontological Society of America.*

Esha Niyogi De is the author of *Empire, Media, and the Autonomous Woman: A Feminist Critique of Postcolonial Thought* (Oxford University Press, 2011) and the co-author and co-editor of *Trans-Status Subjects: Gender in the Globalization of South and Southeast Asia* (Duke University Press, 2002). She has also published articles in a variety of leading international journals including *Diacritics* and *Screen*.

Currently, she holds a Senior Fulbright Regional (Multi-Country) Research Fellowship (2013-14) for her new single-author book project on "Cross-Border Narrative Cinema by Women Film-makers of India, Pakistan, Bangladesh". She teaches at UCLA.

Krishna Menon is an Associate Professor, Department of Political Science at Lady Shri Ram College, Delhi. Her areas of interest include Political Theory, Indian Politics and Feminist Theory and

Politics. She has published books, papers and articles on debates within political theory, issues in Indian politics, and feminist theory and politics. Her publications include *Political Theory: An Introduction*(Penguin Pearson, 2008), *Human Rights, Gender and Environment* (Penguin Pearson, 2009), *Applied Ethics and Human Rights* (Anthem Press, 2010), *Gender and Identity: A Case Study of Nurses from Kerala in Delhi* (National Labour Institute, 2008) among others. She has presented papers in international and national seminars. She was awarded the Teacher of Distinction Award by the University of Delhi in 2009. She is a trained Carnatic musician and a Bharata Natyam dancer with a long record of performances.

Lucinda Joy Peach (Late) was the Associate Professor in the Department of Philosophy and Religion at American University, New York. Her areas of research and teaching included gender and religion, religion and law, women's human rights and applied ethics (including bioethics, feminist ethics and legal ethics). She was the author of *Legislating Morality: Religious Identity and Moral Pluralism* (Oxford University Press, 2002). She had also edited *Women and World Religions* (Prentice Hall, 2002), *Women in Culture: An Anthology* (Blackwell Publishers, 1998), and co-edited (with April Morgan and Colette Mazucelli) *Ethics and Global Affairs: An Active Learning Sourcebook* (New York: Kumarian Press, 2004).

Madhu Vij is Professor of Finance at the Faculty of Management Studies, University of Delhi, where she teaches Financial and Management Accounting and International and Corporate Finance. Her research, professional and teaching interests include banking, international financial management, management of financial services and behavioural finance. She had been the Director, Women's Studies and Development Centre, University of Delhi for one year (June 2012 to July 2013). She is actively involved in working on gender issues, has delivered special talks in this area and has also been sanctioned a project on 'Microfinance and Gender' by University of Delhi.

Professor Vij has also participated and attended the global colloquium on 'Participant Centered Learning' at Harvard Business School, Boston, USA. She was on the Panel of Judges for award of PM's trophy for selecting the best steel plant for the years, 2010-2011 and 2011-2012. She has also been an independent

Director of MOIL Limited for three years. Currently, she is the member of Ad Hoc Task Force (ATF), Result Framework Document (RFD), Performance Management Division, Cabinet Secretariat, Government of India.

Malashri Lal is a writer and a critic with interest in literature for social change. Her specialization is in Women and Gender Studies on which she has 10 books. Her early book *The Law of the Threshold: Women Writers in Indian English* was widely acclaimed. Recently, she has co-edited *In Search of Sita: Revisiting Mythology* and *Chamba-Achamba: Women's Oral Narratives*. She is currently the Dean of Colleges and Dean, Academic Activities and Projects at the University of Delhi and has also held other senior administrative positions in the same university, including Head, Department of English (2000-2003), Director, Women's Studies (2000-2006) and Joint Director, South Campus (2006-2011).

Manjeet Bhatia is a senior faculty member of the Women's Studies & Development Centre (WSDC) at the University of Delhi. She holds degrees in pure sciences, philosophy and political science. She has been working in the interdisciplinary area of Women's Studies for more than two decades. She offers the advanced course in Gender Studies at WSDC and is consultant on other such courses run by the WSDC. She has convened and coordinated several UGC refresher courses in Women's Studies and made presentations in several such courses. She has also completed several research projects, including a Delhi-based study of cases registered in the Delhi courts under the domestic violence law and on the issue of 'honour killings' in North-West India. She regularly presents papers at local, national and international forums. She has been a visiting scholar at the Indian Institute of Advanced Study, Shimla and at the University of Hull, UK.

Mary E. John is currently Senior Fellow at the Centre for Women's Development Studies, New Delhi. She was Director of the Centre from 2006 to 2012 and before that Deputy Director of the Women's Studies Programme at JNU from 2001 to 2006. Her recent book is *Women's Studies in India: A Reader*. She is currently doing a study on the adverse child sex ratio, and is also writing a book on feminism.

Nilima Srivastava is a trained social worker from University of Delhi. She was awarded Ph.D. in 1993 from University of Lucknow. At present, she is Reader with IGNOU in School of Gender and Development Studies. Earlier, she had been on faculty with Department of Social Work and Women's Studies and Development Centre, University of Delhi. Her areas of specialization are women and work and child welfare with special focus on the issue of girl child. Her publications include a book (*Women on the Path of Progress: A Study of Decadal Change in Role Conflict among Women Professionals*) and several papers in national and international journals.

Sanjukta Dasgupta, Professor and former Head, Department of English and former Dean, Faculty of Arts, Calcutta University, teaches English Literature, American Literature and New Literatures in English. She is a poet, critic and translator and her articles, poems, short stories and translations have been published in journals of distinction in India and abroad. Her published books include *The Novels of Huxley and Hemingway: A Study in Two Planes of Reality, Responses: Selected Essays Snapshots* (poetry), *Dilemma* (poetry), *First Language* (poetry), *More Light* (poetry) *Her Stories* (translations), *Manimahesh* (translation), *The Indian Family in Transition* (co-edited SAGE), *Media, Gender and Popular Culture in India: Tracking Change and Continuity* (co-authored, SAGE, 2012) *Tagore: At Home in the World* (co-edited, SAGE, 2012), *Abuse and other Short Stories* (short stories in English, 2013), *Radical Rabindranath Nation, Family and Gender in Tagore's Fiction and Films* (co-authored, Orient Blackswan, 2013). She is the Managing Editor of *FAMILIES: A Journal of Representations*. Her areas of interest are Colonial and Postcolonial Women's Writing, Women and/in Indian Films, Migration and Diaspora Studies, Translation Studies, Media Studies and Creative Writing.

Shefali Moitra is a retired Professor of Philosophy at the Centre of Advanced Study, Jadavpur University, Kolkata. She has been one of the most valuable visiting scholars of WSDC. Her contributions to the academic pursuits of the centre during her visits have remained very rewarding. She is co-editor of *Communication, Identity and Self-expression* (Oxford University Press, 1984), and the editor of *Women Heritage and Violence* (Papyrus, 1996). Her areas of specialization are ethics, philosophy of language and feminist studies.

Shelly Pandey is presently working as Senior Fellow in the Women's Studies and Development Centre, University of Delhi, Delhi. Her Ph.D. from the Indian Institute of Technology (IIT), Delhi is on unmarried women call-centre agents, which explores gendered experiences in a globalized work world. Her research interests cover gender, space, globalization, ICT and work. She is the recipient of M.N. Srinivas Memorial Prize 2012 awarded by Indian Sociological Society for her paper "Private Space in Public Transport: Locating Gender in Delhi Metro", published in *Economic and Political Weekly*.

Sukrita Paul Kumar is an Honorary Fellow of the prestigious International Writing Programme, University of Iowa (USA), and also a former Fellow of the Indian Institute of Advanced Study, Shimla. Recipient of many international fellowships and residencies, she has lectured and read poems in many institutions in India and abroad. She has published several collections of poems in English including *Without Margins, Apurna, Folds of Silence* and *Oscillations*. Her two bilingual collections are *Poems Come Home* (with Hindustani translation by Gulzar) and *Rowing Together* (with Hindi translation by Savita Singh). She was the Guest Editor of *Crossing Over*, a special issue of "Manoa" (University of Hawaii, USA).

Sukrita's major works include *Narrating Partition, Conversations on Modernism, The New Story* and *Man, Woman and Androgyny. Speaking for Herself: Asian Women's Writings* (Penguin), *Ismat, Her Life, Her Times* (Katha) and *Interpreting Homes in South Asian Literature* (Pearson). As Director of a UNESCO project on "The Culture of Peace", she edited *Mapping Memories*, a volume of Urdu short stories. She has two books of translations too *Stories of Joginder Paul* and the novel *Sleepwalkers*. She is the chief editor of the book on *Cultural Diversity in India* (Macmillan India). Deeply interested in oral traditions of India, her most recent co-edited book is *Chamba Achamba: Women's Oral Culture from Chamba and Bharmour*, published by Sahitya Akademi.

Currently, she is on deputation as Programme Coordinator of B.Tech Humanities, Cluster Innovation Centre, University of Delhi.

Susheela Kaushik was the first director of WSDC and had remained on this position for about 13 years. She is an eminent political scientist and worked extensively on the areas of girl child and political participation of women, especially at panchayat levels. She has authored two remarkable books titled *Family and Right of Girls* and *Panchayati Raj in Action: Challenges to Women's Role*. She continues to be a guide to the UGC Women's Studies Centres.

Tanya Caulfield was awarded her Ph.D. in the field of Anthropology by the University of Queensland. Her doctoral research considered different female sexualities and lived experiences with regard to unmarried women in India. She obtained her Master's degree, which focused on the dowry violence phenomenon in India, from Monash University in the field of Women's Studies. She has also worked with many women's organizations and NGOs in India and several international agencies, undertaking research on humanitarian and development issues. Her research interests include sexuality, gender, difference and identity in India. She is currently working at the Nossal Institute for Global Health, University of Melbourne, Australia.

Veena Poonacha is Professor and Director of the Research Centre for Women's Studies (RCWS), and the Project Director of the Dr. Avabai Wadia Archives for Women at the SNDT Women's University, Mumbai. With a Ph.D. in Sociology from SNDT Women's University, her research interest in Women's Studies straddles the interdisciplinary areas of History, Sociology and Social Anthropology. She has undertaken research across India, particularly in Gujarat, Maharashtra, Tamil Nadu and Karnataka for national/international agencies to investigate state/community responses to domestic violence, self-help groups, gender issues in educational, scientific and private sectors and development deficits in urban slums.

Vibha Chaturvedi is a professor of philosophy at University of Delhi. She has also been holding the charge of Director of Women's Studies and Development Centre at University of Delhi since 2006. She did her Doctorate in Philosophy from University of Lucknow, and began her teaching career at the Department of Philosophy, University of Lucknow. Later she joined University of Delhi. She has authored two books and published several research papers and articles in academic journals and anthologies. Her areas of special interest include Modern Western Philosophy, Analytic Philosophy, Ethics, Philosophy of Religion and Gender Studies.

Zarina Bhatty is President, Indian Association for Women's Studies, of which she is also a founder member. Earlier, she taught Sociology at Jesus and Marry College for ten years. She has conducted research on Muslim women and on women in the unorganized sector of Indian economy. She has over two dozen publications in academic journals and books. Her study, "Women in the Beedi Industry" was sponsored and published by the International Labour Office. She conceptualized and wrote a distant education course on gender sensitization for grassroots workers in Hindi. This course has been translated into four other languages. She is currently member of the national executive of the YMCA of India.

Index